PALIMPSESTIC MEMORY

PALIMPSESTIC MEMORY

The Holocaust and Colonialism in French and Francophone Fiction and Film

Max Silverman

berghahn
NEW YORK · OXFORD
www.berghahnbooks.com

First edition published in 2013 by

Berghahn Books

www.berghahnbooks.com

© 2013 Max Silverman

Library of Congress Cataloging-in-Publication Data

Silverman, Maxim.
 Palimpsestic memory : the Holocaust and colonialism in French and
francophone fiction and film / Max Silverman. -- 1st ed.
   p. cm.
 Includes bibliographical references and index.
 ISBN 978-0-85745-883-4 (hardback : alk. paper) -- ISBN 978-0-85745-884-1
(ebook)
 1. French fiction--20th century--History and criticism. 2. French
fiction--French-speaking countries--History and criticism. 3. Colonies
in literature. 4. Colonies in motion pictures. 5. Holocaust, Jewish (1939-
1945), in literature. 6. Holocaust, Jewish (1939-1945), in motion pictures.
I. Title.
 PQ673.S55 2013
 843'.91409358405318--dc23

                                                                            2012032935

British Library Cataloguing in Publication Data

A catalogue record for this book is available from the British Library

Printed in the United States on acid-free paper

ISBN 978-0-85745-883-4 (hardback)
ISBN 978-0-85745-884-1 (ebook)

CONTENTS

List of Illustrations

ACKNOWLEDGEMENTS

Earlier versions of parts of this book were first published in the following books and journals: the founding argument of chapter 1 and some examples used in chapter 4 appeared as 'Interconnected Histories: Holocaust and Empire in the Cultural Imaginary', *French Studies* 62, 4 (2008), 417–428; parts of chapter 1 appeared as 'Trips, Tropes and Traces: Reflections on Memory in French and Francophone Culture' in Peter Collier, Anna Magdalena Elsner and Olga Smith (eds), *Anamnesia: Private and Public Memory in Modern French Culture* (Oxford: Peter Lang, 'Modern French Identities Series' 83, 2009), pp. 17–28; the section 'Fearful Imagination' in chapter 2 appeared as 'Fearful Imagination: *Night and Fog* and Concentrationary Memory' in Griselda Pollock and Max Silverman (eds), *Concentrationary Cinema: Aesthetics as Political Resistance in Alain Resnais's 'Night and Fog'* (Oxford and New York: Berghahn, 2012), pp. 199–213; the section 'Michael Haneke: *Caché'* in chapter 5 appeared as 'The Violence of the Cut: Michael Haneke's *Caché* and Cultural Memory', *French Cultural Studies* 21, 1 (2010), 57–65; the section 'Hélène Cixous's "Pieds nus" and Jacques Derrida's *Le Monolinguisme de l'autre, ou le prothèse de l'origine'* in chapter 6 appeared as 'Knotted Intersections: Cixous and Derrida', *Wasafiri*, special issue on 'Jewish/Postcolonial Diasporas', 57 (2009), 9–13; and the section 'Patrick Chamoiseau and Rodolphe Hammadi: *Guyane: Traces-mémoires du bagne'* in chapter 6 appeared as 'Memory Traces: Patrick Chamoiseau and Rodolphe Hammadi's *Guyane: Traces-mémoires du bagne'* in Michael Rothberg, Debarati Sanyal and Max Silverman (eds), *'Noeuds de mémoire*: Multidirectional Memory in Post-war French and Francophone Culture', *Yale French Studies* 118/119 (2010), 225–238.

I would like to thank the School of Modern Languages and Cultures at the University of Leeds for granting me sabbatical leave for the writing of parts of this book, and the Arts and Humanities Research Council of Great Britain for the award of a Fellowship to complete the manuscript. I would also like to thank the following friends and colleagues for their help, support and conversation: Zygmunt Bauman, Bryan Cheyette, Marianne Hirsch, Matthew John, Bill Marshall, Griselda Pollock, Michael Rothberg, Nigel Saint, Debarati Sanyal, John Schwarzmantel, Susan Suleiman and the anonymous readers of the manuscript.

My thanks and love go to Nina, Rosa, Sam, Anna and Joe and my parents Len and Lili.

Introduction

Staging Memory as Palimpsest

Scenario 1

In François Emmanuel's novella *La Question humaine* the narrator, a psychologist working in the French branch of a large German firm in the 1990s, is given the task of investigating the strange behaviour of the company's Chief Executive Officer, Mathias Jüst.[1] In the course of his investigation he unearths details linking Jüst's father to the Nazi policy of the extermination of the Jews in the Second World War. More disturbing still for the narrator are anonymous letters that he receives linking his own role in the selection of employees for redundancy in the company's recent 'down-sizing' operation to the Nazis' Final Solution. The device employed by the sender of the letters to suggest this link between different events, separated in time by over fifty years, is to insert parts of the famous SS memorandum of 5 June 1942 on technical modifications needed to improve the efficiency of the so-called 'gas-vans' operating at Kulmhof and Chelmno extermination camps (which Claude Lanzmann reads out in his film *Shoah*) into technical documents drafted by the narrator justifying his company's selection process in 'down-sizing'.

> Certain sentences revealed a different origin; they were founded on the first text and seemed to push the logic of this text to its extreme, introducing evil connotations and thus corrupting its texture, to the point that certain familiar technical terms became charged with a meaning that one would not normally have associated with them.[2]

The narrator describes the effect created by this device as follows: 'I immediately had a feeling of "doubling" and found myself hesitating over words whose meaning had suddenly become strange';[3] 'it appeared (and here the comparison of the two letters left no doubt) that the first technical text had been invaded and as if devoured by the *other* text'.[4]

Scenario 2

The novel by the crime fiction writer Didier Daeninckx *Meurtres pour mémoire* ends with a short epilogue in which the narrator, Inspector Cadin, and Claudine pass the metro station Bonne-Nouvelle in the second *arrondissement* in Paris.

> A dozen workmen on scaffolding were busy tearing off the successive layers of posters covering the advertising hoardings. Further down, at the end of the platform, two other workmen were scraping the white ceramic tiles with metal spatulas. As they were torn away, the posters revealed old advertisements pasted up ten or twenty years before …. Claudine stopped in front of the wall. She pointed to a tile still partly covered in shreds of yellowing paper that an Algerian workman was having trouble getting rid of. Only some of the text was visible but its overall meaning was not affected: '… *prohibited in France … guilty liable to be sentence … court mart … Ger … Anyone carrying … Jewish natio … maximum sentence of … irresponsible eleme … support for the enemies of Germany. … ilance … guilty themselves and the population of the occupied territories. Signed: the Militaerbefehlshaber Stulpnagel.*'[5]

This superimposed layering of posters recalls an earlier moment in the text when a wall opposite the police headquarters is described by Cadin as covered with traces of different political slogans to constitute a sort of collage of letters, each one referring to a distinct moment of violence (Indo-China in the 1950s, Iran after the Revolution of 1979, Israel-Palestine) but, when overlaid in this fashion, producing a dense condensation of meaning.[6]

Daeninckx uses these images of superimposed adverts and slogans as a metaphor for the interconnections between the two major events at the heart of the book, the massacre in Paris of peacefully demonstrating Algerians on 17 October 1961 at the height of the Algerian War of Independence and the round-up of Jews in France by French police for dispatch to the extermination camps during the Second World War (hence the uncovering of the posters from the Occupation by an Algerian workman in the passage cited above). In the text, it is the character of André Veillut – a barely-concealed portrayal of the real French official intimately connected with both events, Maurice Papon – who provides the link between the two different moments of racialized violence. In the novel, Veillut is the administrator charged with dealing with 'Jewish affairs' in Toulouse in 1942/3 (Papon himself was in Bordeaux) and, nearly twenty years later, is head of a team whose mission is to liquidate leaders of the Algerian Front for National Liberation (FLN) in Paris (Papon was Prefect of Police in Paris at the time and responsible for the events of 17 October 1961).

Scenario 3

A novel influenced by Daeninckx's themes and, more specifically, his device for drawing together different events of racialized violence is *La Seine était rouge* by the Franco-Algerian writer Leïla Sebbar.[7] This work also deals with the events of 17 October 1961 and puts them into contact with not only the Second World War but also other moments of violence and trauma. In the course of the documentary film he is making on 17 October 1961, Louis visits different sites in Paris and superimposes commemorations of the Algerian War of Independence onto official memorial plaques to the Second World War. In the rue de la Santé, where there are commemorative plaques to the Republic and to heroes of the French resistance to the Germans ('On this site were imprisoned, on 11 November 1940, pupils and students who were the first to respond to the call by General de Gaulle to resist the occupier'),[8] Louis adds and then films his own commemoration: '1954–1962. In this prison were guillotined Algerians who resisted the French occupiers'.[9] He repeats this act at the Place de la Concorde ('On this site Algerians were savagely machine-gunned by the police under the command of the prefect Papon on 17 October 1961),[10] at Saint-Michel ('On this site Algerians died for the independence of Algeria on 17 October 1961')[11] and so on in the streets of Paris.

These examples demonstrate two major aspects of the work of memory that I wish to explore in this book. First, the present is shown to be shadowed or haunted by a past which is not immediately visible but is progressively brought into view. The relationship between present and past therefore takes the form of a superimposition and interaction of different temporal traces to constitute a sort of composite structure, like a palimpsest, so that one layer of traces can be seen through, and is transformed by, another. Second, the composite structure in these works is a combination of not simply two moments in time (past and present) but a number of different moments, hence producing a chain of signification which draws together disparate spaces and times. A significant part of the intrigue in *Meurtres pour mémoire* derives from the fact that the investigation into one buried memory (the events of 17 October 1961) turns out to be an investigation into another (the round-up of Jews during the Second World War). Or, rather, the two are shown to be profoundly connected, so that what one might have thought of as distinct moments in time and space are recomposed to create a different spatio-temporal configuration. The overlaying of different texts in *La Question humaine* and of different inscriptions in *La Seine était rouge* creates a similar straddling of multiple moments in time and space. The 'history which returns' to shadow the present is therefore not a linear history but one that condenses different moments, and recreates each due to the connection between them, to resemble Walter Benjamin's famous 'constellation'.[12]

It is my contention that, in the vast field of memory studies of recent years, insufficient attention has been devoted to these features of the work of memory. I will argue that, in the immediate post-war period when returnees from the camps, commentators on the catastrophe that had just occurred and the victims of colonial dehumanization were attempting to understand the nature of racialized violence and horror, the perception of interconnections between different moments of violence was an important part of the reappraisal of the human in the wake of extreme terror. In more recent decades, however, histories of extreme violence have tended to compartmentalize memory on ethno-cultural lines and, hence, blinker the attempt to see multiple connections across space and time. The superimposed traces of different histories at the heart of the works by Emmanuel, Daeninckx and Sebbar are a model for a concept of cultural memory which re-engages with the post-war attempt to seek interconnections. I will argue that, in a sense, art has never lost track of this fact, despite the sociological and historical turn towards more reductive readings of extreme violence and horror. Many of the works that I consider testify to this ongoing engagement with the hybrid and dynamic nature of memory, though they are not always read in this way. This version, like any other, is not without its dangers, a number of which I will outline in the course of my discussion. However, I believe that the aesthetic, political and ethical lessons that we can draw from this understanding of memory far outweigh the dangers. This book is therefore an intervention in the debate around cultural memory in a transnational age, not in order to contribute to the memory wars which beset us (and which are a source of much conflict around the globe) but, on the contrary, to propose a different way of viewing past violence and its relation to the present and future.

I have chosen the term 'palimpsestic memory' to discuss this hybrid form because, of all the figures which connect disparate elements through a play of similarity and difference (analogy, metaphor, allegory, montage and so on), the palimpsest captures most completely the superimposition and productive interaction of different inscriptions and the spatialization of time central to the work of memory that I wish to highlight. I will, at different times, talk of composite memory, 'concentrationary' memory, Gilles Deleuze's *mémoire-monde*, *noeuds de mémoire*, memory traces and a Benjaminian understanding of memory as 'image'. The link between all these terms, as will become apparent, is their palimpsestic structure whereby one element is seen through and transformed by another. There are obvious dangers in applying the same model to literature and film. Yet I believe the notion of the palimpsest can bring into focus the dynamic activity of interconnecting traces common to both media without necessarily obliterating the differences between them.

Chapter 1 sets out the broad scope of the book in more detail. I discuss how the perception of interconnections between different forms of racialized violence in the post-war period has given way to a comparative and competitive view of histories of violence. I challenge this concept of memory to propose an approach which neither universalizes nor particularizes histories but views memory between sameness and difference. I suggest that the politics of this non-competitive concept of memory is dependent on a poetics of memory. The staging of memory across different times and spaces works according to a number of poetic 'figures', including metaphor in Proust, condensation and displacement in Freudian dream-work, Freud's notion of the palimpsest as a metaphor for memory, Benjamin's use of allegory and montage to inform his ideas on history (which are 'crystalized' in his notion of 'the constellation'), and Jacques Derrida's (non-)concept, or concept 'under erasure' ('sous rature') of the trace. The notion of memory as palimpsest provides us with a politico-aesthetic model of cultural memory in that it gives us a way of perceiving history in a non-linear way and memory as a hybrid and dynamic process across individuals and communities.

Chapter 2 considers three films of the 1950s and early 1960s by Alain Resnais, Jean Cayrol and Chris Marker through the prism of what I call 'concentrationary memory'. I consider Resnais's *Nuit et brouillard* from the point of view of Cayrol's ideas on 'concentrationary' or 'Lazarean' art, by which the present is haunted by the past and life is haunted by death to create an overlapping layering of time and space. I suggest that the concentrationary art of *Nuit et brouillard* institutes a notion of memory as the haunting of the present and an uncanny superimposition of the visible and the invisible. This version of memory, detached from a linear notion of time to open up the becalmed aftermath of the war to the persistence of horror, translates the interconnections between different moments of radical violence proposed by David Rousset, Hannah Arendt and other post-war theorists into a politicized aesthetic in which the present is always contaminated by multiple elsewheres. It can be distinguished from Holocaust memory in that its gesture to other spaces and times and its refusal to define the singularity of the event as the genocide of the Jews means that it is a memory which puts the present into contact not with one past and one ethno-cultural community but (dialectically in a Benjaminian sense) with a complex history.

The second section of this chapter analyses Chris Marker's *La Jetée* and Resnais and Cayrol's *Muriel ou le temps d'un retour* through a similar lens. *La Jetée* epitomizes the idea of the 'Lazarean image' (the concept of images drawn from a life after death) and is also founded on a superimposition of layers of time. Memory – in which dream, imagination and the historical 'real' are no longer distinguishable – is transformed into a present process of questioning the image after catastrophe. This is not a 'psychological' memory but, like Deleuze's notion of 'mémoire-monde', one in which individual consciousness and history are profoundly related. Like *La Jetée*, *Muriel* blurs the distinction between the present and different moments of catastrophe, especially those connected with the Second World War and the Algerian War of Independence. The commodified objects of post-war modernization are invested with the charge of different traumas and a complex history. In this way, Resnais proposes a political rather than a purely formal aesthetic as the film raises fundamental questions about the relationship between post-war consumer society and different moments of horror.

In chapters 3 and 4 I read a number of works 'against the grain' of habitual interpretations. Chapter 3 considers three 'anti-colonial' or 'post-colonial' works to highlight the intersections between colonial violence and other forms of racialized violence. Frantz Fanon's *Peau noire masques blancs* stages multiple encounters between different histories of violence, especially between anti-semitism and anti-Black racism, to constitute an intertextual and transcultural poetics and politics. My analysis of Mohammed Dib's *Qui se souvient de la mer* explores Dib's poetic language of memory in the light of his question in the postscript to the novel, 'How should we speak about Algeria after Auschwitz, the Warsaw Ghetto and Hiroshima?'.[13] As in Marker's *La Jetée*, Dib's novel blends science fiction and dream to create a new post-apocalyptic language of trauma and desire. In the final section of chapter 3 I consider how Assia Djebar's *Femmes d'Alger dans leur appartement* overlays the critique of Delacroix's orientalist painting with other stories from elsewhere. Djebar's poetic language transforms a monologic version of History into the pluralized, transcultural and transgenerational voice of memory.

Chapter 4 reverses the gaze of the previous chapter by viewing three works that have become central to the canon of 'Holocaust literature' in French – Charlotte Delbo's trilogy *Auschwitz et après*, Georges Perec's *W ou le souvenir d'enfance* and Patrick Modiano's *Dora Bruder* – to show that 'Holocaust literature' is always in dialogue with other stories of racialized violence (a lesson we can take from Cathy Caruth's groundbreaking work on trauma, *Unclaimed Experience*). Delbo's 'testimony' is a polyphonic play in which the voice of memory is a layering of the subjective and the inter-subjective and only emerges through the connections between different traumas. The poetics of Perec's text, consisting of constant substitutions and displacements of meaning, stages catastrophe in terms of an endless deferral of meaning from one site to another. Perec's use of Rousset's *L'Univers concentrationnaire* at the end of the text not only refers to the concentration camps of the Second World War but to a broader 'concentrationary' mentality in our cultural and political imaginary. *Dora Bruder* transforms Parisian city space into a palimpsest of traces of violence and loss in which the Occupation and the Holocaust are connected not only with colonialism (especially Algeria) but also with dehumanizing modernity in general. Seeing the intersections of different traumatic moments in these three works displaces the singularity of Holocaust memory across different sites, not in order to conflate them in a universal theory of trauma or to efface the specificity of the event, but to define a tension between one and another, and between singularity and generality inevitably contained in representations of trauma.

In chapter 5 I use the term 'the memory of the image' as a way of redefining Benjamin's notion of the dialectical image and apply it to Jean-Luc Godard's *Histoire(s) du cinéma* and Michael Haneke's *Caché*. Godard's use of montage aligns his non-linear approach to history with Benjamin's notion of the image as a constellation in which past and present collide in a flash. Godard creates literal palimpsests in which different images are overlaid and dissolve into each other, connecting the disparate in fascinating and provocative ways. Though very different in practice from Godard's approach in *Histoire(s)*, Haneke's technique also reinvests the image with a hidden memory composed of intersecting histories of violence and trauma and, consequently, provokes us into reading history in the moment of the image. I compare the first and final scenes of *Caché* to demonstrate how the return of a complex history is related to a sort of pedagogy of the image, 'the image that is read' as Benjamin puts it.

Chapter 6 applies Freud's notion of the memory trace refashioned by Jacques Derrida to discuss intersections between histories and memories in works by Hélène Cixous, Derrida, and Patrick Chamoiseau and Rodolphe Hammadi. In the first section I compare two texts by Cixous and Derrida which both refer to their childhood as French Jews in Algeria and both evoke the abrogation by the Vichy state in October 1940 of the Crémieux decree of October 1870 (which had granted full citizenship to the Jews of Algeria) as a mark of the other (and history) inscribed on the self. In her story 'Pieds nus' Cixous transforms her Algerian childhood into a complex personal and historical conjuncture in which colonialism, anti-semitism and patriarchy intersect in conflicting ways. In Derrida's *Le Monolinguisme de l'autre* the trace or mark of the other disturbs the singularity of language and renders problematic all essentialist accounts of the self and the community. The tension in both works between the singular and the plural, and the individual and the collective, opens up the possibility of viewing 'different' histories in terms of interconnecting sites in which the trace of one is always in the other.

In their collaborative photo-text *Guyane: Traces-mémoires du bagne* Chamoiseau and Hammadi view the remains of the famous penal colony in French Guiana through the lens of the memory trace. Their approach opens up monolinear, 'monumental' national history to a pluralized space of memories of transportation, imprisonment and dehumanization. The memory trace is a hybrid network of echoes and reverberations across space and time (a *'noeud de mémoires'* as opposed to Pierre Nora's famous *'lieux de mémoire'*).[14] Many of these echoes are of the concentrationary universe evoked by Resnais and Cayrol in *Nuit et brouillard* so that memories of French penitentiary practice, French colonialism and the Nazi camps are connected to create an image-constellation of meaning.

The final chapter considers the politics and poetics of cultural memory in a transnational, transcultural and information age. Not only are we beset by an invidious competition between memories as part of an identity politics; we are also challenged by the deterritorialization of memories as they are increasingly mediatized on the global stage and, conversely, a new amnesia as information overload risks reducing our capacity to remember to that of the zombie. Palimpsestic memory offers a vision of memory which has always been deterritorialized in the sense of being a hybrid rather than pure category. But it is also a critical space in that it opens up the bland surface of the present to the 'knotted intersections' of history. Derrida proposed a post-Enlightenment 'cosmopolitics' to replace the Enlightenment cosmopolitanism of Kant, and challenge the binary distinction between universalism and particularism and the notion of the self-presence of the human on which Kant's vision is premised. I argue that palimpsestic memory offers us a non-foundational approach to the human in keeping with Derrida's 'cosmopolitical' vision of the 'democracy-to-come'. It would be a dynamic and open space composed of interconnecting traces of different voices, sites and times, and it would hold out the prospect of new solidarities across the lines of race and nation.

Notes

1. François Emmanuel, *La Question humaine* (Stock, 2000).
2. 'Certaines phrases trahissaient une autre provenance, elles se fondaient au premier texte et semblaient pousser à l'extrême la logique de celui-ci, constituant des inclusions malignes qui tendaient à en corrompre la trame, au point que certains mots d'un vocabulaire technique pourtant familier se retrouvaient chargés d'une potentialité de sens que l'on ne leur soupçonnait pas', Emmanuel, *La Question humaine*, p. 74. All translations from the French are my own, except where otherwise stated.
3. 'J'éprouvais brusquement une impression de dédoublement, je me voyais hésiter sur des mots dont le sens m'était soudain étranger', Emmanuel, *La Question humaine*, p. 76.
4. 'il apparaissait ici (et la comparaison des deux lettres ne faisait aucun doute) que le premier texte technique avait été envahi et comme dévoré par *l'autre* texte', Emmanuel, *La Question humaine*, pp. 77–78. Emmanuel's novella makes explicit links between past and present but not between the Holocaust and colonialism. However, in their 2007 film of Emmanuel's text, Nicolas Klotz and Elisabeth Perceval overlay the links between the Holocaust and contemporary management systems with references to a colonial imaginary and present immigration controls. For an excellent discussion of these connections in the film, see Libby Saxton, 'Horror by Analogy: Paradigmatic Aesthetics in Nicolas Klotz and Elisabeth Perceval's *La Question humaine*' in Michael Rothberg, Debarati Sanyal and Max Silverman (eds), '*Noeuds de mémoire*: Multidirectional Memory in Post-war French and Francophone Culture', *Yale French Studies* 118/119 (2010), pp. 209–224.

5. 'Une dizaine d'ouvriers, grimpés sur des échafaudages étaient occupés à arracher les couches successives d'affiches qui recouvraient les panneaux publicitaires. Au bout du quai, deux autres ouvriers grattaient les carreaux de céramique blanche à l'aide de spatulas métalliques. En se déchirant, les papiers laissaient apparaître de vieilles réclames collées dix, vingt années auparavant. ... Claudine s'arrêta devant un coin de mur. Elle me montra un carré de céramique à demi recouvert de lambeaux de papier jauni qui résistaient aux efforts d'un travailleur algérien : « ... *est interdite en France ... coupable à être condamn ... cour martia ... lemande ... personne qui porte ... sortissants jui ... peine allant jusqu'à la mo ... éléments irrespon ... à soutenir les ennemis de l'Allemagne ... met en garde ... coupables eux-mêmes et la population des territoires occupés. Signé : le Militaerbefehlshaber Stulpnagel.* »', Didier Daeninckx, *Meurtres pour mémoire* (Gallimard, 1984), pp. 215–216. (*Meurtres pour mémoire* was translated by Liz Heron as *Murder in Memoriam* (London: Serpent's Tail, 2005).)
6. Daeninckx, *Meurtres pour mémoire*, pp. 158–159.
7. Leïla Sebbar, *La Seine était rouge* (Thierry Magnier, 1999).
8. 'En cette prison le 11 novembre 1940 furent incarcérés des lycéens et des étudiants qui à l'appel du Général De Gaulle se dressèrent les premiers contre l'Occupant', Sebbar, *La Seine était rouge*, p. 29.
9. '1954–1962. Dans cette prison furent guillotinés des résistants Algériens qui se dressèrent contre l'occupant français', Sebbar, *La Seine était rouge*, p. 30.
10. 'Ici des Algériens ont été matraqués sauvagement par la police du préfet Papon le 17 octobre 1961', Sebbar, *La Seine était rouge*, p. 88.
11. 'Ici des Algériens sont tombés pour l'indépendance de l'Algérie le 17 octobre 1961', Sebbar, *La Seine était rouge*, p. 118.
12. I have taken the term 'the history which returns' from the article 'L'Histoire qui revient: La Forme cinématographique de l'histoire dans *Caché* et *La Question humaine*' by Antoine de Baecque. (In the case of *La Question humaine*, it is the film by Klotz and Perceval of Emmanuel's novella that he discusses rather than the original text.) De Baecque uses the idea of the palimpsest to demonstrate how cinema can represent a buried or repressed history: 'The primary form of the porous nature of historical time is comparable to the phenomenon of the palimpsest in that the present of these films seems to be constantly printed over by a hidden past which, however, returns according to specific cinematic techniques. Just as transcribers would use a parchment already written on but whose previous inscriptions they would efface by techniques of scraping or washing, so, in *Caché* and *La Question humaine*, the film-narrative of the present (omnipresent) covers a past narrative of trauma and guilt which constitutes a buried history'. ('La première forme de cette porosité des temps historiques est comparable au phénomène du palimpseste, car le présent de ces films semble constamment enregistré par recouvrement d'un passé enfoui qui pourtant revient selon des modes propres au cinéma. De même que les copistes réutilisaient un parchemin déjà écrit, mais dont ils savaient effacer l'écriture précédente par grattage ou par lavage, de même dans *Caché* et *La Question humaine* le film-récit du présent, omniprésent, recouvre un récit passé, traumatisant, culpabilisant, qui est une histoire enfouie'.) (*Annales. Histoire, Sciences sociales* 63, 6 (2008), 1279). De Baecque's argument is illuminating throughout and his use of terms like 'le spectre revenant' ('the returning ghost'), taken from Jacques Derrida's *Spectre de Marx*, and 'le palimpseste secret' ('the secret palimpsest', p. 1281) will inform my own argument in this book. Yet my interpretation of the palimpsest and ghosting is slightly different. As is clear from the passage above, de Baecque talks of the return of one buried memory in each work, the Holocaust in *La Question humaine* and 17 October 1961 in Michael Haneke's *Caché* (which I discuss in chapter 5). However, my use of the palimpsest is to suggest

that it represents the condensation of a number of different spatio-temporal traces. It is strange that, in his exhaustive account of works dealing with 17 October 1961, de Baecque does not mention Daeninckx's *Meurtres pour mémoire* (although the reason for this is possibly because de Baecque is dealing with the relationship between history and cinema rather than fiction too). As I say above, Daeninckx's text complicates the 'history which returns' by rendering visible the interconnections between disparate sites of extreme violence. Saxton's article 'Horror by Analogy' detects a similar superimposition in the film *La Question humaine*. (I discuss *Meurtres pour mémoire* and *La Seine était rouge* in more detail in 'Hybrid Memory in the City', *Moving Worlds* (special issue on 'Postcolonial Europe' ed. Graham Huggan) 11, 2 (2011), 57–66.)

13. 'Comment parler de l'Algérie après Auschwitz, le ghetto de Varsovie et Hiroshima ?', Mohammed Dib, 'Postface' in *Qui se souvient de la mer* (Editions de la différence, 2007 [1962]), p. 218.

14. Pierre Nora (ed.), *Les Lieux de mémoire* (Gallimard, 3 volumes: 1984, 1986, 1992). For a critique of Nora's concept through the idea of '*noeuds de mémoire*', see Michael Rothberg, 'Introduction: Between Memory and Memory. From *Lieux de mémoire* to *Noeuds de mémoire*' in Michael Rothberg, Debarati Sanyal and Max Silverman (eds), '*Noeuds de mémoire*: Multidirectional Memory in Post-war French and Francophone Culture', *Yale French Studies* 118/119 (2010), 3–12.

Chapter 1

THE POLITICS AND POETICS OF MEMORY

The Concentrationary Universe and Total Domination

In the immediate aftermath of the Second World War, the study of the camps by the political deportee David Rousset entitled *L'Univers concentrationnaire* was, above all, a warning to 'normal' men and women that now 'everything is possible' ('tout est possible').[1] The limits that had circumscribed the human had been destroyed by the Nazi experiment of total domination. Rousset exhorts us to integrate this knowledge into our understanding of the human, however unbelievable that knowledge might appear. For, once unleashed on the world, and despite the defeat of its Nazi incarnation, the concentrationary universe will reappear unless we are permanently vigilant. Rousset's call for a new understanding of the relationship between the normal and the unimaginable is therefore premised on the belief that the concentrationary universe is profoundly connected to the world outside the camps rather than isolated from it. As he says at the end of his essay:

> it would be easy to show that the most characteristic traits of both the SS mentality and the social conditions which gave rise to the Third Reich are to be found in many sectors of world society .... It would be blindness – and criminal blindness, at that – to believe that, by reason of any difference of national temperament, it would be impossible for any other country to try a similar experiment. Germany interpreted, with an originality in keeping with her history, the crisis that led her to the concentrationary universe. But the existence and the mechanism of that crisis were inherent in the economic and social foundations of capitalism and imperialism. Under a new guise, similar effects may reappear tomorrow. There remains therefore a very specific war to be waged. The lessons learned from the concentration camps provide a marvellous arsenal for that war.[2]

For Rousset, the analogical potential of the unimaginable experiment designed to eradicate whole peoples (the word 'analogue' appears twice in the above passage in the original French) stems from the fact that it has its roots in the familiar soil of capitalism and imperialism. Rousset's contention that one must see, at one and the same time, the interconnections between the concentrationary universe and the outside world and understand the absolute novelty of an experiment which means that now (as never before) 'everything is possible' might seem paradoxical, even contradictory. One of the fascinating features of Rousset's work is, precisely, the perception of a new monster produced from old ingredients, and the search for (pre-existing) words and images to define an unknown world. We know how this tension between the known and the unknown (which his fellow deportee Robert Antelme describes as '[t]his disproportion between the experience we had lived through and the account we were able to give of it')[3] will be at the heart of much survivor testimony and critical work on the representation of the Holocaust. Rousset's own attempt in *L'Univers concentrationnaire* to find a language adequate to the task includes a mixture of Marxist analysis, biblical references and surrealist imagery. What this shows is that intertextual references and the location of the roots of the concentrationary universe in the soil of capitalism and imperialism are an inevitable part of the attempt to define the novelty of the experience. In the same chapter in which Rousset says '[i]t is a universe apart, totally cut off, the weird kingdom of an unlikely fatality' he uses an imagery derived from the slave trade to try to conjure up the experience ('the slave market', 'Kapos and Vorarbeiter, slave traders').[4] The resources for defining the indefinable have to be sought in the familiar but stretched so that they no longer resemble what we already know.

Rousset's writings on the concentrationary universe (and those of other political deportees to the camps) were a major inspiration for Hannah Arendt's understanding of totalitarian rule expressed in *The Origins of Totalitarianism*. Arendt takes from Rousset the lesson that 'everything is possible' and that this marks the absolute novelty of totalitarian rule, despite a pre-history of violence and massacre which comprises 'the extermination of native peoples', slavery and even the concentration camps in South Africa and India earlier in the twentieth century.[5] However, like Rousset's *L'Univers concentrationnaire*, Arendt's text also demonstrates (if only implicitly) a profound tension between the novelty, unimaginable nature and unique quality of the Nazi camps and the more familiar political landscape from which they have sprung. For example, Arendt challenges the 'isolation' of the camps which creates the illusion that they are distinct from the surrounding context. Instead, she maintains, the camps are 'the guiding social ideal of total domination in general' and can only be understood as such if we see them in terms of their relations with the surrounding context:

the experiment of 'total domination' in the concentration camps depends on sealing off the latter against the world of all others, the world of the living in general, even against the outside world of a country under totalitarian rule. This isolation explains the peculiar unreality and lack of credibility that characterize all reports from the concentration camps and constitute one of the main difficulties for the true understanding of totalitarian domination, which stands or falls with the existence of these concentration and extermination camps; for unlikely as it may sound, these camps are the true central institution of totalitarian organizational power.[6]

Arendt's whole argument in the book – which locates the origins of totalitarianism in capitalism, the rise of the modern nation-state (and, with it, 'stateless' people), imperialism and anti-semitism – could be said to be in tension with the idea of the absolute novelty of totalitarian rule. Yet, as with Rousset, rather than see this as a contradiction, we should note instead the anxious relationship at play in the text between the unique and the interconnected, similarity and difference, and repetition and singularity. A crucial aspect of the works of both Rousset and Arendt is their attempt to defamiliarize the banality of the everyday to show the persistence of unimaginable horror and a radical reshaping of the idea of the human in post-war life; hence, to appeal to our slumbering consciousness by exposing the *'hidden potential of the so-called "normal" world'* (*'potentialité cachée du monde dit "normal"'*),[7] and the overlap between apparently 'different' worlds. Much of the discussion in this book will be situated in this disturbing 'in-between' zone between horror and the everyday, between camps and non-camps, and between apparently 'different' spatio-temporal sites. What, more recently, has been framed in terms of an opposition between the notion of the uniqueness of the Holocaust, on the one hand, and its emergence from rationalizing modernity, on the other, is presented by Rousset and Arendt in more ambivalent terms. As I shall later argue, the difference between the concentrationary universe (and system of total domination that it represents) and the more recent focus on the specificity of the Holocaust is that the former, by its very nature, requires an analysis based on connections across space and time to show the general nature of the transformation of the idea of the human, whereas the latter presents the extreme horror of the event as an isolated experiment related to specific racialized targets. The 'analogical' approach by Rousset and the intersections between the concentration camps, imperialism and modern racial science perceived by Arendt open out the space of 'total domination' onto the 'normal' world and provide us with a model for understanding memory and history across sites of violence.

The Politics of Memory: Between the Holocaust and Colonialism

The responses by Rousset and Arendt to the concentrationary universe and the experiment of 'total domination' are indicative of a more general attempt, in the immediate post-war period, to relate the camps to the broader history of human subjection in the modern world. Capitalism, imperialism, the rise of the modern nation-state and racial theory were interconnected processes responsible, according to Theodor Adorno and Max Horkheimer, for the production of 'interchangeable' victims, 'Frenchman, Negro, or Jew'.[8] Anti-colonial theorists and activists of the time understood this only too well. In his *Discours sur le colonialisme*, Aimé Césaire states provocatively that Hitler's real crime, in the eyes of the European humanist, 'is not *the crime* in itself, *the crime against man*, it is not *the humiliation of man as such*, it is the crime against the white man, the humiliation of the white man, and the fact that he applied to Europe colonialist procedures which until then had been reserved exclusively for the Arabs of Algeria, the "coolies" of India and the "niggers" of Africa'.[9] Césaire's influence on Frantz Fanon is evident in Fanon's understanding of Nazism as 'the apparition of "European colonies", in other words, the institution of a colonial system in the very heart of Europe'.[10] Fanon's theorization of anti-Black colonial racism in *Peau noire, masques blancs* is largely based on Sartre's model of anti-semitism in *Réflexions sur la question juive*, while the Jewish Tunisian anti-colonial writer Albert Memmi (also profoundly influenced by Sartre) applied the same analytical model of domination to the situation of the colonized under colonialism and that of the Jew in non-Jewish society.[11]

These analogies and borrowings should not surprise us given the interconnectedness of those struggling to come to terms with the catastrophe of the Second World War, the barbarity of colonialism and news about the Soviet camps in the immediate post-war period. Although it does not treat colonial violence, Simone de Beauvoir's *Les Mandarins*, published in 1954, deals with the passionate debates in France after the war about the connections between different camps, especially the Nazi concentration camps and the camps of the Soviet gulag. Rousset himself was bitterly denounced by communists for using his experience as a political deportee in Buchenwald as the reason for condemning the camps in the Soviet Union. As Tzvetan Todorov observes,

> in making concern for the other the priority, [Rousset] chooses to transform past experience into a reason for acting in the present, in a new situation in which he is not the central character and can only understand through analogy or from the outside.[12]

Todorov draws attention to others who used one experience in exemplary fashion to denounce another, be it analogies between the Nazi and Soviet camps (Vassily Grossman), or between anti-semitism and slavery (André Schwarz-Bart).[13] In a short article on the publication in 1950 of Jean Cayrol's *Lazare parmi nous* (see chapter 2), Maurice Blanchot relates Cayrol's experience of the Nazi concentration camps to that of victims of the Soviet gulag.[14] '*Le concentrationnat*' was a term used at the time to describe the camp system in general.

Analogies, transfers, interconnections and intertextual borrowings particularly abound during the Algerian War of Independence. The extraordinary career of Maurice Papon as collaborationist bureaucrat, colonial administrator and Paris police chief demonstrates the ways in which the same administrative practices of surveillance, classification, round-up, deportation and violence were developed and applied in different contexts, circulating freely between France and the colonies and between the Nazi and colonial eras.[15] Studies of the Algerian War often note the frequent references to and analogies with the 'dark years' (*années noires*) by metropolitan politicians and intellectuals of all persuasions. For some, this is a classic case of what Freud defined as 'screen memory', whereby one memory is really a screen hiding another. In his celebrated book *Le Syndrôme de Vichy* on the belated reappearance of discussion of the Vichy era in France, Henry Rousso shows how the events in Algeria during the 1950s were frequently understood by French observers in terms of the occupation of France, resistance, and the struggle for national liberation during the war. He sees this as an anachronism whose effect is to 'evacuate' the true 'memorial dimension' of both events. He concludes that 'the Algerian War, seen from the metropolis, is therefore really just a replay of the Franco-French War'.[16] Philip Dine has developed this approach to argue that French fiction and film which deals with the Algerian War of Independence through the lens of the Liberation 'must ultimately be reckoned a reduction, and thus part of a wider occultation of the radical ideological challenge of militant colonial nationalism'.[17] Seen in this light, the constant association by Sartre and others on the Left between colonialism and fascism and between French army torture in Algeria and German torture during the war ('[c]olonialism there, fascism here: one and the same thing'),[18] and allegorical works like Sartre's *Les Séquestrés d'Altona* would then appear to be well-intentioned indictments of racialized violence in the colonial situation but, ultimately, denials of the specificity of the Algerian War, in Dine's words instances of 'the limitations of the francocentric perspective, even in its most apparently sympathetic and committed forms'.[19] Dominic LaCapra's reading of Camus's *La Chute* is also in terms of a screen memory that effaces the specificity of Algeria:

> Camus's turn to the Holocaust in *The Fall* … may function to obscure or displace interest in a more recent series of events: the Algerian war and its troubled aftermath in Franco-Algerian relations … . Indeed the attention paid to earlier events may even serve as a screen to conceal both the significance of recent, and, in certain respects, more pressing events and the limitations or inadequacy of one's response to them.[20]

However, even if we accept that, for some, the Algerian war was understood through the deeper frame of the Second World War, it would be hasty to dismiss the dynamic at play here underlying the work of memory. Freud's screen memory certainly maintains that one memory is a substitute for another more troubling experience but suggests that this only comes about through a complex process of condensation and displacement which connects the initial trauma and its substitute.[21] Substitution is not simply effacement, although it may have that effect; it creates a doubling process by which the displaced object continues to haunt a visible site. Furthermore, the use of the analogy between different events has a very different function when employed by victims of colonial oppression from when it is employed by French metropolitan commentators. It would be rather difficult to suggest, for example, that the indictments of colonialism by Césaire and Fanon are simply screen memories for the fight against fascism. The instrumentalization of memory for narrow political purposes should not blind us to the unconscious aspects of memory work, as the process of condensation and displacement does not necessarily respect national frontiers or political agendas. Beyond the different *prises de position* adopted through the use of the analogical mode lies an imaginary (at once political, historical, cultural and psychic) in which colonial and fascist 'spaces' are overlapping, intertwined and inextricable. Rousso's 'Franco-française' model does not capture the complexities of this other space.

For post-war theorists and political activists like Rousset, Arendt, Césaire, Fanon, Sartre and others, the interconnections between the histories of genocide in Europe and European colonialism seemed to be self-evident (although, as Richard H. King and Dan Stone point out, this 1950s debate in the French metropolis and colonies was not duplicated by left-wing intellectuals in other countries).[22] Today, however, this is not necessarily the case. In those post-war years, the Holocaust was not perceived in the way that we presently understand the event. Many point to the trial of Adolf Eichmann in 1961 as a crucial moment in defining the Jewish victim (rather than the political deportee) as the central focus of Nazi brutality, and the genocide of the Jews as the defining event of the war. The 'Judeocentric' reading of the event – premised on the critique of the failure to specify the genocide of the Jews in the early post-war years by (amongst others) Elie Wiesel in the late 1960s – has been accompanied by the notion of its uniqueness. Today, to relate the Holocaust to other genocides, least of all to other moments of racialized violence, is a fraught issue and is immediately caught up in an invidious comparative and relative framework of understanding. The end of colonialism, the rise of post-colonial voices and the rediscovery of oppressed pasts (together with the breakdown of grand universal narratives of explanation) have, like Jewish memory of the Holocaust, also heralded a particularization and ethnicization of memory which is similarly premised on the rejection of the grand universal narratives of old (seen as a cover for a Eurocentric understanding of history and Man) and a recognition of memories formerly suppressed. The rise of difference has ushered in a new politics of memory which is premised predominantly on the ethno-cultural identity of the group, constitutes a counter-memory to official (national) history, and is often accompanied by a competition for recognition and victim status.[23] The backlash against this invasion of different (private) memories into the (public) sphere formerly occupied by history aims to reinforce the clear distinction between memory and history which is today under threat: memory is concerned with the 'subjective' and 'lived' relationship with the past of the individual or the group; history is concerned with the 'objective', 'scientific' and 'universal' interpretation of the past. Pierre Nora's huge undertaking to read the national past of France through different 'sites' of memory, which resulted in the three volumes entitled *Lieux de mémoire*, is one such project wedded to maintaining the dividing line between memory and history; other intellectuals have rallied to the same cause (for example, Pascal Bruckner, Alain Finkielkraut and the phalanx of republican intellectuals who regard the fragmentation of a single universal history into a plurality of particular memories as part of the breakdown of Enlightenment universalism). However, as the historian Enzo Traverso points out, the distinction between history and memory was always an illusion, for not only is history itself a selective narrative process full of holes (as critics of *Lieux de mémoire* have observed), but

> we [also] need to take into account the influence of history on memory itself, for there is no such thing as a literal, original and non-contaminated memory: memory is always constructed within public space, and therefore subject to collective modes of thought, but also influenced by the established paradigms for representing the past.[24]

The challenge to the dichotomies which held a particular view of history in place may have exposed the Western version of the past but has, simultaneously, led to the present memory wars, as republican commentators argue. In this context of postmodern relativism, comparisons are frequently odious. The famous 'historians' debate' in Germany in the 1980s is a classic case of using the comparative argument to deflect attention from specific crimes against humanity (in this case, the comparison by neo-conservative historians of Soviet and Nazi murders to downplay the specificity of the Nazi crimes). A similar relativizing of the Holocaust for revisionist ends can be seen in the argument used by the lawyer Jacques Vergès in defence of his client, the Nazi Klaus Barbie, in his trial of 1987, by creating an equivalence between Barbie's crimes and those of France as a colonial power in Algeria. The fact that comparisons between crimes against humanity are frequently manipulated for political ends in this way gives support to those who maintain the absolute quality and uniqueness of the Holocaust, and who regard any comparison as, at best, devaluing its status and, at worst, dangerous revisionism.[25] Moreover, the rise of Holocaust Studies and Post-colonial Studies in the American and British academies as separate and distinctive forms of study has tended to nourish this comparative and relative framework for analysis.

However, should the fact that analogies can be exploited for political ends, or that new doxas in the academy have institutionalized a separation between the histories and memories of (supposedly) homogeneous groups, be allowed to place a veto on seeking relations of any sort between different moments of extreme violence? The intertextual connections between a Holocaust and colonial imaginary explored in the works by Daeninckx and Sebbar suggest a more nuanced perspective on this debate. It is not so much a question of parallel histories for the purposes of comparison (and often conflict); it is more a question of overlapping realms of history, memory and imagination so that the historical and psychical base of cultural memory is a genuinely composite affair.

In recent years, several commentators have indeed attempted to challenge the relative and comparative framework and seek a paradigm that neither takes us back to an old universalism nor supports a reductive ethnic particularism; the effort here is rather to seek overlaps and tease out similarities and differences. The historian Omer Bartov relates the industrial killing of the Holocaust not only to nightmare scenes from the fronts in the First World War and to the instrumental rationality of modernity but also to a wider European imagination of hell and destruction.[26] The Ugandan political philosopher Mahmood Mamdani highlights the similarities between the Rwandan and Nazi genocides in terms of a settler–native logic inherited from colonialism.[27] The historian A. Dirk Moses urges us to consider the 'dynamic historical relations' between the Holocaust and other genocides rather than think in terms of a competitive logic that prevails in much discussion, while in his fascinating work *Hitler's Empire* Mark Mazower analyses Hitler's campaigns on the eastern front in terms of an imperial project in Europe.[28] The reappraisal of Hannah Arendt by historians Richard H. King and Dan Stone is in the spirit of exploring 'the "subterranean stream" that linked imperialism in Asia and Africa with the emergence of genocidal, totalitarian regimes in Europe'. They point up the strange paradox whereby Arendt's work can be central to post-colonial studies and genocide studies (especially Holocaust studies) but is rarely the catalyst for bringing these two forms of study together.[29]

In France, Traverso's work takes us back to the tradition of Weber, Arendt and the Frankfurt School (and more recently articulated powerfully by Zygmunt Bauman) to show how the Holocaust must be situated within the wider structures of rationalizing modernity:

> If, at the origin of this crime, there is an intention to annihilate, it also implicates certain fundamental structures of industrial society. Auschwitz was the realization of the fusion of anti-semitism and racism and the prison, the capitalist factory and rationalized bureaucratic administration. To study such an event, we can call on thinkers from Hannah Arendt to Michel Foucault, from Karl Marx to Max Weber. In this sense, the genocide of the Jews constitutes a paradigm of modern barbarism.[30]

While recognizing the potential problems with both the singularity and comparative arguments about the Holocaust, Traverso nevertheless argues cogently for an understanding of the dialectical process at play between different moments of racialized violence:

> Those who deny the singularity of Auschwitz are not all 'revisionists'; those who argue for its singularity are sometimes blind to other sites of violence. On both sides of the argument the event can be instrumentalized for dubious purposes. The best way to preserve the memory of a genocide is neither to deny other genocides, nor to erect a religious cult. Today, the Holocaust has its dogmas – its incomparability and its inexplicability – and also has its formidable and fervent advocates. The recognition of the singularity of Auschwitz only has a meaning if it helps to found a fruitful dialectical understanding of the relationship between a memory of the past and a critique of the present, with the ultimate aim of shedding light on the multiple links between our world and the recent past, since which, in the words of Georges Bataille, the image of Man can no longer be dissociated from that of a gas chamber.[31]

Traverso is aware of the dangers of a universalizing discourse on modernity in which the specificities of different moments of catastrophe are fused into a single narrative; hence his insistence on the dialectical nature of the relationship between each moment of catastrophe and catastrophe in general. As Catherine Coquio and Irving Wohlfarth remark, it is not a question of effacing

> the differences between camps and genocides but [an attempt] to understand them better by putting them in relation to each other. In this way, research on these questions in France can catch up on that undertaken elsewhere, while also suggesting a clear line of enquiry: to seek out the human through the inhuman and the 'universal' through the 'particular', or, to put it another way, 'unity' through 'difference'.[32]

Alain Brossat is also critical of the universalizing discourse on modernity. He highlights the way in which the argument on the uniqueness of the Holocaust reinforces, ironically, the idea of the universality of European history by asserting itself as the 'dominant discourse in memories of catastrophe today'.[33] Brossat's approach is an inverted form of Dine's 'screen memory' argument; instead of the use of the comparative argument to screen out the specificity of colonial violence, Brossat offers us a vision of the use of the specificity argument (the uniqueness of the Holocaust) to screen out the comparison between different forms of disaster.[34] Brossat takes a fairly extreme position with regard to the instrumentalization of the memorialization of the Holocaust (especially in Israel). Yet his argument raises important questions about how we conceptualize extreme forms of violence.

In their different ways, these works challenge reductive and globalizing approaches to history and force us to rethink the complex relationship between specificity and generality. Yet these are predominantly works of historians who are beginning to look across separate conceptual frameworks for understanding colonialism and the Holocaust.[35] They can be of great use to theorists of cultural memory (just as, it is hoped, the work of theorists of cultural memory can influence new historical approaches). Two works that have perhaps done more than most to shift the paradigm of memory studies (and have significantly influenced the present study) are Paul Gilroy's *Between Camps* and Michael Rothberg's *Multidirectional Memory*. Gilroy's work, though not specifically about memory, challenges ethnic essentialism of all kinds and seeks intercultural complicities between apparent opposites, and hybrid formations where others see separate histories. At the end of *The Black Atlantic* he describes how the literature on Jews under conditions of modernity has been central to his own formulation of Black experience, and maintains that 'the complicity of rationality and ethnocidal terror' affecting both Jews and Blacks should be an enriching line of enquiry rather than one that necessarily negates the uniqueness of the Holocaust. He suggests that Jewish and Black histories can be discussed together 'without the development of an absurd and dangerous competition and without lapsing into a relativizing mode that would inevitably be perceived as an insult'.[36] His aptly-named book *Between Camps* pursues this approach further.[37] In this Arendtian enquiry into the connections between a fascist and a colonial imaginary, and the grounding of both within modern race-based thinking, he bemoans the relative absence of approaches of this kind and asks 'Why does it remain so difficult for so many people to accept the knotted intersection of histories produced by this fusion of horizons?'.[38]

Rothberg's book is a hugely significant response to this question. His concept of multidirectional memory is a challenge to what he calls the 'zero-sum struggle for preeminence' involved in competitive memory.[39]

Rejecting the idea that the public space is simply a forum for a battle for recognition by different groups, and that the recognition of one memory is necessarily at the cost of another, Rothberg argues lucidly and convincingly for a notion of memory which is not an already constituted appendage of a group identity but is 'subject to ongoing negotiation, cross-referencing, and borrowing; as productive not privative'.[40] This approach not only allows him to read a variety of post-war French and Francophone works across the fault lines of the Holocaust and colonialism, and between individual and collective memory; it also opens up new ways of understanding how memory emerges into the public sphere (which, like identity, is not pre-given but 'a malleable discursive space'),[41] not at the expense of other memories but profoundly articulated with them. By avoiding the reductive teleologies which competitive memory often entails, Rothberg's approach perceives 'dynamic transfers' between different spaces and times,[42] solidarities across lines of ethno-cultural division, and new possibilities for the negotiation of justice. It opens up a different way of perceiving the relationship between memory and the acting out/working through of trauma: subjects are not simply victims burdened with the melancholic repetition of a particular traumatic moment in the past but actively work through the interconnections between that moment and others.

Not only do I endorse Rothberg's important intervention in the political and ethical stakes of cultural memory; I also echo his nuanced reading of Freud's screen memory. Rothberg rightly emphasizes the fact that the substitutions and displacements that operate to produce a screen memory do not simply hide a more disturbing truth (in instrumentalist fashion) which the conscious mind has repressed; it links this 'truth' with its substitutions in a complex and dynamic process of conscious and unconscious work: 'While screen memory might be understood as involving a conflict of memories, it ultimately more closely resembles a remapping of memory in which links between memories are formed and then redistributed between the conscious and the unconscious.'[43] This will be an important feature of my own analyses of works that deal with overlapping layers of meaning. The brief introductions to the works by Emmanuel, Daeninckx and Sebbar highlight the complex interconnections between the visible and the hidden, the 'deep' truth and the substitute, and hence the fluid relationship between conscious and unconscious processes. This is not the same as treating the screen simply as a cover for political ends.[44]

The memory wars of recent years are the consequence of an invidious politicization of memory in the age of (often) crude cultural differences. However, critics of the reductive link between memory and cultural identity point us in the direction of a different politics of transversal, transnational and transcultural solidarities. The analyses in this book are in this spirit of reappraising the connections between memory, cultural identity and politics today. Drawing on a number of the approaches outlined above, I will propose that memory fundamentally works according to a principle of transversal connections across time and space which disrupt essentialist readings of cultural identity and ethnic and national belonging. But I will also argue that memory is always 'staged' in a particular way so that one cannot talk of what it records without also talking about how it records. I will suggest that what distinguishes the notion of palimpsestic memory from other non-essentialist accounts of memory is a figurative 'staging' of memory by which memory traces overlap, intersect and are transformed – what I will call a 'poetics of memory'. The focus on the figure of the palimpsest reveals how time and space are reconfigured through a ceaseless process of straddling and superimposition of elements, and condensation and displacement of meaning. LaCapra asks, 'Does art itself have a special responsibility with respect to traumatic events that remain invested with value and emotion?'.[45] My response to that question is that the poetics of memory with regard to traumatic events has a crucial role in determining 'the shapes of memory' (to use Geoffrey Hartman's phrase) and is fundamental to any renewal of the politics of memory today. Palimpsestic memory is therefore a politics of memory founded on a poetics of memory.

The Poetics of Memory

In *Le Temps retrouvé*, the last volume of Marcel Proust's *A la recherche du temps perdu*, Proust's narrator, Marcel, is in the courtyard of the grand *hôtel* of the Duchesse de Guermantes in Paris when, in order to avoid a carriage entering the courtyard, he stumbles and finds himself standing on two uneven paving stones. At that moment he is suddenly overwhelmed by an intense sensation which springs from his body as it senses being in a similar posture at another time. Almost at once he realizes when and where this was:

> it was Venice, of which my efforts to describe it and the supposed snapshots taken by my memory had never told me anything, but which the sensation which I had once experienced as I stood upon two uneven stones in the baptistery of St Mark's had, recurring a moment ago, restored to me complete with all the other sensations linked on that day to that particular sensation, all of which had been waiting in their place – from which with imperious suddenness a chance happening had caused them to emerge – in the series of forgotten days.[46]

The stumble in the courtyard allows the buried memory to come flooding back involuntarily. Suddenly, and by pure chance, spatial and temporal distinctions dissolve as Paris merges with Venice and the present merges with the past. This is like the other famous episodes in the book when a remembered experience from the past is triggered by a similar experience in the present: the chink of a spoon against a plate (which immediately follows the incident with the uneven paving stones), the roughness of a napkin and, of course, the most famous of them all, the taste of the *madeleine* dipped in tea (except that, this final time, Marcel is intent on discovering the exact nature of this 'dazzling and indistinct vision [which made] death a matter of indifference to me').[47]

These *moments bienheureux* in Proust, which signal the possibility of rediscovering lost time, have of course generated vast amounts of critical commentary. My intention is not to add to this body of work but to draw out three related points concerning the poetics of memory which will be germane to my argument. The first is that we learn that the present contains traces of the past and that these traces could be anywhere – in everyday objects, in a piece of music, in a sound, in a taste – because they are, in fact, in ourselves. Habit, as Samuel Beckett wrote of Proust, has dulled the senses and normalized the world but, if we are lucky enough to stumble upon the traces of our past, these objects will act as triggers to release us from the constraints of clock time and social spacing, from our habitual apprehension of reality and our selves, and re-enchant the world.[48] Involuntary memory (indeed art in general) has the power to transform our habitual reality into something more profound, involving body and mind, something more complex, ambiguous and intangible, by opening up the invisible elsewhere which haunts the present. The second point, closely linked to the first, is that the activation of this elsewhere through memory, which converts the blandness of the everyday into something beyond 'common sense', is a performative and transformative act in the present. The lesson that Rothberg draws from Richard Terdiman's notion of memory as 'the past made present' is that 'memory is a contemporary phenomenon, something that, while concerned with the past, happens in the present'.[49]

The third and final point concerns the mechanism, or figure, itself for effecting this transformation of and in the present. The technique which most closely captures the experience – drawing together two separate elements through a perceived similarity – is that of metaphor, perhaps the quintessential trope. The true power of metaphor is not that it simply substitutes one thing for another (as in the crude understanding of the screen memory) but that, by drawing together two distinct elements through a perceived similarity, it connects them (or, to use Baudelaire's term, creates 'correspondences' between them) and, in the process, reinvents both. The 'staging' of memory in Proust works fundamentally through the mechanism of metaphor. Metaphor is a creative and transformative process in that it unsettles or defamiliarizes habitual meanings, connects the most unlikely elements and reshapes our perceptions. In relation to memory, metaphor allows a past sensation, and, as Proust says, all its metonymic associations, to flood into the present, creating new relationships between past and present and, hence, forcing us to rethink both. Metaphor does not simply collapse one element into the other so that they become the same; nor does it leave both elements intact and separate. Its beauty lies in the fact that it creates unstable correspondences by means of similarity and difference.

Metaphor becomes the tool *par excellence* for the journeys in space, time and identity explored in modernism. Metaphor contains within it the classic modernist devices of juxtaposition, relationality and *simultanéisme* which could pierce the accumulating layers of rationalization of modernity and open up the (irrational) buried world of desire and fear. It resembles the process of condensation which (with displacement) Freud located at the heart of dream-work and, indeed, the unconscious itself. In the heyday of structuralist poetics, when Jacques Lacan famously stated that the unconscious is structured like a language, the seminal work by the Czech linguist Roman Jakobson on aphasia was often used as evidence that Freud's condensation and displacement were equivalent to the tropes of metaphor and metonymy respectively, the former conflating different elements through similarity (which Jakobson equated with poetry) and the latter displacing meaning from one element to another through contiguity (which Jakobson equated with prose).[50] However, Proust's description of involuntary memory as the emergence of a chain of contiguous associations which accompany the initial shock of similarity across space and time suggests that metonymy is not distinct from but part of the work of metaphor, or rather that the two processes are more tightly imbricated than a rigid structural analysis sometimes foresaw.

A different though profoundly related figure also employed by Freud which perhaps captures more precisely the tight imbrication of metaphor and metonymy, and condensation and displacement, involved in the work of memory is that of the palimpsest. Freud develops the idea of memory as palimpsest in his 'A Note upon the "Mystic Writing-pad"' which was published in 1925. In this brief paper Freud describes how the children's writing toy captures the dual mechanism of memory – infinite reception and permanent retention of information. Writing on paper or a slate has the disadvantage of either having a limited capacity for reception (notes on paper) or no capacity for permanent retention (the slate must be wiped clean to make way for new information). Freud observes, therefore, that 'an unlimited receptive capacity and a retention of permanent traces seem to be mutually exclusive properties in the apparatus which we use as substitutes for our memory: either the receptive surface must be renewed or the note must be destroyed'.[51] The mystic writing pad, however, is able to perform both these functions: inscriptions made on the thin sheet of celluloid covering which forms the top part of the pad can be erased by lifting the sheet, thus leaving the sheet free for the recording of new inscriptions, but their traces are nevertheless preserved as marks left on the wax surface below. However imperfect as a metaphor, the writing pad thus provided Freud with a simple way of confirming his thoughts on perception and memory that he first formulated as long ago as 1900 with the publication of *The Interpretation of Dreams*: although the psyche does not retain, at a surface level, sense impressions received from the outside world, and is therefore able to receive an infinite number of fresh impressions, at a deeper level these impressions have left their mark – as unconscious memory.

Jacques Derrida would later criticize what he perceived as the rather static, and even essentialist, model proposed by Freud (which I will discuss in chapter 6). However, the principle of the superimposition of different traces to condense surface and depth, present and past, and the visible and the invisible remains a powerful way of envisaging the work of memory.[52] It implies a psychic rearrangement of space and time which subverts the authority of the rationalizing categories of modernity. Surrealism exploited the Freudian principle of the palimpsest to construct new composite images which transformed the normalized everyday into an uncanny blend of the familiar and the strange, the here and the elsewhere, and the conscious and the unconscious. The formulations by both Rousset and Arendt in the post-war period (and those of Jean Cayrol, as we shall see) owe much to the influence of surrealist distortions of the familiar during their formative years in France in the 1930s. Their search for a new language which could defamiliarize everyday life was already at hand.

It was, of course, Walter Benjamin who brought together a Proustian concept of involuntary memory, the Baudelairean and surrealist tradition of the defamiliarization of the everyday in the figure of the *flâneur*, and Freud's description of memory-traces left in the unconscious to theorize the conjoining of personal (psychic) and historical memory. In his monumental *Arcades Project* on Paris and the nineteenth century Benjamin writes the following of the *flâneur*:

> For him, every street is precipitous. It leads downward – if not to the mythical Mothers, then into a past that can be all the more spellbinding because it is not his own, not private. Nevertheless, it always remains the time of a childhood. But why that of the life he has lived? In the asphalt over which he passes, his steps awaken a surprising resonance. The gaslight that streams down on the paving stones throws an equivocal light on this double ground.[53]

The 'double ground' that Benjamin talks of here is constituted by the physical footsteps in the city street and the mental journey they trigger (in involuntary fashion through shock) into the past; or, indeed, the individual *and* collective journey in time that the *flâneur* undergoes through chance encounter in the city. Benjamin's description of the gaslight that 'throws an equivocal light' is evocative of the Proustian stumble in the courtyard of the grand *hôtel* of the Duchesse de Guermantes, for the firm ground is suddenly withdrawn from beneath the feet of the *flâneur* and he (for the *flâneur* is indeed an untheorized 'he')[54] finds himself in an ambivalent state composed of a complex layering of consciousness (as the unconscious flows in to the conscious mind). In another memorable passage from *The Arcades Project*, Benjamin calls this moment an 'image', a 'constellation' or a 'critical point':

> It is not that what is past casts its light on what is present, or what is present its light on what is past; rather, image is that wherein what has been comes together in a flash with the now to form a constellation. In other words: image is dialectics at a standstill. For while the relation of the present to the past is purely temporal, the relation of what-has-been to the now is dialectical: not temporal in nature but figural 'bildlich'. Only dialectical images are genuinely historical – that is, not archaic – images. The image that is read – which is to say, the image in the now of its recognizability – bears to the highest degree the imprint of the perilous critical moment on which all reading is founded.[55]

Like the Freudian palimpsest which it clearly resembles, Benjamin's 'image' or 'constellation' is one of the most profound descriptions of this overlapping of spatio-temporal sites in which personal and collective memory and the conscious and unconscious collide.[56] Like the palimpsest, the image/constellation (or 'idea', as Benjamin calls it elsewhere) brings together past and present not in a teleological way but through a superimposition of different traces in the same space. First, this image is a weaving together of these traces (as Benjamin says, the central element of recollection in Proust is the way 'in which memory issues strict weaving regulations').[57] This process draws together and creates correspondences between different elements so that the 'oppositions' between the fragment and the totality, past and present, here and elsewhere, and movement and stasis are not in fact oppositions but in permanent tension, or rather that one can be seen within the other, just as history must be made visible (recognizable) in the present moment.[58]

Second, Benjamin spatializes time so that dialectical movement is as if held in the instant. Montage therefore becomes another figure which can capture this weaving together of elements in the same space. Montage allows Benjamin to make the case for showing the dialectical movement of history in visible form:

> A central problem of historical materialism that ought to be seen in the end: Must the Marxist understanding of history necessarily be acquired at the expense of the perceptibility of history? Or: in what way is it possible to conjoin a heightened graphicness "Anschaulichkeit" to the realization of the Marxist method? The first stage in this undertaking will be to carry over the principle of montage into history. That is, to assemble large-scale constructions out of the smallest and most precisely cut components. Indeed, to discover in the analysis of the small individual moment the crystal of the total event. And, therefore, to break with vulgar historical naturalism. To grasp the construction of history as such.[59]

By spatializing the dialectic, montage transforms a 'vulgar historical naturalism' into a poetic materialism. In her introduction to Benjamin's collection of essays *Illuminations*, Arendt notes that Adorno and Horkheimer considered Benjamin 'undialectic' and that Adorno's perception of 'the static element in Benjamin' was a clear sign of this.[60] Referring both to Benjamin's figure of the *flâneur* and to his discussion (in his ninth thesis on the philosophy of history) of the angel of history in Paul Klee's painting 'Angelus Novus', Arendt concurs with Adorno's view that Benjamin's propositions show no signs of dialectical thinking. What Adorno points to instead in Benjamin's thought is a metaphorical imagination. However, as I suggest above, the metaphorical imagination does not so much abandon dialectical thinking as convert it from its linear, syntagmatic, and teleological axis to its vertical, paradigmatic axis, so that events are 'piled up' one on the other rather than ordered in a chain. This is how the angel of history perceives the past: 'Where we perceive a chain of events, he sees one single catastrophe which keeps piling wreckage upon wreckage and hurls it in front of his feet'.[61]

Arendt goes on to make the distinction, in Benjamin's work, between metaphor and allegory.[62] Yet this, too, seems an odd reading of Benjamin's work, for Benjamin's fascination with Baudelaire and modern art is, to a large extent, premised on Baudelaire's exploration of the allegorical mode ('Baudelaire's genius, which is nourished on melancholy, is an allegorical genius').[63] Rather than perceiving an opposition between metaphor and allegory, Benjamin saw their proximity in that both operate on the paradigmatic, spatial axis by which one thing is seen in terms of another. In an essay on allegory in postmodern art, Craig Owens brings together a number of the features of the poetics of memory discussed above:

> [A]llegory superinduces a vertical or paradigmatic reading of correspondences upon a horizontal or syntagmatic chain of events ... . This projection of structure as sequence recalls the fact that, in rhetoric, allegory is traditionally defined as a single metaphor introduced in continuous series. If this definition is recast in structuralist terms, then allegory is revealed to be the projection of the metaphoric axis of language onto its metonymic dimension. Roman Jakobson defined this projection of metaphor onto metonymy as the "poetic function," and he went on to associate metaphor with poetry and romanticism, and metonymy with prose and realism. Allegory, however, implicates both metaphor and metonymy.[64]

We have already noted how Jakobson's discussion of metaphor and metonymy and the structuralist mapping of these tropes onto Freud's condensation and displacement respectively were, perhaps, a rather hasty compartmentalization of terms and processes that may be more tightly imbricated. This would suggest that it is not only allegory that 'implicates *both* metaphor and metonymy', as Owens argues, but that metaphor itself is a hybrid term which involves a metonymic input as part of its activity.

Be that as it may, Owens is surely right when he describes allegory as 'a vertical or paradigmatic reading of correspondences upon a horizontal or syntagmatic chain of events'. Indeed, it is precisely this paradigmatic reading which is at play in all the figures discussed here and that we see so clearly in the staging of memory in the texts by Emmanuel, Daeninckx and Sebbar.

In his essay, Owens observes that '[i]n allegorical structure ... one text is *read through* another, however fragmentary, intermittent, or chaotic their relationship may be; the paradigm for the allegorical work is thus the palimpsest'.[65] Andreas Huyssen talks of 'urban palimpsests' in his work on memory and describes contemporary Berlin in a spirit clearly informed by the Baudelairean and Benjaminian perception of city space:

> What is now emerging is the more intriguing notion of Berlin as palimpsest, a disparate city-text that is being rewritten while previous text is preserved, traces are restored, erasures documented, all of it resulting in a complex web of historical markers that point to the continuing heterogeneous life of a vital city that is as ambivalent of its built past as it is of its urban future.[66]

Huyssen champions the palimpsestic idea of the city as an open, ambivalent and diverse space in preference to the city with 'a physical and psychological center'.[67] This suggests that the sedimentation of different layers of meaning in the city is not simply the endless repetition of the same in a reductive harmonization of difference but a dynamic interplay 'resulting in a complex web'. Thus, the spatialization of a dialectical process, at play in all the figures mentioned above, reformulates time and history by connecting diverse elements to form a dynamic, unstable, multivalent and ambivalent 'image'.

It is my contention in this book that the poetics of palimpsestic memory can be the basis of a new politics of memory. Palimpsestic memory brings to the politics of memory the challenging idea that memory does not function according to the linear trajectory of a particular ethno-cultural group and lead inexorably to the distinction (and often competition) between different groups; it functions, instead, according to a complex process of interconnection, interaction, substitution and displacement of memory traces in which the particular and the universal, and memory and history, are inextricably held in an anxious relationship. Rather than see them as opposites, leaving us with a choice of either 'objective' (universal) history or 'personal' (relative) memory, the ambivalent space of the palimpsest, which overlays individual and collective meanings, gives us a different way of understanding this relationship.

I will argue that artistic works may be more suited than historical or sociological method to making visible the complex interaction of times and sites at play in memory, as a fundamental feature of imaginative (poetic) works is to overlay meaning in intertextual space and blur the frontiers between the conscious and the unconscious, the present and the past, and the personal and the collective. Correspondences, substitutions and transformations – the very substance of the literary imagination – can open up an alternative history (though one announced by the post-war generation of theorists of modern forms of violence) which challenges the compartmentalized narratives that we habitually receive.

Interconnecting Memories

The complexities of memory have long been the subject of a number of works by writers, filmmakers and other creative artists in the post-war Francophone world, yet their works are not always received from this point of view. A number of the readings which follow will attempt to rediscover interconnected memories when more reductive versions are sometimes the orthodoxy. So, for example, Alain Resnais's classic 1955 film on the concentration camps *Nuit et brouillard*, that I discuss in the following chapter, is both an evocation of the radical nature of the horror of the camps and, as Resnais himself observed, an allegory for the war in Algeria. In the same year, *Les Boucs* by the Moroccan writer Driss Chraibi, one of the first post-war novels treating the North African immigrant experience in France, places anti-Arab racism alongside the horrors of the war (in the figure of Isabelle).[68] It is true that these works were part of the same climate in which Arendt, Fanon and Sartre were writing. But even when theory had turned another way in the 1960s, and the interconnections between a fascist and colonial imaginary were giving way to more reductive ethno-cultural versions of memory, cultural practitioners continued to evoke 'the knotted intersection of histories' sought by Gilroy. In her book on the reordering of French culture in the 1960s, *Fast Cars, Clean Bodies*, Kristin Ross uncovers one of these histories (that of decolonization) at the heart of post-war modernization.[69] Ross demonstrates convincingly how new consumerism and the privatization of desire in metropolitan France can only be sensibly understood in the light of withdrawal from Empire and post-war immigration. Two of the works from the period that Ross considers at some length, Simone de Beauvoir's *Les Belles images* and Georges Perec's *Les Choses*, are reread to great effect through this prism. Yet one could argue that a post-Holocaust narrative is also visible in these works, establishing an even more intricate set of connections traversing the French and Francophone landscape.

In *Les Belles images*, for example, one of the key moments in a repressed past which returns to haunt the present of the central character Laurence is the existence of the concentration camps. This knowledge of trauma will return through the figure of Brigitte, the Jewish friend of Laurence's daughter Catherine, whose absent mother and grandparents in Israel suggest a history of violence, death, exile and the camps.[70] Like the suppressed accounts of Algeria which will flicker spasmodically through Laurence's anaesthetized consciousness, this moment acts as another memory of the dark and violent underside to new consumerism's glossy surface. As for *Les Choses*, there is no explicit mention of anything to do with Jews or the Holocaust in the text. Yet a post-Holocaust reading of the novel could allow us to understand Jérôme and Sylvie not simply as the products of new consumer society and decolonization but also as rootless individuals in the wake of the destruction of Jewish tradition brought about by the Holocaust. Claude Burgelin's reading of *Les Choses* along these lines, which echoes Alain Finkielkraut's description of the post-Holocaust 'imaginary Jew' ('juif imaginaire'), offers us a text in which the unconscious subtext of French post-war modernization is determined by the aftermath of the Holocaust as much as by decolonization.[71]

Didier Daeninckx's *Meurtres pour mémoire* is, as we have observed, more explicit in exploring the linked themes of Holocaust and empire. In a different vein, François Maspero's journey through the suburbs of Paris in *Les Passagers du Roissy-Express* (1990) also reveals interconnected histories of violence beneath the surface of contemporary life. In the section dealing with Drancy (chapter 7), overlapping layers of histories and memories emerge in the course of the narrative (the Holocaust, post-war immigration from the former colonies, utopian social housing projects of the 1960s, and so on) which challenge the compartmentalization of French metropolitan history, colonial history and the history of European genocide. In giving a material existence to connections that are, at first glance, invisible (especially to those for whom the suburbs are simply a 'shapeless mass'),[72] Maspero's real and imaginative journey across Paris constitutes a significant rewriting of the French and Francophone *patrimoine*. Why should immigrants from Africa today living in the Cité de la Muette housing estate in Drancy know of the fate of Jews during the Second World War, when the estate was a transit camp for deportation to the death camps of Eastern Europe, unless the connections are rendered visible?[73]

By retrieving a largely repressed past in post-war France and formerly colonized Francophone countries, these works (and others to be analysed in this study) reveal a complex landscape of extreme and racialized violence in which traces of different histories intertwine. My purpose in this book is not simply to seek out narratives which deal with colonialism and the Holocaust together. It is rather an attempt to unearth an overlapping vocabulary, lexicon, imagery, aesthetic and, ultimately, history shared by representations of colonialism and the Holocaust. A hybrid iconography, an intertextual web and a palimpsestic *modus operandi* give us a different paradigm for understanding memory, one to which the post-war theorists of extreme violence pointed the way and that the rise of more reductive (and sometimes essentialist) concepts of cultural difference has tended to obscure. However, if memory is to be renewed in a less compartmentalized way, to allow the perception of solidarities across national and ethno-cultural borders, we need to consider the stakes of such a proposition in a transnational and postmodern age.

Notes

1. David Rousset, *L'Univers concentrationnaire* (Minuit, 1965 [1946]), p. 181 / *The Other Kingdom*, trans. Ramon Guthrie (New York: Reynal and Hitchcock, 1947), p. 168.
2. 'il serait facile de montrer que les traits les plus caractéristiques et de la mentalité S.S. et de soubassements sociaux se retrouvent dans bien d'autres secteurs de la société mondiale … . Ce serait une duperie, et criminelle, que de prétendre qu'il est impossible aux autres peuples de faire une expérience analogue pour des raisons d'opposition de nature. L'Allemagne a interprété avec l'originalité propre à son histoire la crise qui l'a conduite à l'univers concentrationnaire. Mais l'existence et le mécanisme de cette crise tiennent aux fondements économiques et sociaux du capitalisme et de l'impérialisme. Sous une figuration nouvelle, des effets analogues peuvent demain encore apparaître. Il s'agit, en conséquence, d'une bataille très précise à mener. Le bilan concentrationnaire est à cet égard un merveilleux arsenal de guerre', Rousset, *L'Univers concentrationnaire*, pp. 186–187 / *The Other Kingdom*, p. 173.
3. 'Cette disproportion entre l'expérience que nous avons vécue et le récit qu'il était possible d'en faire', Robert Antelme, *L'Espèce humaine* (Gallimard, 1957 [1947]), p. 9 / *The Human Race*, trans. Jeffrey Haight and Annie Mahler (Marlboro, Vermont: The Marlboro Press, 1992), p. 3. Both Rousset and Antelme make the distinction between what can be communicated to others by survivors and what they alone can feel in their bones. Rousset says '[n]ormal men do not know that everything is possible. Even if the evidence forces their intelligence to admit it, their muscles do not believe it. The concentrationees do know' ('Les hommes normaux ne savent pas que tout est possible. Même si les témoignages forcent leur intelligence à admettre, leurs muscles ne croient pas. Les concentrationnaires savent'), *L'Univers concentrationnaire*, p. 181 / *The Other Kingdom*, p. 168. Antelme expresses the same sentiment as follows: 'it seemed impossible to us to bridge the gap between the words at our disposal and this experience which, in the case of most of us, we were still experiencing in our bodies' ('il nous paraissait impossible de combler la distance que nous découvrions entre le langage dont nous disposions et cette expérience que, pour la plupart, nous étions encore en train de poursuivre dans notre corps'), *L'Espèce humaine*, p. 9 / *The Human Race* (trans. modified), p. 3.
4. 'c'est un univers à part, totalement clos, étrange royaume d'une fatalité singulière' (Rousset, *L'Univers concentrationnaire*, p. 36 / *The Other Kingdom*, p. 41); 'le marché des esclaves', 'Kapos et *Vorarbeiter*, des négriers' (Rousset, *L'Univers concentrationnaire*, p. 33 / *The Other Kingdom*, pp. 38–39). See also the title to chapter 9, 'Slaves Give Only Their Bodies' / 'Les esclaves ne donnent que leur corps' (Rousset, *L'Univers concentrationnaire*, p. 81 / *The Other Kingdom*, p. 81).
5. Hannah Arendt, *The Origins of Totalitarianism* (London: Allen and Unwin, 1967), p. 568.
6. *The Origins of Totalitarianism*, p. 566. Giorgio Agamben pursues an Arendtian logic in *Homo Sacer*: 'Historians debate whether the first camps to appear were the *campos de concentraciones* created by the Spanish in Cuba in 1896 to suppress the popular insurrection of the colony, or the "concentration camps" into which the English herded the Boers toward the start of the century. What matters here is that in both cases, a state of emergency linked to a colonial war is extended to an entire civil population. The camps are thus born not out of ordinary law … but out of a state of exception and

martial law', *Homo Sacer: Sovereign Power and Bare Life* (Stanford: Stanford University Press, 1998 [1995]), pp. 166–167.

7. Catherine Coquio, 'Parler au camp, parler des camps: Hurbinek à Babel' in Catherine Coquio (ed.), *Parler des camps, penser les génocides* (Albin Michel/Idées, 1999), p. 611.

8. Max Horkheimer and Theodor Adorno, *Dialectic of Enlightenment* (New York: Continuum, 2001 [1944]), pp. 171 and 183.

9. '[Ce] n'est pas *le crime* en soi, *le crime contre l'homme*, ce n'est pas *l'humiliation de l'homme en soi*, c'est l'humiliation de l'homme blanc, et d'avoir appliqué à l'Europe des procédés colonialistes dont ne relevaient jusqu'ici que les arabes d'Algérie, les coolies de l'Inde et les nègres d'Afrique', Aimé Césaire, *Discours sur le colonialisme* (Présence Africaine, 2004 [1955]), p. 14 / *Discourse on Colonialism*, trans. Joan Pinkham (New York: Monthly Review Press, 2000 [1972]), p. 36.

10. 'l'apparition de "colonies européennes", c'est-à-dire l'institution d'un régime colonial en pleine terre d'Europe', Frantz Fanon, 'Racisme et culture' in *Pour la révolution africaine: Écrits politiques* (La Découverte, 2001 [1956]), p. 40 / 'Racism and Culture' in *Toward the African Revolution*, trans. Haakon Chevalier (New York: Grove Press, 1967), p. 33. See also similar statements in 'Unité et solidarité effective sont les conditions de la libération africaine', in *Pour la révolution africaine: Écrits politiques* (La Découverte, 2001 [1956]), p. 198 and *Les Damnés de la terre* (Gallimard/Folio, 1991 [1961]), p. 135.

11. See *Portrait du colonisé* (Gallimard, 1957) and *Portrait d'un juif* (Gallimard, 1962). Fanon's *Peau noire masques blancs* will be discussed in more detail in chapter 3.

12. 'en privilégiant le souci pour autrui [Rousset] choisit de transformer l'expérience passée en raison d'agir dans le présent, à l'intérieur d'une situation nouvelle dont il n'est pas un acteur, qu'il ne connaît que par analogie ou de l'extérieur', Tzvetan Todorov, *Mémoire du mal, tentation du bien: Enquête sur le siècle* (Robert Laffont, 2000), p. 165.

13. Tzvetan Todorov, *Les Abus de la mémoire* (Arléa, 2004), pp. 46–49.

14. Maurice Blanchot, 'Les Justes', *L'Observateur* (20 July 1950), reprinted in Jean Cayrol, *Jean Cayrol: Œuvre lazaréenne* (Seuil, 2007), pp. 759–760.

15. In their excellent scholarly study of the events surrounding 17 October 1961 in Paris, James House and Neil Macmaster make the following observation: 'First, historians have failed to note that the techniques deployed by the Vichy regime to locate and identify the tens of thousands of Jews who could conceal themselves by merging into the vast, anonymous crowds of the towns and cities were similar to the methods later used to track Algerian nationalists and to locate members of the minority community embedded in the total French population. Both systems of control shared the following features: the creation of specialized intelligence agencies for the policing of target groups (Jews, Algerians); the total census of minority populations; elaborate card-index files (*fichiers*) to identify and locate individuals; mass round-up operations involving street-level stop-and-search checks or the surrounding and isolation of urban sectors, with house-to-house searches; special police intervention units; mass holding centres and camps for those rounded up, often with screening/identification units (*triage*); exceptional and discriminatory legislation aimed to identify and detain minorities (night curfew, special identity cards, administrative arrest).

Second, the convergence between the methods of policing Jews and Algerians was more than superficial: in many instances we find senior police officers or administrators, who during the course of their career were involved in both forms of repression, drawing on a shared body of practices. A key role was played by the Interior Ministry which constantly circulated top officials between the Maghreb and metropolitan France. In Bordeaux, Papon was closely associated with a circle of senior administrators who had significant past connections with Algeria', *Paris 1961: Algerians, State Terror and Memory* (Oxford: Oxford University Press, 2006), p. 34.

16. 'la guerre d'Algérie, observée en métropole, est donc bien un rejeu de la guerre franco-française', Henry Rousso, *Le Syndrôme de Vichy (1944–198...)* (Seuil, 1987), pp. 87 and 94 respectively. Elsewhere Rousso, with Eric Conan, has described the obsessive fascination with the Second World War as itself a screen memory effacing present and future concerns: 'But today does the duty of memory give us the right to teach history as a perpetual trial of the war generation, especially as, for our generation, the obsession with the past – more specifically this particular past – can be simply a substitute for the pressing problems of the present, or, worse still, a refusal of the future?' ('Mais aujourd'hui le devoir de mémoire donne-t-il le droit d'instruire un procès perpétuel à la génération de la guerre ? D'autant que, pour la nôtre, l'obsession du passé, de ce passé-là, n'est qu'un substitut aux urgences du présent. Ou, pis encore, un refus de l'avenir.'), *Vichy: Un Passé qui ne passe pas* (Fayard, 1994), p. 286. For a wider discussion of the response of French intellectuals to the Algerian War, see Hervé Hamon and Patrick Rotman, *Les Porteurs de valises: La Résistance française à la guerre d'Algérie* (Seuil, 1982), and Jean-Pierre Rioux and Jean-François Sirinelli (eds), *La Guerre d'Algérie et les intellectuels français* (Brussels: Éditions Complexe, 1991).

17. Philip Dine, 'The Inescapable Allusion: The Occupation and the Resistance in French Fiction and Film of the Algerian War' in H.R. Kedward and Nancy Wood (eds), *The Liberation of France: Image and Event* (Oxford: Berg, 1995), p. 280. Dine sets out his argument in the following way: '[I]n many cases we shall encounter what we might, with apologies to Henry Rousso and with obvious reference to Camus's *La Peste* (1947), call "the Oran syndrome", in which Algeria becomes for French writers and film-makers a mere backdrop for the reliving of the Second World War, and, in many cases, for settling its old scores. For in the Algerian context, one war may all too easily hide another. More than this, in the imagined Algeria of French fiction and film, one liberation from foreign occupation may actually serve to deny another' (pp. 269–270). Dine develops this argument by suggesting that associations made between colonial violence and fascist violence are instances of 'the limitations of the francocentric perspective, even in its most apparently sympathetic and committed forms' (p. 280).

18. 'Colonialisme là-bas, fascisme ici : une seule et même chose', Jean-Paul Sartre, *Situations, V: Colonialisme et néo-colonialisme* (Gallimard, 1964), p. 163. In his famous book *La Question* on being tortured in Algeria, Henri Alleg states, '[e]ach blow brutalized me further but, at the same time, strengthened my conviction not to give in to these brutes who prided themselves on emulating the Gestapo' ('Chaque coup m'abrutissait davantage mais en même temps me raffermissait dans ma décision : ne pas céder à ces brutes qui se flattaient d'être les émules de la Gestapo'), *La Question* (Minuit, 1961), p. 36.

19. Dine, 'The Inescapable Allusion', p. 280.

20. Dominic LaCapra, *History and Memory after Auschwitz* (Ithaca and London: Cornell University Press, 1998), pp. 73–74. In this essay on *La Chute*, LaCapra does, however, draw attention to Steven Ungar's reading of the text, which approaches the question of 'screen memory' in a slightly more nuanced way: 'The true objective of Clamence's elaborate confession was disclosure, not of the incident on the Pont Royal, but of the incident in the detention camp in North Africa that he let slip at the beginning of the novel's last chapter when he referred with understatement to the malaria he thought he had first caught at the time he was pope ...[. A]cts of exclusion and violence perpetrated under Vichy toward internal minorities brought home to France practices that had been instituted abroad through colonial rule', p. 82, quoted from Steven Ungar, *Scandal and Aftereffect: Blanchot and France since 1930* (Minneapolis: University of Minnesota Press, 1995).

21. 'Through the processes, already familiar to you, of condensation and more specifically of displacement, what is important is replaced in memory by something else which

appears unimportant. For this reason I have called these childhood memories "screen memories", and with a thorough analysis everything that has been forgotten can be extracted from them', Sigmund Freud, *Introductory Lectures on Psychoanalysis*, vol. 1 (Harmondsworth: Penguin, 1978), p. 237.

22. Richard H. King and Dan Stone, 'Introduction' in Richard H. King and Dan Stone (eds), *Hannah Arendt and the Uses of History: Imperialism, Nation, Race and Genocide* (Oxford and New York: Berghahn, 2007), p. 4.

23. The French historian Annette Wieviorka characterizes this post-war development as one that leads from an indifference to Jewish testimony to the genocide in the immediate post-war period to the contemporary era in which Jewish testimony has become the model for testimonies by other victims of extreme violence (*L'Ère du témoin* (Plon, 1998)). For a comprehensive account of how this development is also an evolution towards a politics of competitive memory, see Jean-Michel Chaumont, *La Concurrence des victimes: Génocide, identité, reconnaissance* (La Découverte, 1997) and Olivier Wieviorka, *La Mémoire désunie: Le Souvenir politique des années sombres, de la Libération à nos jours* (Seuil, 2010).

24. 'il faudrait prendre en compte l'influence de l'histoire sur la mémoire elle-même, car il n'y a pas de mémoire littérale, originaire et non contaminée : les souvenirs sont constamment élaborés par une mémoire inscrite au sein de l'espace public, soumis aux modes de penser collectifs mais aussi influencés par les paradigmes savants de la représentation du passé', Enzo Traverso, *Le Passé, modes d'emploi: Histoire, mémoire, politique* (La Fabrique, 2005), p. 29. For excellent analyses of the anxious relationship between history and memory in relation to traumatic experience, see (amongst others) Saul Friedlander (ed.), *Probing the Limits of Representation: Nazism and the 'Final Solution'* (Cambridge, Mass.: Harvard University Press, 1992); Geoffrey Hartman (ed.), *Holocaust Remembrance: The Shapes of Memory* (Oxford: Blackwell, 1994); and LaCapra, *History and Memory after Auschwitz*.

25. See for example Richard Golsan's discussion of the trial of Maurice Papon for crimes against humanity in 1997–1998. Referring to the final scene in Daeninckx's *Meurtres pour mémoire*, he also highlights the dangers of confusing distinct historical periods: 'the crucial issue was ... whether it was possible to return to a precise point in the past and interpret and judge it without reference to subsequent events – subsequent *pasts* – in which the accused was involved. ... To ask the same question metaphorically, as does Didier Daeninckx in *Meurtres pour mémoire*, does it require an Algerian worker to peel away the layers of the past encrusted on the metro walls to put us in the presence, once again, of the horrors of Nazi hegemony? What this perspective suggests, in many respects, is a dangerous parallel between the implementation of the Final Solution in France and the excesses of *la guerre sans nom*', *Vichy's Afterlife: History and Counterhistory in Postwar France* (Lincoln: University of Nebraska Press, 2000), p. 177. However, as Todorov points out, the uniqueness argument inevitably contains a comparative element within it: 'in effect, how can I confirm that a phenomenon is unique if I have never compared it to anything else?' ('comment, en effet, affirmer qu'un phénomène est unique si je ne l'ai jamais comparé à rien d'autre ?'), *Les Abus de la mémoire*, p. 36; see also Dan Stone, *Histories of the Holocaust* (Oxford: Oxford University Press, 2010), p. 210.

26. Omer Bartov, *Mirrors of Destruction: War, Genocide, and Modern Identity* (Oxford and New York: Oxford University Press, 2000).

27. Mahmood Mamdani, *When Victims Become Killers: Colonialism, Nativism and the Genocide in Rwanda* (Princeton, NJ: Princeton University Press, 2001).

28. A. Dirk Moses, 'Conceptual Blockages and Conceptual Dilemmas in the "Racial Century": Genocides of Indigenous Peoples and the Holocaust', *Patterns of Prejudice* 36, 4 (2002), 19. Mark Mazower, *Hitler's Empire: Nazi Rule in Occupied Europe* (London: Allen Lane, 2008).

29. Richard H. King and Dan Stone, 'Introduction' in *Hannah Arendt and the Uses of History*, p. 2. As regards historical studies of connections between colonialism and genocide in Europe, see also Sven Lindkvist, *Exterminate All the Brutes: One Man's Odyssey into the Heart of Darkness and the Origins of European Genocide* (London: Granta, 2002 [1997]), and the work of Jurgen Zimmerer, for example, 'Colonialism and the Holocaust: Towards an Archaeology of Genocide' in A. Dirk Moses (ed.), *Genocide and Settler Society: Frontier Violence and Stolen Indigenous Children in Australian History* (Oxford and New York: Berghahn Books, 2004), pp. 49–76, and 'The Birth of the *Ostland* out of the Spirit of Colonialism: A Postcolonial Perspective on the Nazi Policy of Conquest and Extermination', *Patterns of Prejudice* 39, 2 (2005), 202–224.

30. 'Si à l'origine de ce crime il y a une *intention* d'annihiler, il implique aussi certaines *structures* fondamentales de la société industrielle. Auschwitz réalise la fusion de l'antisémitisme et du racisme avec la prison, l'usine capitaliste et l'administration bureaucratico-rationnelle. Pour étudier un tel événement, on peut bien faire appel à Hannah Arendt, à Michel Foucault, à Karl Marx et à Max Weber. En ce sens, le génocide juif constitue un *paradigme* de la barbarie moderne', Enzo Traverso, 'La Singularité d'Auschwitz: Hypothèses, problèmes et dérives de la recherche historique' in Catherine Coquio (ed.), *Parler des camps, penser les génocides* (Albin Michel/Idées, 1999), p. 134. See also Zygmunt Bauman, *Modernity and the Holocaust* (New York: Cornell University Press, 1989), and Enzo Traverso, *La Violence nazie: Une Généalogie européenne* (La Fabrique, 2002).

31. 'Les négateurs de la singularité d'Auschwitz ne sont pas tous des « révisionnistes » ; ses partisans peuvent parfois faire preuve d'un grand aveuglement à l'égard d'autres violences. Les uns et les autres peuvent instrumentaliser cet événement à des fins douteuses. La meilleure façon de préserver la mémoire d'un génocide n'est certes pas celle qui consiste à nier les autres, ni celle qui consiste à ériger un culte religieux. La Shoah a aujourd'hui ses dogmes – son incomparabilité et son inexplicabilité – et ses redoutables gardiens du Temple. Reconnaître la singularité historique d'Auschwitz peut avoir un sens seulement si elle aide à fonder une dialectique féconde entre la mémoire du passé et la critique du présent, dans le but de mettre en lumière les fils multiples qui relient notre monde à celui bien récent depuis lequel, selon les mots de Georges Bataille, l'image de l'Homme ne pourra plus être dissocié de celle d'une chambre à gaz', Traverso, 'La Singularité d'Auschwitz', pp. 137–138.

32. 'les différences entre *les* camps ni entre *les* génocides, mais de les mieux saisir en les mettant en relation – et de combler ainsi le retard pris en France par la recherche, tout en indiquant une voie propre: celle qui s'assignerait la tâche de chercher l'humain à travers l'inhumain, l'"universel" dans le "particulier", ou bien, pour parler autrement, l'"unité" dans le "reste"', Catherine Coquio and Irving Wohlfarth, 'Avant-propos' in Coquio (ed.), *Parler des camps, penser les génocides*, p. 14.

33. 'discours dominant de la mémoire contemporaine des catastrophes', Alain Brossat, 'Massacres et génocides: Les Conditions du récit' in Coquio (ed.), *Parler des camps, penser les génocides*, p. 168.

34. See especially Alain Brossat, *L'Épreuve du désastre: Le XXe siècle et les camps* (Albin Michel, 1998). For an overview of the critique of the argument on the uniqueness of the Holocaust from this perspective, see Moses, 'Conceptual Blockages and Conceptual Dilemmas in the "Racial Century"'.

35. According to Dan Stone, '[m]any historians now accept the fact that the German occupation of Europe during World War II was a colonial enterprise' (*Histories of the Holocaust*, p. 205). For a detailed account of recent work by historians theorizing the connections between colonialism and the Holocaust, see Stone's *Histories of the Holocaust*, pp. 222–242.

36. Paul Gilroy, *The Black Atlantic: Modernity and Double Consciousness* (London: Verso, 1993), p. 213. See also his 'Afterword: Not Being Inhuman' in Bryan Cheyette and Laura Marcus (eds), *Modernity, Culture and 'the Jew'* (Cambridge: Polity, 1998), pp. 282–297, and Cheyette's own earlier attempts to break the dividing line between 'different' histories in his analysis of George Eliot and Frantz Fanon: 'Far from seeing the history of anti-Black racism or Orientalism as mutually exclusive in relation to the history of anti-semitism, I want to attempt to establish some of the ways in which these various histories may be interrelated' ('Jews and Jewishness in the Writings of George Eliot and Frantz Fanon', *Patterns of Prejudice* 29, 4 (1995), 5.)

37. The American title of the book, *Against Race: Imagining Political Culture beyond the Color Line*, fails to capture the significance of Gilroy's transversal study across the fault lines of fascism and imperialism.

38. Paul Gilroy, *Between Camps: Nations, Cultures and the Allure of Race* (London: Routledge, 2004[2000]), p. 78. Gilroy's answer to his own question ('Of course, occupying a space between camps means also that there is danger of encountering hostility from both sides, of being caught in the pincers of camp-thinking', p. 84) illustrates the bold nature of his approach.

39. Michael Rothberg, *Multidirectional Memory: Remembering the Holocaust in the Age of Decolonization* (Stanford: Stanford University Press, 2009), p. 3. See also Moses, 'Conceptual Blockages and Conceptual Dilemmas in the "Racial Century"', p. 18.

40. Rothberg, *Multidirectional Memory*, p. 3.

41. Rothberg, *Multidirectional Memory*, p. 5.

42. Rothberg, *Multidirectional Memory*, p. 11.

43. Rothberg, *Multidirectional Memory*, p. 14. In his discussion of 'the culture of memory' today, Andreas Huyssen interprets the global presence of Holocaust memory as effacing the specificities of other instances of extreme violence rather than interacting with them in a more complex way: 'While the comparison with the Holocaust may rhetorically energize some discourses of traumatic memory, it may also serve as a screen memory or simply block insight into specific local histories', *Present Pasts: Urban Palimpsests and the Politics of Memory* (Stanford, California: Stanford University Press, 2003), p. 14.

44. It is often said that the memory of the massacre of Algerians on 17 October 1961 was 'screened out' by the killing of nine French trade unionists at a demonstration against the OAS (Organisation de l'armée secrète) at the *métro* station of Charonne in Paris on 8 February 1962, and that this then became the '"dominant" memory on the left [symbolizing] police violence during the Algerian War', (House and Macmaster, *Paris 1961*, p. 256; see also Jean-Luc Einaudi, *La Bataille de Paris: 17 octobre 1961* (Seuil, 1991)). This is undoubtedly true, yet a Freudian approach to screen memory might reveal, even in a case like this, a highly complex dynamic at play in memory construction.

45. LaCapra, *History and Memory after Auschwitz*, p. 1. I have taken the term 'poetics of memory' from Susan Suleiman's discussion of the 'crises of memory' in her excellent book of the same name (see Susan Rubin Suleiman, *Crises of Memory and the Second World War* (Cambridge, Mass.: Harvard University Press, 2006), p. 9).

46. 'c'était Venise, dont mes efforts pour la décrire et les prétendus instantanés pris par ma mémoire ne m'avaient jamais rien dit, et que la sensation que j'avais ressentie jadis sur deux dalles inégales du baptistère de Saint-Marc m'avait rendue avec toutes les autres sensations jointes ce jour-là à cette sensation-là et qui étaient restées dans l'attente, à leur rang, d'où un brusque hasard les avaient impérieusement fait sortir, dans la série des jours oubliés', Marcel Proust, *Le Temps retrouvé* (Gallimard, 1954), p. 222 / *Time Regained*, trans. Andreas Mayor (London: Chatto and Windus, 1972), p. 224.

47. 'vision éblouissante et indistincte … à me rendre la mort indifférente', Proust, *Le Temps retrouvé*, p. 222 / *Time Regained*, p. 224.

48. Samuel Beckett and Georges Duthuit, *Proust, and, Three Dialogues* (London: Calder, 1965).

49. Rothberg, *Multidirectional Memory*, pp. 3–4. See also Richard Terdiman, *Present Past: Modernity and the Memory Crisis* (Ithaca, NY: Cornell University Press, 1993).

50. Roman Jakobson, 'Two Aspects of Language and Two Types of Aphasic Disturbances' in Roman Jakobson and Morris Halle (eds), *Fundamentals of Language* (The Hague: Mouton, 1971 [1956]), pp. 67–96.

51. Sigmund Freud, 'A Note upon the "Mystic Writing Pad" (1925)' in *General Psychological Theory* (New York: Touchstone, 1997), p. 208.

52. Gérard Genette also uses the figure of the palimpsest (in *Palimpsestes: La Littérature au second degré* (Seuil, 1982)) to describe the 'transtextual' layering of texts in which one can be seen through another.

53. Walter Benjamin, *The Arcades Project* (Cambridge, Mass.: Belknap Press of Harvard University Press, 1999), p. 416.

54. For a gender critique of the *flâneur*, see Griselda Pollock, *Vision and Difference: Femininity, Feminism and the Histories of Art* (London: Routledge, 1988), p. 71, and Janet Wolff, 'The Invisible *Flâneuse*: Women and the Literature of Modernity', *Theory, Culture and Society* 2, 3 (1985), 37–48.

55. Benjamin, *The Arcades Project*, p. 463.

56. In one of his discussions of Proust's 'mémoire involontaire', Benjamin observes, '[w] here there is experience in the strict sense of the word, certain contents of the individual past combine with material of the collective past' ('On Some Motifs in Baudelaire' in *Illuminations* (London: Collins-Fontana Books, 1973), p. 156).

57. Walter Benjamin, 'The Image of Proust' in *Illuminations*, p. 198.

58. Benjamin's notions of the 'monad', the 'crystal' and the 'mosaic' also refer to the general principle by which fragments contain the totality of which they are a part in mutually reinforcing fashion. See Graham Gilloch, *Walter Benjamin: Critical Constellations* (Cambridge: Polity, 2002), pp. 68–73.

59. Benjamin, *The Arcades Project*, p. 461.

60. Hannah Arendt, 'Introduction. Walter Benjamin: 1892–1940' in Walter Benjamin, *Illuminations*, pp. 16 and 18 respectively.

61. Walter Benjamin, 'Ninth Thesis on the Philosophy of History' in *Illuminations*, p. 249.

62. '[A] metaphor establishes a connection which is sensually perceived in its immediacy and requires no interpretation, while an allegory always proceeds from an abstract notion and then invents something palpable to represent it almost at will. The allegory must be explained before it can become meaningful, a solution must be found to the riddle it presents, so that the often laborious interpretation of allegorical figures always unhappily reminds one of the solving of puzzles even when no more ingenuity is demanded than in the allegorical representation of death by a skeleton', (Arendt, 'Introduction. Walter Benjamin: 1892–1940', p. 19).

63. Benjamin, *The Arcades Project*, p. 21.

64. Craig Owens, 'The Allegorical Impulse: Toward a Theory of Postmodernism', *October* 12 (1980), 72–73.

65. Owens, 'The Allegorical Impulse', p. 69. Owens also talks of 'the essentially allegorical nature of all Benjamin's work – the "Paris Arcades" project, for example, where the urban landscape was to be treated as a sedimentation in depth of layers of meaning which would gradually be unearthed' (p. 84).

66. Huyssen, *Present Pasts*, p. 81.

67. Huyssen, *Present Pasts*, p. 84.

68. Driss Chraibi, *Les Boucs* (Denoel, 1955), p. 174.

69. Kristin Ross, *Fast Cars, Clean Bodies: Decolonization and the Reordering of French Culture* (Cambridge Mass.: MIT Press, 1995).

70. Simone de Beauvoir, *Les Belles images* (Gallimard, 1966), p. 57.
71. Claude Burgelin, 'Perec et la Judéité: Une Transmission paradoxale', *Revue d'Histoire de la Shoah* 176 (2002) (special issue 'La Shoah dans la littérature française'), 167–182; Alain Finkielkraut, *Le Juif imaginaire* (Seuil, 1980).
72. 'magma informe', François Maspero, *Les Passagers du Roissy-Express* (Seuil, 1990), p. 24.
73. A similar juxtaposition to create connections of this kind occurs in the documentary *Chronique d'un été* (1961) by Jean Rouch and Edgar Morin. During a conversation on colonialism, African interviewees are unaware of the significance of the tattooed number on Marceline's forearm from her war experience in a concentration camp. (For interesting analyses of this encounter, see Steven Ungar, 'In the Thick of Things: Rouch and Morin's *Chronique d'un été* Reconsidered', *French Cultural Studies* 14, 1 (2003), 5–22; Joshua Hirsch, *Afterimage: Film, Trauma and the Holocaust* (Philadelphia: Temple University Press, 2004), pp. 64–68; and Rothberg, *Multidirectional Memory*, chapter 6.) Maspero's career trajectory – from champion of 'Third World' publications in France in the 1960s through his radical bookshops and publishing house to his later writing career – is a lesson itself in post-war intersections between genocide and colonialism. For a detailed account of his work in the 1960s and the development of his 'third-worldist perspective' (p. 85), see Kristin Ross, *May '68 and its Afterlives* (Chicago and London: University of Chicago Press, 2002), especially pp. 82–88.

Chapter 2

CONCENTRATIONARY MEMORY

Fearful Imagination

In an essay entitled 'The Concentration Camps' published in 1948 (and incorporated later into *The Origins of Totalitarianism*) Hannah Arendt criticizes the way in which the stock responses to those returning from the camps simply assimilate their stories to psychological and other normalizing narratives of understanding:

> There is a great temptation to explain away the intrinsically incredible by means of liberal rationalizations. In each one of us, there lurks such a liberal, wheedling us with the voice of common sense. We attempt to understand elements in present or recollected experience that simply surpass our powers of understanding. We attempt to classify as criminal a thing which, as we all feel, no such category was ever intended to cover. What meaning has the concept of murder when we are confronted with the mass production of corpses?[1]

Arendt likens this process to the resurrection of Lazarus. To all intents and purposes a man has returned to the human world with 'personality or character unchanged'. However, 'the reduction of a man to a bundle of reactions separates him as radically as mental disease from everything within him that is personality or character'.[2] Lazarus is the living dead, not a man as we know him. No psychological rationalization is sufficient to describe him and no reportage (like that of the Allied films of the opening of the camps) can fully represent the horror of where he has been,[3] just as the word 'murder' fails miserably to comprehend 'the mass production of corpses'. Arendt's response to the way in which the absolute novelty of 'totalitarian rule' (of which 'the concentration camps are the most consequential institution')[4] poses a fundamental challenge to our habitual modes of understanding is to propose the approach of 'fearful anticipation' founded on a 'fearful imagination'.[5] 'Fearful imagination' must be as far removed from 'normal' imagination as the concentration camp is from our known world: the 'mad unreality' of the camps 'can be described only in images drawn from a life after death, that is, a life removed from earthly purposes'.[6] In the rest of her essay, Arendt employs her 'fearful imagination' to define how a life can be 'removed from earthly purposes' to produce, ultimately, 'living corpses'. The process comprises, first, the murder of the juridical person in man, then the moral person, and, finally, his individuality, uniqueness and spontaneity 'to establish the superfluity of man'.[7] What remains might resemble a man outwardly but, inwardly, has been stripped of everything that we know to be constitutive of the human. How, then, to capture the uncanny idea that what seems familiar on the surface in fact resembles nothing that we already know?[8]

Jean Cayrol's 'concentrationary art', and the 1955 film directed by Alain Resnais *Nuit et brouillard*, for which Cayrol wrote the spoken text, both constitute a remarkable response to Arendt's challenge to portray the 'mad unreality' of the camps 'in images drawn from a life after death'. Like Arendt, Cayrol also uses the figure of Lazarus as the symbol of the new art in his work *Lazare parmi nous*:[9] an art which will show human life shocked out of its familiar contours through revealing the 'invisible thread' ('fil invisible') that ties it to the presence of death, humanity haunted by its inhuman double, the known always subject to its deformation into the grotesque.[10] Lazarean art will therefore be founded on a 'doubling' (and troubling) effect ('this doubling of the Lazarean being'),[11] to cast us into a state of the 'in-between', '*between* two universes …, into a sensation of *floating*, a state of mental and rootless wandering'.[12] Cayrol states:

> [t]he Lazarean hero is never there where he finds himself … because he has lived in a world which is situated nowhere and whose frontiers are not marked out since these are the frontiers of death. He permanently mistrusts the place at which he has just arrived.[13]

In an early article on Cayrol's *Lazare parmi nous*, Roland Barthes relates Cayrol's 'man who has escaped from a great fear and who still bears its stigmata' to Camus's Sisyphus and the literature of the absurd.[14] René Prédal describes Cayrol's Lazarus as follows:

> Lazarus is a man who has been raised from the dead, a man who has known death and can no longer be the man he was prior to this experience. In the same way, modern man has known the awful death of the camps and is also no longer the same as he was before the war, as he, too, is marked forever by the presence of these atrocities. To be affected, he does not need to have actually been interned. It is sufficient that this imprisonment and death have taken place to transform humanity completely. The Lazarean hero is therefore the archetypal hero of our era: solitary, anonymous, held in a place of instability, traumatized and consumed by the affliction of the world.[15]

This figure will be at the heart of a new art – that of the 'waking dream' ('rêve éveillé')[16] – whose duty it is to alert us (the unbelieving, those who want to re-establish the comfort of 'ordinary life') to a radically altered reality. As Daniel Oster says, 'these dreams opened onto a knowledge of the real'.[17] Cayrol's concentrationary art is therefore imbued with an imagination whose duty is to 'make present what is absent'.[18] This is a vision of humanity in the wake of the camps in which time and place are haunted by an elsewhere, and life is permanently haunted by death.[19]

In this chapter I will propose that Cayrol's discussion of Lazarean 'doubling' is central to what I am calling 'concentrationary memory'. I will suggest that the concentrationary art of Resnais's *Nuit et brouillard* and *Muriel* and Chris Marker's *La Jetée*, which transforms 'the image of man' into the living corpse, institutes a notion of memory as the haunting (and hence disturbance) of the present, a site of the in-between, of doublings and overlappings, of an uncanny superimposition of the visible and the invisible. Like the Lazarean hero, detached from his entrapment within the humanistic version of Man and split across space and time, memory in the wake of the camps and Hiroshima is not psychological memory (that is, centred within the 'known' psychology of the individual) but de-individualized, de-temporalized and de-spatialized. Concentrationary memory is never there where it finds itself, both here and elsewhere, the present disfigured, tainted permanently by the presence of death and oblivion. These films transform the Lazarean 'in-between' into a politicized aesthetic which will radically open up the becalmed aftermath of the war to the persistence of horror.

Alain Resnais's *Nuit et brouillard*

Fearful Vision

The opening shots of *Nuit et brouillard* announce the aesthetic and political vision of 'concentrationary art'. As the camera pans down to show that the first image of sky and land is being filmed through (from behind) the barbed wire of the camp, and as the next tracking shot from left to right similarly disturbs the clear vision of the countryside beyond by filming through the same fencing close up, we are presented with a world that can no longer be apprehended in a pure and uninterrupted fashion (could it ever or was this not always just Western utopian hubris?). Now, in the wake of the camps, the world can only be seen through the prism of camp barbed wire (see Figure 2.1). The filmmakers (like us?), who have come from the world outside to look into the camp of horror, present a perspective from the inside of the camp looking out. A multiple splitting and doubling takes place as the barbed wire acts as an ambivalent conduit for a new vision: the vision from the present looking in at the past is doubled by the vision from the past looking back at the present, outside and inside the camp are no longer mutually exclusive, and filming itself is composed of a vision

Figure 2.1 Auschwitz-Birkenau, Alain Resnais, *Nuit et brouillard* (1955)

split by the barbed wire. The panning and tracking shots on a vertical and horizontal axis, which will subsequently guide us through the camp, are thus, from the very beginning, incorporated into a new scopic regime of the 'in between' of the post-concentrationary universe. This is a fearful vision of doublings, hauntings and contaminations in which the filmic representations of people, objects, places and times are forever shadowed by their ghosts from elsewhere. The text which accompanies the tracking shot across the ruins of Birkenau in shot 5 – 'the only visitor to the blocks is a camera', grass has covered the former 'tread of the inmates' so that now there are 'no steps other than our own'[20] – makes explicit the link between material traces in the present and superimposed layers (invisible but present) of different times, spaces and looks to construct a palimpsest or Benjaminian 'double ground'.[21] Emma Wilson observes how the tension between 'material remains' and elsewhere is a constant feature of Resnais's films:

> Resnais seeks to know or understand a relation between the unimaginable (the invisible, the unsayable) and the very matter that remains – the material remains, the relics and traces of past experience. His films work at that difficult junction between events that cannot be known, seen, or felt (in their occurrence or in retrospect) and the matter, the images and objects, which seem conversely to offer material proof and evidence.[22]

The disturbance of time, space and vision effected in this way in the opening sequences means that when the cut occurs to the first black-and-white 'flashback' to the past (although, as I argue below, 'flashback' is not the right word to describe the temporal confusion here), it is not only steps which are made to carry an ambivalent charge (the steps of the Nazi jackboots in shot 6 echoing the steps of the film crew and those of the inmates mentioned in the previous shot). The horizontal movement of the Nazi camera to record the process of the machine 'starting up' also seems to mimic the tracking shots of the opening of the film to establish a troubling complicity between the look in the present of filming the disused camp and the sweeping embrace of Leni Riefenstahl's camera filming the crowd cheering Hitler in those images taken from her 1935 film *Triumph of the Will*.[23] Furthermore, the remnants of the 'machine' (the ruins of Auschwitz-Birkenau that we see in the present) and its initial stirrings ('the machine gets under way') are also drawn together to unsettle beginnings and endings and challenge the way in which the teleological reading of History becomes intelligible.[24] Does the present (the opening) trigger the past or vice versa? Does the filming of bearing witness to the concentrationary universe trigger the filming of its construction and celebration, or vice versa? Is our look in the present so different from the look that recorded the celebration of the dictator in the past?[25] To accommodate this blurring of 'different' temporal sequences, Gilles Deleuze quite rightly eschews all talk of 'flashback' in the cinema of Resnais, grounded as it is in a chronological notion of time. What we have instead are overlapping and superimposed 'layers' or 'sheets' of time, not a teleology which allows us to talk of 'past' and 'present' as separate categories or the present as the major organizing principle of time:

> *Night and Fog* could even be thought of as the sum of all the ways of escaping from the flashback, and the false piety of the recollection-image …. In Resnais' case, however, this inadequacy of the flashback does not stop his work as a whole being based on the coexistence of sheets of past, the present no longer even intervening as centre of evocation.[26]

This temporal dislocation matches visual and spatial dislocation: centred visual and spatial fields (the distinctions between objective and subjective points of view and between here and there, inside and outside respectively) are disrupted by a similar 'coexistence of sheets' which denies the specificity and singularity of each. The haunting quality of the Lazarean derives from the repetitions and similarities that cut across demarcated temporal, spatial and scopic regimes.

Hence, the following shots which develop the theme of the 'machine' of the concentrationary universe (the drawing up of plans for the construction of the camps, the styles employed in their design, the round-up and transportation in cattle trucks of those who will populate this universe and eventually perish there) continue to trace multiple connections between the world of the camp and 'everyday life'. The film draws a web of interconnecting and overlapping lines, like the rail tracks which draw diverse European locations and people to their concentrationary destination. The cut back to the tracks leading up to Birkenau in the present (shot 72) once again juxtaposes and overlays past and present (especially through the draining of the colour filming of the present to resemble the black and white of the past) and, similarly, overlays our present vision of the camp with that of the past through the shared connections between camera and rail track.[27]

When we return once again to Birkenau in the present (shot 91), the inter-penetration of different regimes of time, space and vision already created means that the 'known' surfaces over which the camera glides are now rendered strange and unknowable (because haunted by an elsewhere), or rather 'uncanny' in the Freudian sense of being both familiar and strange at the same time:

> this reality of the camps ...[is] unattainable for those who endure it and beyond the grasp of we who, in turn, seek to convey its meaning. These wooden barracks, these bedsteads on which three would lie, these holes in which they hid and where they ate illicitly and in fear, where sleep itself was a threat – no description, no image can render their true dimension: that of interminable fear.[28]

A fearful vision is, precisely, one of permanent anxiety and 'interminable fear'. Stripped of its habitual apparatus for perceiving and making sense, a fearful vision knows that the familiar appearance of objects is like a husk or stage set hiding unimaginable horror (like Lazarus whose external appearance tells us nothing of the living corpse that he has become).

> Of this brick dormitory, this threatened sleep, we can but show you the shell, the surface. Here is the décor: these buildings which could be stables, barns or workshops, impoverished land turned into wasteland, an autumn sky now indifferent. These are all we have left to imagine this night of piercing cries, of checking for lice, of chattering teeth.[29]

The 'doubling' regime of the Lazarean transforms all 'known' objects into deceptive surfaces and sites of fear: familiar activities like drinking soup and going to the lavatory are life or death events; words hide the truth rather than reveal it, as in the Nazi slogans "CLEANLINESS IS HEALTH" – "WORK IS FREEDOM" – "EVERYONE HIS DUE" – "A FLEA MEANS DEATH";[30] for the deportee 'the real world, that of peaceful countryside and of former times' is an illusory image;[31] and hospital is a torture chamber ('at a glance, you could have imagined that you were in front of a real clinic').[32] Fearful vision is not fooled by this deception. It asks, 'there is a décor, but behind?';[33] it knows that the SS's 'life-like town with hospital, red-light district, residential area and even – yes – a prison' is a sham;[34] it is sceptical of the ways in which what we take to be the real are, in fact, screens and images ('A crematorium could be the opportunity for a postcard. Later – today –, tourists take pictures of themselves there');[35] it knows that death lurks behind the most banal of objects ('Nothing distinguished the gas chamber from an ordinary building');[36] and it is aware of Man's capacity, now that 'everything is possible',[37] to turn fellow humans into everyday objects (fabric, fertilizer, soap…). The everyday has become a façade hiding the most unimaginable of crimes.[38]

Resnais's technique of disturbing demarcated regimes of sense produces an anxious apprehension of the real throughout.[39] By destabilizing the familiar, Resnais refuses to allow meaning to congeal into a fixed image (like the postcard) and opens up the surface to the superimposed layering of history. Hence, when the atrocity images are shown (especially shots 272–292), the lifeless corpses should not simply be seen as objects or *'figuren'*, as was the intention of Nazi dehumanization, or be allowed to disappear without trace, as was the intention of the policy of Nächt und Nebel, but are themselves returned to the land of the living through their palimpsestic relationship with other times and spaces.[40] Resnais's fearful imagination disturbs the discrete nature of life and death (and indeed all binary opposites): it breathes life into the dead and shows life haunted by death; it overlays the familiar with the concentrationary but also reminds us that the corpse was a living being; it reawakens us to the ever-present threat of disappearing without trace into the night and fog, and reverses the very policy which attempted to put this into effect by making the traces speak.

Resnais's fearful vision is a new way of seeing in the light of the camps. 'An interminable fear' requires keeping an eye open to survey the permanently open eye of the dormant (but certainly not extinct) concentrationary universe ('war dozes, one eye always open').[41] The concentrationary eye (or 'I') is split, doubled, in part formed (contaminated) by the concentrationary itself (looking out from inside the camp), in part aware of the machine that dehumanized the world and able to read the surface as a trace or sign (looking in from outside the camp): 'They closed the doors. They watched. The only sign – but you must know how to recognise it –, is the ceiling scored by nails. Even the concrete was torn'.[42] The key to the political consciousness of this vision is in the words 'il faut le savoir'. Like Benjamin's 'readability of the image', this part of the vision at least allows the possibility of reading the flat surface of the image in terms of a multi-layered history. As Georges Didi-Huberman observes, '[i]n the parallelism of the archival images and the marks of the present, it was a question of convoking a *critical time* – in the manner of Brecht – that would encourage not identification but political reflection'.[43]

The final shots of the film (303–306) leave us in that in-between state conjured up at the beginning: between the known world and the world of horror ('an abandoned village still bristling with danger', 'nine million dead haunt this landscape');[44] between the perpetrator, the victim and the bystander ('who amongst us watches over this strange observatory to warn us of the coming of the new executioners? Do they really have a different face to our own? Somewhere amongst us there remain duplicitous kapos, re-assimilated leaders, unknown informers');[45] between the spatio-temporal context of Auschwitz-Birkenau during the

Second World War and other times and places ('we who fool ourselves into believing that all that happened in one country and who do not think to look around us, and who fail to hear the endless cry');[46] between the unconscious immersion in the concentrationary and the conscious awareness of its eternal presence. 'Our bad memory',[47] which assumes that 'the old concentrationary monster has died beneath the ruins ... as if one can be cured of the concentrationary plague',[48] must be jolted into recognition of humanity's new state of concentrationary contamination, and replaced by concentrationary memory.

Concentrationary Memory

Resnais famously stated that he preferred to talk of his work in terms of imagination rather than memory.[49] As is evident from his early films, both of these terms are jolted out of their familiar definitions to create something far more fluid, for memory and imagination are not mutually exclusive categories. *Nuit et brouillard* reworks memory so that it is no longer what we thought it was. Detached from its framing within an individualist, humanist and teleological context, memory is incorporated into a Lazarean regime of doubling, splitting and overlapping to propose a radical transformation of our ways of seeing in the light of the concentrationary experience. In this sense, Resnais's treatment of memory and imagination seems to correspond closely to Arendt's plea for a 'fearful imagination' by which perception is forever shocked out of its familiar apprehension of the real, the present is haunted by the past, the self is haunted by its own otherness and the visible is haunted by the elsewhere. We can call this 'concentrationary memory' – rather than 'traumatic memory' – because this haunting is the indelible (invisible but ever-present) trace of the concentrationary universe. Yet, as I mention above, it also brings with it the political charge of permanent surveillance of its ruses. Palimpsestic, concentrationary memory is, therefore, not only an aesthetic device but also becomes the model for a politics of representation. The merging and re(e)merging of traces[50] gives us a way of understanding the concentrationary not as belonging to any one time or place nor as a universal phenomenon but as occupying a new space and time in-between the two, composed of overlapping or superimposed sheets of time (or, to use the Lazarean metaphor, a time always haunted by its own elsewhere). Employing Bergson's concept of *'souvenir pur'*, a form of atemporal memory as opposed to the *'image-souvenir'* which maintains the distinction between past and present, Deleuze compares Resnais's treatment of memory with dream-work in a way that also evokes a palimpsestic concept of time:

> In a dream, there is no longer one recollection-image which embodies one particular point of a given sheet; there are a number of images which are

embodied within each other, each referring to a different point of the sheet. Perhaps, when we read a book, watch a show, or look at a painting, and especially when we are ourselves the author, an analogous process can be triggered: we constitute a sheet of transformation which invents a kind of transverse continuity or communication between several sheets, and weaves a network of non-localizable relations between them. In this way we extract non-chronological time.[51]

In this new space, repetitions and similarities across time disturb the singularity of the event by splitting it between its presence in the here and now and its dispersal across time and space. Andrew Hebard is right to suggest that the uncanny in *Nuit et brouillard* 'forces a reconsideration of the possibility that an event can be contained within a "certain" time or place. To question this possibility is also to question the temporality of the event, a temporality no longer contained by a historical telos.'[52] Sylvie Lindeperg suggests something similar when, referring to the last line of the spoken text, she states, '[t]his endless cry, substituting for the incantatory "never again" of monuments to the dead, captures the floating definition of victims and executioners'.[53] Time and space being out of joint – both of one place and multiple places, of one time and multiple times – means that palimpsestic concentrationary memory draws the present (no matter how banal) into the realm of history and politics by revealing its complicitous concentrationary shadow.

The indeterminate nature of concentrationary memory not only merges present and past, here and elsewhere, and the particular and the universal but also unsettles the boundaries between the individual and the collective and between public and private. As we float between the pronouns *on*, *ils*, *nous* and *je* in the film (caught up in what Lindeperg has called 'a slippage of meaning'),[54] and as vision fragments across different regimes of point of view, each fixed demarcation of identity is decentred through its confusion with the others, and individual psychology and collective memory are revealed as categories (like life and death, the human and the inhuman, and so on) ill-equipped to meet the challenge of the non-binary, post-concentrationary world. Deleuze once again highlights the way in which this memory confuses a conventional psychological understanding: 'Throughout Resnais' work we plunge into a memory which overflows the condition of psychology, memory for two, memory for several, memory-world, memory-ages of the world.'[55] This floating concept of memory is central to the political and ethical charge starkly articulated at the end of the film through the question 'Who is responsible?' ('qui est responsable?'). A Lazarean aesthetic has disturbed the dichotomy between individual and collective guilt and blurred the boundaries between victim, perpetrator and witness to such an extent that this now becomes an unanswerable question in conventional 'psychological' terms (though, of course, no less urgent in judicial and moral terms).

Resnais's palimpsestic memory is thus a radical post-concentrationary aesthetic which incorporates a new (non-humanist and resolutely anti-psychological) post-concentrationary politics and ethics. Cayrol's spoken text and Resnais's montage invoke multiple connections, continuities and ruptures that convert the physical traces in the present into the new field of a non-teleological history. This (fundamentally modernist) practice transforms Auschwitz-Birkenau in the present of filming into a site of superimposed inscriptions of other places and times to suggest that the present is always contaminated by other scenes and that questions of responsibility for unimaginable crimes against humanity haunt seemingly innocent everyday life. Seen in this light, concentrationary memory provides a model of cultural memory which resembles Benjamin's 'constellation' in which the moment is forever in dialectical tension with history ('dialectics at a standstill' indeed capturing the paradoxical relationship between movement and stasis explored in the film). Concentrationary memory does not simply bring back the memory of one specific event (in fact, it counters the very idea of the singularity of the event); instead, it puts each event into contact with a complex history, in the way that Rousset and Arendt contextualize the concentrationary universe.

Concentrationary memory is therefore not the same as what we normally understand today as 'Holocaust memory', which specifies the event as the genocide of the Jews. By its very definition (or rather its refusal of any conventional definition), concentrationary memory escapes any such ethno-cultural or religious particularization.[56] The criticisms that have been made of *Nuit et brouillard* for its silence on the genocide of the Jews (which are, I believe, inaccurate in any case)[57] are not only based on an anachronistic reading of the film (that is, reading the film through the contemporary lens of the Holocaust paradigm) but also ignore the principles of doubling and haunting of Lazarean art underpinning the film's aesthetic and political purpose. Concentrationary memory denies specificity by showing us how the particular is always haunted by its absent other ('the Lazarean hero is never there where he finds himself'). In this way (and as the final sequence of the film so powerfully demonstrates), we are all contaminated by the concentrationary gaze and the concentrationary plague but can be, simultaneously, shocked into a recognition of (and hence challenge to) the hidden complicity and continuities that post-war modernization has repressed by reading 'normality' through a 'fearful imagination'. Mixing and splitting, rather than historical verisimilitude, are both aesthetic and political strategies: they interrupt the self-presence of the present by making visible its hidden elsewhere, they create the connections between times and places which disturb the innocence of 'a peaceful countryside' ('un paysage tranquille'), they make the unimaginable part of our normalized reality, and they give us the means to read a buried history.[58]

Concentrationary memory presents a model of cultural memory as a mongrel process: it politicizes the aesthetic strategies of modernism to capture the strangeness, ambivalences and historical interconnections of a post-concentrationary reality. It belongs to that post-war moment of refusal of the objectification of human relations and the normalization of reality that inspired Rousset, Arendt, Césaire and Fanon, all of whom naturally saw the overlaps between different sites of racialized violence and dehumanization, especially between Western capitalism and extermination and between fascism and imperialism, within Europe and outside its frontiers. My reading of the aesthetic and political practice of concentrationary memory is therefore with a view to reinscribing its radical message into the field of cultural memory at a time when this has often become dominated by monolinear histories of ethno-cultural difference. Reading *Nuit et brouillard* as an allegory of the Algerian War, and thereby recognizing the overlaps and interconnections between the concentrationary universe and colonialism, is not simply one way of understanding the film; it is a required reading because of the formal structures of complicity that the film establishes.[59] Concentrationary memory is itself a blueprint for what I am terming palimpsestic memory. Seeing *Nuit et brouillard* as the first (or the first major) Holocaust film therefore blurs its innovatory treatment of time, space, memory and imagination. Relocating it within Cayrol's concept of the Lazarean and concentrationary art, and Arendt's plea for a fearful imagination in the wake of the camps, allows us, on the contrary, to recognize its palimpsestic character and its radical political aesthetic.

In words that echo the last spoken words of the film, Cayrol suggests that, in the realm of the Lazarean, 'the mouth will always be open, not for the word but for the cry'.[60] *Nuit et brouillard* overlays the here and now of the known world with the endless cry of suffering to produce a disturbing vision of the human condition in the wake of the camps. This is truly a 'fearful imagination' composed, in Arendt's words once again, of 'images drawn from a life after death'.

Mémoire-monde

The Lazarean Image: Chris Marker's La Jetée

At the end of Chris Marker's film *La Jetée* (1962) we learn that the death that the hero witnesses at the beginning of the film, while standing on 'la jetée' of Orly airport as a child, is his own. The concept of 'images drawn from a life after death' is therefore particularly applicable to this film. However, this only makes sense if, as with Cayrol's notion of the Lazarean, time is not linear ('an "atemporal" time'),[61] the distinction between life and death is not clear, and memory, dream, imagination and the real are profoundly interconnected.

The parallels between *La Jetée* and *Nuit et brouillard* do not stop there. The post-apocalyptic scenario, in which an unnamed Lazarean hero is selected as a guinea pig in experiments in time travel by the victors of the Third World War due to his attachment to an image from his past, is the setting for an exploration of memory, imagination, time and, ultimately, humanity. The ruins of Paris resemble images of destroyed cities in the Second World War or Hiroshima after the atom bomb ('after the camps, after the bomb' / 'après les camps, après la bombe'), and the underground passages of the Palais de Chaillot where the experiments take place and where Resistance fighters hid during the Occupation of France ('where, during the war, Langlois saved many films censored by the Nazis and where the Cinémathèque française had recently opened in 1963'), resemble a concentration camp or torture chamber filled by wide-eyed inmates.[62] The references to the Second World War and Hiroshima are clear, but there are also references to the apparatus of torture used in Algeria by the French army.[63] Like Lazarus, the hero is a ghost ('She calls him her Ghost' / 'Elle l'appelle son Spectre') who returns to life after destruction only to be the puppet of the new time lords who control his moves. Memory is both the lure to entrapment ('this man was chosen from a thousand men because of his fixation on an image from the past', intones the nameless narrator)[64] and the catalyst for quickening the dead, as it brings back scenes from his childhood and the woman who is the desired image from his past. In this ambivalent sense, memory (that is, memory/imagination/dream) either fails to bring about a Proustian apotheosis, because the quest to reconquer time can never release itself from the present control of the torturer and the certainty of death, or, viewed the other way round, succeeds in reawakening the embalmed nature of the past (as, for example, the quickening of statues or the stuffed animals in the museum), and offers a glimpse of a path out of the void of the present. The circularity of the film – in which the image at the beginning which triggers desire is also the image at the end of the hero's own death – denies any definitive answer to this question.

Circularity is, indeed, the structural key to the ambivalence of memory in the film. There is no narrative development and resolution in the conventional sense; instead, there is simply a spiraling effect which leads out from and back to the point of departure, so that that point – the initial image – is also the point of termination. The fact that the setting is an airport – a point of both departure and return – is a fitting metaphor for circularity. The rings on the cross-section of the sequoia tree that the man and woman look at and the spiralling 'chignon' of the woman's hair, which clearly reference Hitchcock's *Vertigo* (and of course, through Kim Novak's character Madeleine, Proust), are further *'mises en abyme'* of the circular structure of the film as a whole.[65] The indication at the beginning of the film that the initial image refers to a moment three years before the outbreak of World War Three and is 'the only image from peace-time to survive the period of war' ('la seule image du temps de paix à traverser le temps de guerre') cannot orient us in linear time when we are dealing with an atemporal imagination fixated on, obsessed with and spiralling around *ad infinitum* an unattainable object of desire.[66] Narrative development and linear time are collapsed into a spatial (metaphorical) reworking of certain elements. Instead of a remembrance of a lost past, the film is a present discourse in the process of fabricating an image-text (hence Marker's description of his work as a *'photo-roman'*).

Let us take, for example, the way in which the initial image will generate a text. The film opens on *la jetée* at Orly where the images of the planes are accompanied by the sound of their engines, followed by choral music. It is here where the first image of the woman will be located, contextualized by the sight and sound of planes. Desire (for the woman, for his mother?) and death (his own) – hence, Eros and Thanatos – will also be located in this context. As such, it is a site at which the most intimate aspects of life and death are embedded in public traffic. We are therefore presented at the beginning of the film with a sort of collage which will provide the matrix for what will subsequently spiral out from that point. A crucial moment later is the only time in the film that the still images give way to a moving image. At the end of a sequence of stills showing the face of the woman in bed, she looks directly at the camera and flutters her eyes to the accompaniment of a cacophony of bird-song. The association between woman and flight at the beginning – which is repeated when one of the first images that comes back to the man through the experiment before the image of the woman herself is that of 'real birds' ('de vrais oiseaux') – returns in the scene in bed (she flutters

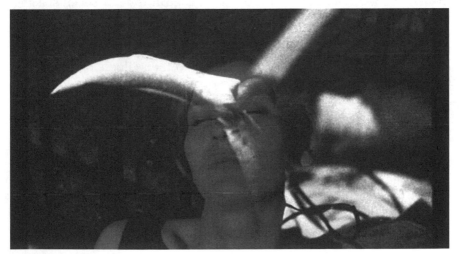

Figure 2.2 Montage of woman and bird, Chris Marker, *La Jetée* (1962)

her eyes like a bird in flight). However, in this scene the sound from the machine world at the beginning (reminiscent of an air raid siren, as Griselda Pollock suggests)[67] has given way to the sound from the natural world, the planes having become birds (an association which has been rendered visible shortly before when the outstretched arms and hands of the couple resemble the wings of a bird prior to a dissolve of the woman's face into the image of a bird in flight (see Figure 2.2)) . The sexual desire (or Oedipal impulse) which prompted the initial image of the woman is clearly returned in her look to camera from her bed. But the presence of death in the first scene is also reintroduced here through metonymic association (hence repeating the overlaying of Eros and Thanatos), as is the presence of totalizing power and fear, given that this Orphic search is a controlled experiment in time travel ('the camp police even spied on one's dreams' / 'la police du camp épiait jusqu'aux rêves'), and that the personal journey cannot take place outside collective history.[68]

In other words, elements which comprise the initial images are reassembled in the sequence of the woman in bed; they are present behind the visible images of this sequence through associations of similarity and contiguity already established. The words that accompany the opening scene as the woman sees the death of the man – 'this sudden noise, the woman's gesture, this falling body, the clamour of those on the jetty, cast into confusion by fear'[69] – therefore haunt this moment of awakening, movement and life. This image of movement is contaminated by the stillness of death due to the 'invisible thread' ('fil invisible', in Cayrol's words) that link all images and every moment with others from elsewhere. The 'journey' that is taken, then, which leads from the airport to the bed – *la jetée d'Orly* morphing, through a play on words, into *là, j'étais au lit?* – is produced by the latent signs present in the first scene and will guarantee their repetition elsewhere. It is not chronological time or social spacing which regulates the flow of image and sound but rather the circular play of sights and sounds themselves as they 'take flight' from their 'grounded' positions on the tarmac at Orly, become dynamic (hence making the eyes move and 'see' while still being connected to the stillness of death) and generate new meanings around a cluster of elements.[70]

In this sense, *La Jetée* is a poetic photomontage: it produces movement from the static photographs by a spatialized reworking of image and sound. The different sites in the film – Orly, scenes of destruction, statues, the museum and so on – are images piled on top of each other, following a dream-like pattern of condensation and displacement of meaning. The image is consequently transformed from its flat, two-dimensional surface into a palimpsest of superimposed traces. Janet Harbord observes that 'as a memory, *La Jetée* is a series of superimpositions, images that surface variously' and, relating Marker to Freud, notes that 'the present is a condition of multiple temporalities with its concomitant dangers, and pleasures, of overlap'.[71] Patrick Ffrench notes the vertical rather than horizontal organization of images in the film to constitute what he terms 'the memory of the image':

> The images of the destruction of Paris in *La Jetée* thus 'remember' in a certain sense the images of the devastation of Hiroshima; the images of the underground tunnels remember those of the camps. The montage of *La Jetée* is effected not only syntagmatically, in terms of the horizontal sequence of images, but also paradigmatically, in terms of their imagined superimposition on a vertical level on images of the historical real.[72]

As Ffrench implies, *La Jetée* is not simply a poetic experiment in formalism, a common critique of the spatialized, circular and labyrinthine *récits* of contemporary *nouveaux romanciers* such as Alain Robbe-Grillet, Claude Simon, Michel Butor and, especially, Jean Ricardou.[73] Marker uses the poetic imagination to explore the very real anxieties in the wake of apocalyptic disaster, for these too are registered, in Sarah Cooper's words, in 'the political unconscious of *La Jetée*'s photographic images'.[74] As Jean Louis Schefer observes, Marker is exploring the unconscious of a particular generation,

> [t]he imperfect but generative memory of a large part of our sensibility, or the memory of mutilation derived from the war that tainted our childhood: the first consciousness of an era of global destruction which lodged like a spirit in us, as if it was a lead bullet or the explosion of a bomb which penetrated us, found by chance a place within us in which it installed itself and continued to live after having only struck a city or killed someone other than us.[75]

Marker mobilizes modernist devices for the purposes of a personal/ political aesthetic that, as Schefer says, is permanently damaged by the catastrophe that has befallen humanity. Highlighting the idea of post-apocalyptic art as a sort of 'survivor memory', Pollock interprets Schefer's insight in the following way:

> This curious formulation catches the notion of the 'survivor' of something traumatic who seems, by virtue of being still alive, to have escaped damage. Yet the survivor is precisely the site of the damage – mnemonic damage. Death hit somewhere else but it nonetheless has wounded those it just missed, leaving a world never again innocent of its reality. Death lives within the survivor as the just-missed encounter.[76]

Like Cayrol's concept of Lazarean art following catastrophe, Marker's film is a sort of generalized 'survivor memory'. As in *Nuit et brouillard*, this is memory dislocated from its entrapment within a limited psychological and individualized framework (that of the sovereign subject) and transformed into a present process of sifting through the private/public fragments, obsessively searching through the ruins, and restlessly questioning the images that inform an individual and collective unconscious in the wake of disaster. This is closer to Deleuze's *'mémoire-monde'* than a humanistic understanding of memory: a bank of overlapping images that neither belongs to the hero (nameless because de-individualized, 'he whom one hesitates to call both hero and narrator' / 'celui que l'on hésite à la fois à nommer héros et narrateur') nor simply to the realm of (objective) history but incorporates both and in which both are inevitably enmeshed.[77] Ffrench is again correct, then, to read memory in Marker as going beyond the specificity of the singular: '[t]his memory is not that of specific events, nor that of a specific subject; it is ... a trans-historical memory of the gestural life inherent to humanity'.[78] However, it might be more appropriate to say that it refashions the specific and the general, for one is always in the other. Perceived in this way, memory is inhabited by and generative of multiple traces and contaminations from other places. It is not bound in space and time or contained within subjects; it is not where it finds itself but always gestures to an elsewhere. Like other work by Marker, *La Jetée* is a portrait of memory as spiralling time and space travel.

Alain Resnais's 'Muriel ou le temps d'un retour'

Montage is the invention of a different reality of the world.[79]

Muriel (1963), like *Nuit et brouillard* directed by Alain Resnais with a script by Jean Cayrol and cinematography by Sacha Vierny, is a further example of Deleuze's description of *'mémoire-monde'*. The intercutting of narrative sequences related to two moments of catastrophic violence – the Second World War and the Algerian War – and the contamination of memories and voices supposedly belonging to different characters denies a psychological interpretation of memory and the self, and subverts a normalized understanding of space and time. Objects and memory fragments seem to circulate in filmic rather than social space; or rather, the film's techniques defamiliarize social space and the social self and constantly rearrange the pieces in new configurations. The result is a sort of collage in the process of being assembled and reassembled, rather like the kaleidoscope through which Marie-Do looks at Bernard, which fragments and rearranges the image with each turn of the cylinder, or Bernard's photographs of Algeria discovered by Alphonse, which fall to the floor in haphazard fashion, one on top of the other. This process of overlapping and interconnection, condensation and displacement of meaning once again blurs the frontiers between memory, imagination, dream and historical reality. However, although this play of signifiers becomes the principal drama of the film, *Muriel* (like *La Jetée*) proposes a political rather than a purely formal aesthetic as it raises fundamental questions about the nature of consciousness in the wake of catastrophe.

Like *La Jetée*, the opening of *Muriel* introduces a number of elements that will be the building blocks for narrative progression. Quick cutting between a gloved hand on a door handle, Hélène smoking a cigarette, and steam from a kettle is accompanied by a woman's voice describing the sort of chest of drawers that she is seeking to buy. When the woman (a customer of Hélène) has left the apartment, Hélène admonishes her stepson Bernard for putting the coffee pot on the table because, as she explains, she cannot sell a piece of furniture with a burn mark on it. Bernard takes the coffee pot into his room and puts it on his own table where we see the pieces of a gun, a tape recorder, a newspaper and a photo (see Figure 2.3). All the objects presented here reappear in the later description by Bernard of the French paratroopers' torture of Muriel in Algeria: Bernard's palms burn, Muriel's hair is soaking wet (the kettle and coffee pot have already introduced the association of 'burning' and 'liquid'), Robert lights a cigarette, Bernard slaps Muriel's face with his hand (an act which is repeated in the present when Bernard slaps Françoise), Muriel has 'burns on her chest' ('des brulûres sur la poitrine'), and so on. Even the association of banal everyday objects with extreme violence is replicated, except that the relationship between image and soundtrack is inverted so that the violence which is contained (implicitly) in the images at the beginning (while the voice consists of the banal business rhetoric of Hélène's customer) is, in the later scene, contained in Bernard's graphic narration (while what we see are the banal, holiday-snap images of French soldiers in Algeria, which parallel Alphonse's depoliticized description of Algeria as 'a beautiful country' / 'un bien beau pays' where 'the sky is always blue' / 'le ciel est toujours bleu').[80]

The formal process central to what I am calling concentrationary memory is once again present here. First, the reappearance of the objects

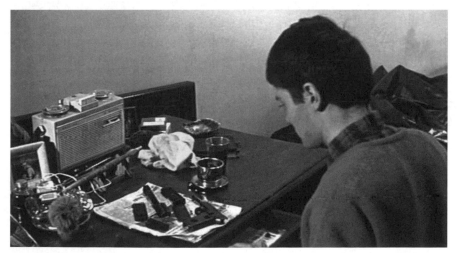

Figure 2.3 Bernard and assorted objects, Alain Resnais, *Muriel* (1963)

first seen in Hélène's flat in the later torture scene in Algeria draws together post-war commercialized modern life in Boulogne-sur-Mer and colonial violence in North Africa. The Proustian model of memory shows that if the initial connection between these apparently separate scenes is through similarity, the invasion of one whole setting into another is due to the chain of metonymic associations (through contiguity) that accompanies the recognition of similarity. The overlaying of Boulogne and Algiers (which, as Celia Britton and Emma Wilson rightly suggest, recalls Resnais's overlaying of Nevers and Hiroshima in the earlier *Hiroshima mon amour*)[81] is therefore a product of metaphor and metonymy, condensation and displacement. A palimpsestic structure is created, in which one scene is visible through another, denying the self-contained nature of each and establishing a constant tension between here and elsewhere, the visible and the invisible.

Second, the constant reappearance of the same, or similar, objects in the film, and the chains of associations attached to them, means that it is not only Hélène's flat in contemporary Boulogne which 'appears' within the account of the torture of Muriel, but other places, times and people as well. The same objects will continue to be reassembled in the remainder of the film, hence weaving an even denser web of overlapping meanings. Let us take, for example, the smoking of cigarettes in the film, whose ubiquity links the major characters and settings with both the torture scene in Algeria and the Second World War.[82] The cigarette smoke and the steam from the kettle at the beginning reappear as smoke from a train going under a bridge in Boulogne (giving the appearance of the aftermath of an explosion). They will be referenced in the name of Hélène's confidant Roland de Smoke (responsible for the demolition of Boulogne after the Second World War) and will make a final appearance billowing out of Bernard's studio after the collapse of the ceiling (which reminds Hélène and Bernard of the time the ceiling fell in during the war when Bernard was a child). The burning of cigarettes and the remains of ash in ashtrays are reflected in the burnt-out appearance of many of the buildings in the town (destroyed by the Allies' bombardments in the war) and the linen transformed into ash in the mind of Bernard as he remembers the childhood incident from the war. Inevitably, they will also conjure up the ashes of the dead from the crematoria of the extermination camps. Alphonse's final act, which involves him entering a tobacconist's shop to buy some cigarettes as a means of escaping the efforts of Ernest to take him back to his wife Simone in Paris, is therefore a heavily over-determined sequence in that it draws into the scene the disparate but interconnected elements with which cigarettes, smoke and ash have been associated throughout the film. The film's construction of these associations (prompting us as spectators to participate actively in the pursuit of connections too) means that Boulogne's blandly modernized and commercialized present of the early 1960s (which, like the ruins of

Auschwitz in *Nuit et brouillard*, is a décor which tells us nothing unless we question the surface) is exposed as a superficial veneer covering a personal and collective past which embraces the war, the extermination camps, torture in Algeria by the French army, lost innocence and dreams of love, and much more. Like *Nuit et brouillard*, *Muriel* constructs chains of associations in image and sound, established through similarity and contiguity, to materialize the 'invisible thread' that links the present to history and the personal to the collective.

Bersani and Dutoit refer to this process as 'the associational mobility among scenes, a mobility that provides a cinematic model, during the time of *Muriel*, of the past as providing textual accretions to the present'.[83] One could point to numerous other examples of this 'associational mobility' and its effects on the filmic staging of memory in the present. In a scene in which Hélène and Alphonse are sitting on a bench overlooking the port and a ship moving slowly past, the camera's focus is, firstly, on the interlocked hands of the two characters. This mimics the intertwined memories/stories they are telling/inventing, but this flight of fancy is itself doubled by the meanings already constructed within the film associated with hands (smoking, torture and so on) which makes the whole scene fragment in numerous directions. Hélène's comment to Alphonse at the end of this sequence – 'the main thing is that you feel at home here, at your ease'[84] – is completely contradicted by the splintering, associational movement of image and sound which disperses meaning rather than drawing it in to a unified place. The inability to fix flux and moor memory is portrayed in miniature later on when passers-by, including Bernard, look through the window of a snack bar following news that a ship has run aground. Bernard's attempt to focus on this sudden ceasing of movement is foiled when a woman's voice shouting 'Muriel!' distracts his attention and introduces the 'elsewhere' associated with that name.

'Associational mobility' thus fragments the wholeness of personal and national identity. In her fascinating discussion of *Muriel*, Celia Britton is right to highlight the centrifugal movement of the film as it splinters any secure space. Yet the emphasis on dispersal of meaning should not obscure the other side of 'associational mobility', namely the creation of new connections. The purpose of the unsettling fragmentation brought about by disjunction between sound and image, fast cutting, strange juxtapositions and so on that early critics perceived (including Claude Ollier, Susan Sontag and Marie-Claire Ropars) is not only to deconstruct linear time, rationalized space and coherent identity; these techniques also create new associations between disparate spatio-temporal elements in Proustian and surrealist fashion, hence contaminating the present with what Naomi Greene has called the interconnected 'national disasters' of the past.[85] The mention of the name 'Muriel' in the Boulogne street is disconcerting because, thanks to the metonymic associations attached to that name, it draws torture in Algeria into the heart of bourgeois France. 'Associational mobility' thus consists of a dual process of fragmentation/ recomposition. The centrifugal structure does not so much replace a centripetal one but works in tandem with it. It is simply that the centripetal structure does not unify associations around a centre but regroups them in a new constellation, establishing a Benjaminian historical dialogue between different moments.[86]

The real drama of the film is therefore displaced from psychological realism onto the filmic process of the dispersal and association of elements, which itself becomes a profound reflection on, and reconfiguration of, memory and history. Memory (like imagination) is de-psychologized, dispersed within the perpetual sliding of meaning between different spatio-temporal sites. The past is incorporated into the present process of production of signification, or, Bersani and Dutoit suggest, 'a textual project of the present'.[87] The question that we asked about the opening of *Nuit et brouillard* – Does the past trigger the present or does the act of filming in the present trigger the past? – can also be asked of the opening of *Muriel*. However, as with the earlier film, the question has no answer because time is not linear but converted into loops. Like Marker in *La Jetée*, Resnais uses Hitchcock's image of the spiral in *Vertigo* as a metaphor for this process:[88] Bernard puts on joke glasses with spiralling eyes and later takes a picture of the rings of a cross-section of a tree. The spiral circles round an absent centre. Boulogne is, indeed, an in-between space without a centre: Alphonse has a baffled expression when looking at a circular plan of Boulogne, as does a visitor to the town whose question to a passer-by 'the centre please' ('le centre s'il vous plaît') receives the reply 'this is the centre' ('vous y êtes'). The town is a point of crossing with no fixed point, 'a location of interwoven connections',[89] traversed by a dizzying sequence of unstable elements from elsewhere. Hence, the constant images of travelling and journeys – the Hôtel des Voyageurs, the ships in the port, the train station, the bikes, the luggage of Alphonse and Françoise, the constant Beckettian talk of leaving with no action following the statements (except perhaps at the end) – and flights of fancy in story-telling, 'remembering' and acting.[90] Cayrol's description of the Lazarean hero ('the Lazarean hero is never there where he finds himself') is reflected visually and verbally in all these ways in the film. The characters are all versions of the Lazarean hero: de-centred, strangers to themselves, disfigured and evacuated of individualizing content (as in Bernard's blacked-out face in the photo) and transformed into the interchangeable containers of the traces of multiple elsewheres (especially of horror and death). As Cayrol said of his intention in *Muriel*, 'what I wanted to show was … how one can become a shattered being who survives'.[91] Ernest repeats the memory of meeting Hélène at the Club d'Or first recounted by Alphonse;[92] Hélène and Bernard share a memory of the war but have different recollections of the details. Once again it is futile to wonder who is telling the truth and who is lying because we are dealing not with personal memory but with a memory which is, at least, 'echoing Deleuze ...', a memory for two'[93] but, more generally, like Deleuze's *'mémoire-monde'*, a memory which floats free of its moorings within a limiting subjectivity and intertwines with a collective imaginary shaped by a concentrationary historical reality. 'Memory', 'imagination' and 'consciousness' are interchangeable terms determined by the dynamic politico-aesthetic process of the filmic work. As Deleuze observes, the present of filming in Resnais thus becomes a meeting place for layers of time and space.[94]

At the heart of the politics of representation of Cayrol's concentrationary art, it will be remembered, is the ambivalent status of objects. The strangeness of life that the Lazarean figure will impart after his return from death will be explored through the interrogation of objects. Objects hide the real and are banal substitutes for it. But they are also the containers of the affective weight of traumatic experience. *Muriel* captures the existential state of anxiety and the traces of destruction and modernization by investing objects with the charge of trauma and history, a charge which is constantly deferred from one object to another and never finally arrives at a sense of closure. The other part of the title of the film – 'the time of a return' ('le temps d'un retour') – is, perhaps, an ironic gesture to what turns out to be the impossibility of a return. Lazarus returns but is never there where he finds himself. The journey is a constant deferral (a spiral) which has no point of return (unless the return is itself redefined as deferral or, in Cayrol's words, 'an "atemporal" time'). It fixes on objects, otherwise it would be free-floating anxiety. Hélène's anxiety is transferred onto her lost keys, the jumbled assortment of objects in her flat, her continual movement and her gambling but cannot be contained by them. Metaphorically, Alphonse's flight at the end (another journey) announces the further deferral of a return but latches onto the object (the packet of cigarettes) as an excuse for flight. Cigarettes are literally and metaphorically a 'smoke-screen' or a means to 'burn out' (erase) the source of anxiety; but they are also the mark of the original event that caused that anxiety. They recall the burnt-out face in the photo of a man standing next to Muriel ('Burn'-ard?), the melting image of veiled Algerian women that Hélène sees on the screen in Bernard's studio which reappears in the destroyed studio at the end, or the stain that Alphonse is attempting to remove from his jacket. The erasure always leaves its mark. Hélène's desire at the beginning of the film not to leave a mark on the table is a hopeless attempt to deny the power of the object to act as a trace of the past, just as the blackened face (indeed, the photograph in general) is a reminder (however imperfect) of something else that went before (Barthes's *'ça-a-été'*),[95] despite its substitution for and erasure of that very thing. Like the screen in Freud's screen memory, objects contain the traces of the reality they screen out. Resnais's framing of the consumer objects in the new shops in Boulogne and the bourgeois diners in the restaurants through reflecting glass highlights the double-edged nature of the object. On the one hand, its seductive surface erases depth and lures us into the delights of modern consumer society (as is clearly the case for Françoise); on the other hand, it is exposed, through what Bersani and Dutoit call 'composed chance correspondences',[96] as a trace of and substitute for the violent history on which that society is built.

In a certain sense, the object is like photography and film. Françoise is not only attracted to the displays in shop windows; she is also transfixed and seduced by the glossy film posters outside a cinema and postcards of Boulogne. Yet the idealized image cannot completely hide its secret memories, just as the tourist version of Auschwitz mentioned in *Nuit et brouillard* cannot completely cover the traces of horror – provided, that is, that we can read the connections (*'il faut le savoir'*) between surface and depth, present and past in a new way. Although Bernard's postcards, photos and film of Algeria dissimulate their dark secrets, and the torture of Muriel is nowhere to be seen, the associations that have been established between objects, violence and death throughout give us a way of reading the violence that has been erased. Bernard's film is, then, a sort of *mise en abyme* of *Muriel* as a whole: a series of apparently bland images (like the scenes of bourgeois Boulogne) contain multiple connections with a dark past. Bernard as Lazarean hero communicates his 'fearful imagination' to the becalmed and commodified post-war world of metropolitan France.

Notes

1. Hannah Arendt, 'The Concentration Camps', *Partisan Review* 15 (1948), 745.
2. Arendt, 'The Concentration Camps', p. 746.
3. Arendt, 'The Concentration Camps', p. 750.
4. Arendt, 'The Concentration Camps', p. 746.
5. Arendt, 'The Concentration Camps', pp. 744 and 746.
6. Arendt, 'The Concentration Camps', p. 749.
7. Arendt, 'The Concentration Camps', p. 762.
8. As noted in the preceding chapter, one of the major areas of interest of *The Origins of Totalitarianism* is precisely the tension in the text (largely unresolved) between, on the one hand, the continuities between anti-Semitism, imperialism and totalitarianism (as apparently announced in the title itself) and, on the other hand, the rupture between totalitarianism and preceding forms of violence. For an excellent discussion of this tension, see Rothberg, *Multidirectional Memory*, chapter 2.
9. *Lazare parmi nous* was first published by Seuil in 1950. It is divided into two parts, 'Les Rêves lazaréens' and 'Pour un romanesque lazaréen' (which had themselves previously been published separately). 'Pour un romanesque lazaréen' was then reprinted as 'De la vie à la mort' to accompany the publication of Cayrol's commentary for *Nuit et brouillard* in 1997. For a complete collection of Cayrol's writing on the Lazarean, see *Jean Cayrol: Œuvre lazaréenne*.
10. Cayrol, 'De la vie à la mort' in *Nuit et brouillard* (Fayard, 1997), p. 67.
11. 'ce dédoublement de l'être lazaréen', Cayrol, 'De la vie à la mort', p. 67.

12. *'entre* deux univers ..., dans une sensation de *flottement*, d'état de vagabondage mental et sans racines', Jean Cayrol, 'Préambule' to 'Les Rêves lazaréens' in *Jean Cayrol: Œuvre lazaréenne*, p. 776.

13. 'Le héros lazaréen n'est jamais là où il se trouve ... car il a vécu dans un monde qui ne se trouvait nulle part et dont les frontières ne sont pas marquées puisque ce sont celles de la mort. Il se méfie toujours de l'endroit où il vient d'arriver', Cayrol, 'De la vie à la mort', pp. 106–107. Cayrol used the same idea of things being 'out of place' on numerous occasions, for example: 'The prisoner was never there where he was beaten, where he was made to eat, where he worked' ('Le prisonnier n'était jamais là où on le frappait, là où on le faisait manger, là où il travaillait'); 'The most insignificant daily acts were never in their place' ('Les moindres actes de la journée n'étaient jamais à leur place'), 'Préambule', pp. 773 and 775 respectively.

14. 'homme échappé de la grande peur dont il porte encore les stigmates', Roland Barthes, 'Un Prolongement à la littérature de l'absurde', *Combat*, 21 September 1950 (reprinted in *Jean Cayrol: Œuvre lazaréenne*, pp. 761–762).

15. 'Lazare est un ressuscité, un homme qui a connu la mort et ne peut plus se retrouver tel qu'il était avant cette expérience. De même l'homme moderne connaît la mort horrible des camps. Aussi n'est-il plus le même qu'avant la guerre, marqué à tout jamais par l'existence de ces atrocités. Il n'a pas besoin, pour être concerné, d'avoir effectivement été interné. Il suffit que cet emprisonnement et cette mort aient existé pour modifier totalement l'humanité. Le héros lazaréen est donc le héros typique de notre époque, solitaire, anonyme, figé dans un équilibre instable, traumatisé et usé par toute la misère du monde', René Prédal, *L'Itinéraire d'Alain Resnais* (Lettres Modernes, 1996), p. 104.

16. Cayrol, 'Préambule', p. 770.

17. 'Ces rêves étaient des ouvertures sur la connaissance du réel', Daniel Oster, *Jean Cayrol et son œuvre* (Seuil, 1967), p. 29. Oster draws attention to the importance of surrealism in Cayrol's concentrationary art. See also Dorota Ostrowska, 'Dreaming a Cinematic Dream: Jean Cayrol's Writings on Film', *Studies in French Cinema* 6, 1 (2006), 17–28, and Max Silverman, 'Horror and the Everyday in Post-Holocaust France: *Nuit et brouillard* and Concentrationary Art', *French Cultural Studies* 17, 1 (2006), 5–18.

18. 'rendre présent ce qui est absent', Alain Parrau, *Écrire les camps* (Belin, 1995), p. 227.

19. The use of the figure of Lazarus in a post-concentrationary definition of art recasts humanism by the spectral haunting of the sovereign and autonomous individual. In his book on the return of the dead, Colin Davis observes that '[t]he entry on superstition in the *Encyclopédie* (1751–1772) lists "spectres, dreams and visions" as the tools of fear and imagination', *Haunted Subjects: Deconstruction, Psychoanalysis and the Return of the Dead* (Basingstoke, Hampshire: Palgrave Macmillan, 2007), p. 6. The classic recent work on *hantologie* is Jacques Derrida's *Spectres de Marx* (Galilee, 1993). For a wide-ranging discussion of 'ghosts in French literature', see the collection of essays in Kate Griffiths and David Evans (eds), *Haunted Presences: Ghosts in French Literature and Culture* (Cardiff: University of Wales Press, 2009).

20. 'les blocks ne sont plus visités que par une caméra', 'piétinement des concentrationnaires', '[p]lus aucun pas que le nôtre', Jean Cayrol, 'Nuit et brouillard (commentaire)' in *Nuit et brouillard* (Fayard, 1997), p. 18. Shot numbers refer to the reassembled shooting script reproduced in Richard Raskin, *Nuit et brouillard by Alain Resnais: On the Making, Reception and Functions of a Major Documentary Film* (Aarhus: Aarhus University Press, 1987).

21. Benjamin, *The Arcades Project*, p. 416.

22. Emma Wilson, 'Material Remains: *Night and Fog*', *October* 112 (2005), 93. For a discussion of the opening images in terms of the Cayrolian 'in-between', see Sylvie Lindeperg, *'Nuit et brouillard', un film dans l'histoire* (Odile Jacob, 2006), pp. 87–90.

23. For overlaps between Resnais's filming and Nazi footage, see André-Pierre Colombat, *The Holocaust in French Film* (Metuchen, New Jersey: Scarecrow Press, 1993), pp. 130–131. Susan Sontag cites Ernst Jünger's observation in 1930 that 'the camera and the gun, "shooting" a subject and shooting a human being … are congruent activities', Susan Sontag, *Regarding the Pain of Others* (London: Penguin, 2003), p. 60. Resnais's montage reveals the inevitable contamination of 'shooting' a film in the present and objectifying and dehumanizing the other in the past.

24. 'la machine se met en marche', Cayrol, 'Nuit et brouillard (commentaire)', p. 18. It is interesting to compare the disturbance of beginnings and endings here with the opening of Charlotte Delbo's *Aucun de nous ne reviendra (Auschwitz et après 1)* (Minuit, 1970). For an excellent analysis of the problematization of arrivals and departures in Delbo's *Auschwitz et après* trilogy, see Michael Rothberg, *Traumatic Realism: The Demands of Holocaust Representation* (Minneapolis: University of Minnesota Press, 2000), pp. 141–145.

25. See Leo Bersani and Ulysse Dutoit, *Arts of Impoverishment: Beckett, Rothko, Resnais* (Cambridge, Mass.: Harvard University Press, 1993).

26. '*Nuit et brouillard* peut même être considéré comme la somme de toutes les manières d'échapper au flash-back, et à la fausse piété de l'image-souvenir …. Dans le cas de Resnais, cette insuffisance du flash-back n'empêche pourtant pas que toute son œuvre soit fondée sur la coexistence des nappes de passé, le présent n'intervenant même plus comme centre d'évocation', Gilles Deleuze, *Cinéma 2: L'Image-temps* (Minuit, 1985), p. 160 / *Cinema 2: The Time-image*, trans. Hugh Tomlinson and Robert Galeta (London: Athlone Press, 1989), p. 122. Resnais himself said, in relation to *Hiroshima mon amour*, 'I don't like using the "flashback" – for me *Hiroshima mon amour* is always in the present' ('Je n'aime pas utiliser le "flash back" – pour moi, *Hiroshima mon amour* est toujours au présent'), cited in Yvonne Baby, 'Un Entretien avec Alain Resnais', *Le Monde*, 11 May 1966, itself cited in Cathy Caruth, *Unclaimed Experience: Trauma, Narrative and History* (Baltimore and London: Johns Hopkins University Press, 1996), n. 10, p. 123. Jean Gruault suggests instead that 'most of the time Resnais uses the flashback not as a form of memory but as a narrative device' ('la plupart du temps, Resnais n'utilise pas le flash-back comme souvenir mais en tant que forme de récit'), cited in Prédal, *L'Itinéraire d'Alain Resnais*, p. 169.

27. For a detailed account of how Resnais subverts the simplistic dichotomy between colour (present) and black and white (past), see Lindeperg, '*Nuit et brouillard', un film dans l'histoire*, p. 8; Sylvie Lindeperg, 'Night and Fog: A History of Gazes' in Griselda Pollock and Max Silverman (eds), *Concentrationary Cinema: Aesthetics as Political Resistance in Alain Resnais's 'Night and Fog' (1955)* (Oxford and New York: Berghahn, 2011), pp. 55–70; and Andrew Hebard, 'Disruptive Histories: Toward a Radical Politics of Remembrance in Alain Resnais's *Night and Fog*', *New German Critique* 71 (1997), 87–113 (reproduced in Pollock and Silverman (eds), *Concentrationary Cinema*, pp. 214–237). Lindeperg shows that Resnais chose quite explicitly to film part of the footage at Auschwitz in black and white, for example 'certain sequences in the museum blocks …: the pan in the kapo's room, the vertical tracking shot of a puppet and the long bleak shot of the huge pile of women's hair preserved in Block 4' ('Night and Fog: A History of Gazes').

28. 'Cette réalité des camps … [est] insaisissable pour ceux qui la subissent, c'est bien en vain qu'à notre tour nous essayons d'en découvrir les restes. Ces blocks en bois, ces chalits où l'on dormait à trois, ces terriers où l'on se cachait, où l'on mangeait à la sauvette, où le sommeil même était une menace, aucune description, aucune image ne peuvent leur rendre leur vraie dimension : celle d'une peur ininterrompue', Cayrol, 'Nuit et brouillard (commentaire)', p. 23.

29. 'De ce dortoir de briques, de ces sommeils menacés, nous ne pouvons que vous montrer l'écorce, la couleur. Voilà le décor : ces bâtiments qui pourraient être écuries, granges,

ateliers, un terrain pauvre devenu terrain vague, un ciel d'automne devenu indifférent : voilà tout ce qui nous reste pour imaginer cette nuit coupée d'appels, de contrôle de poux, nuit qui claque des dents', Cayrol, 'Nuit et brouillard (commentaire)', p. 24.

30. 'LA PROPRETÉ C'EST LA SANTÉ; 'LE TRAVAIL C'EST LA LIBERTÉ'; 'CHACUN SON DÛ'; 'UN POU C'EST LA MORT', Cayrol, 'Nuit et brouillard (commentaire)', p. 28.

31. 'le monde véritable, celui des paysages calmes, celui du temps d'avant', Cayrol, 'Nuit et brouillard (commentaire)', p. 29.

32. 'Pour un peu, on se serait cru devant une vraie clinique', Cayrol, 'Nuit et brouillard (commentaire)', p. 33.

33. 'Il y a un décor, mais derrière ?', Cayrol, 'Nuit et brouillard (commentaire)', p. 33.

34. 'cité vraisemblable avec hôpital, quartier réservé, quartier résidentiel, et même – oui – une prison', Cayrol, 'Nuit et brouillard (commentaire)', p. 36.

35. 'Un crématoire, cela pouvait prendre à l'occasion un petit air de carte postale. Plus tard – aujourd'hui –, des touristes s'y font photographier', Cayrol, 'Nuit et brouillard (commentaire)', p. 37.

36. 'Rien ne distinguait la chambre à gaz d'un block ordinaire', Cayrol, 'Nuit et brouillard (commentaire)', p. 38.

37. Arendt, *The Origins of Totalitarianism*, p. 459.

38. Cayrol, 'Nuit et brouillard (commentaire)', p. 39. I have written about the anxious relationship between horror and the everyday in 'Horror and the Everyday in Post-Holocaust France'. Cayrol draws out the tension between horror and the everyday that one finds in Arendt's work from her very early post-war writings through to *Eichmann in Jerusalem: A Report on the Banality of Evil*.

39. For the purpose of my present argument, I am limiting the discussion of techniques of defamiliarization to certain key aspects. However, one could equally talk of the disjunction between image, music and spoken text, the constant tension between the still and moving image, the uncertain relationship between filmic addressor and addressee, and others.

40. Our perception of the archive images of atrocity in *Nuit et brouillard* (and especially the Sonderkommando image of the smouldering bodies of victims recently gassed) has, more recently, been caught up in the debates about the ethics of representation and the use of the archive. However, the dichotomy 'representation versus anti-representation', in which *Nuit et brouillard* is placed on the side of representation because of its use of archive material and Claude Lanzmann's *Shoah* on the side of anti-representation because of its refusal to use the archive, is, I would suggest, itself a misrepresentation of Resnais's use of archive footage and photographs in the film. These photographs are themselves broken images rather than a direct representation of horror giving us unmediated access to the real. They are, like the split vision announced at the beginning of the film and the traces in the present gesturing to an elsewhere, part of the Lazarean regime by which clarity of vision has been replaced by 'haunted images'. In her excellent book on film, ethics and the Holocaust, Libby Saxton acknowledges this treatment of the archive in *Nuit et brouillard* (and gives a brilliant critique of the false oppositions established in the heated polemical debates in France in recent years about the representation of atrocity): 'in *Nuit et brouillard* the archive images too, in their turn, become haunted, the emaciated, traumatized survivors and the mounds of corpses evoking, but not supplanting, the missing bodies of those who were murdered in the gas chamber, incinerated in the crematoria or recycled in the various appalling ways mentioned', *Haunted Images: Film, Ethics, Testimony and the Holocaust* (London and New York: Wallflower Press, 2008), p. 90.

41. 'la guerre s'est assoupie, un œil toujours ouvert', Cayrol, 'Nuit et brouillard (commentaire)', p. 42.

42. 'On fermait les portes. On observait. Le seul signe – mais il faut le savoir –, c'est ce plafond labouré par les ongles. Même le béton se déchirait', Cayrol, 'Nuit et brouillard (commentaire)', p. 38.

43. 'Il s'agissait, dans le parallélisme des images d'archive et des marques du présent, de convoquer un *temps critique* – à la façon de Brecht – propice, non à l'identification, mais à la réflexion politique', Georges Didi-Huberman, *Images malgré tout* (Minuit, 2003), p. 165 / *Images in Spite of All*, trans. Shane B. Lillis (Chicago and London: University of Chicago Press, 2008), p. 132. See also Georges Didi-Huberman, 'Opening the Camps, Closing the Eyes: Image, History, Readability' in Pollock and Silverman (eds), *Concentrationary Cinema*, pp. 84–125. The *'projet benjaminien'* of *Nuit et brouillard* (Hélène Raymond, *Poétique du témoignage: Autour du film 'Nuit et brouillard' d'Alain Resnais* (L'Harmattan, 2008), p. 62) is in large part constructed by detaching the seeing eye of the film from a personal framing and converting it into a device for asking historical questions. Alain Fleischer captures this well: 'The technique of a subjective tracking-shot without a viewing subject, a movement filmed by a camera whose look belongs to no living being, no survivor, no fictional character created by someone's imagination, but a pure machine for reading and a mechanics of deciphering is a filmic technique that Alain Resnais will apply in new and specific ways elsewhere' ('La figure du travelling subjectif sans sujet regardant, le mouvement filmé par une caméra qui n'est le regard d'aucun être vivant, d'aucun survivant, d'aucun personnage de fiction qu'aucune imagination ait pu inventer, mais pure machine à lire, machinerie de déchiffrage, est une figure de filmage dont Alain Resnais trouvera ensuite quelques nouvelles et spécifiques applications'), *L'art d'Alain Resnais* (Éditions du Centre Pompidou, 1998), p. 34.

44. 'un village abandonné encore plein de menaces'; 'neuf millions de morts hantent ce paysage', Cayrol, 'Nuit et brouillard (commentaire)', p. 42.

45. 'qui de nous veille dans cet étrange observatoire pour nous avertir de la venue de nouveaux bourreaux ? Ont-ils vraiment un autre visage que le nôtre ? Quelque part, parmi nous, il est des kapos chanceux, des chefs récupérés, des dénonciateurs inconnus', Cayrol, 'Nuit et brouillard (commentaire)', pp. 42–43.

46. 'nous qui feignons de croire que tout cela est d'un seul pays, et qui ne pensons pas à regarder autour de nous, et qui n'entendons pas qu'on crie sans fin', Cayrol, 'Nuit et brouillard (commentaire)', p. 43.

47. 'Notre mauvaise mémoire', Cayrol, 'Nuit et brouillard (commentaire)', p. 41.

48. 'le vieux monstre concentrationnaire était mort sous les décombres ... comme si on guérissait de la peste concentrationnaire', Cayrol, 'Nuit et brouillard (commentaire)', p. 43.

49. 'I've always refused the word "memory" a propos my work. I'd use the word "imagination"', cited in James Monaco, *Alain Resnais* (Oxford and New York: Oxford University Press, 1979), p. 11. (See also Prédal, *L'Itinéraire d'Alain Resnais*, p. 161.)

50. Thomas Elsaesser, 'Freud as Media Theorist: Mystic Writing-pads and the Matter of Memory', *Screen* 50, 1 (2009), 5.

51. 'Dans un rêve, il n'y a plus une image-souvenir qui incarne un point particulier de telle nappe, il y a des images qui s'incarnent l'une dans l'autre, chacune renvoyant à un point de nappe différente. Il se peut que, quand nous lisons un livre, regardons un spectacle ou un tableau, et à plus forte raison quand nous sommes nous-mêmes auteur, un processus analogue se déclenche : nous constituons une nappe de transformation qui invente une sorte de continuité ou de communication transversales entre plusieurs nappes, et tisse entre elles un ensemble de relations non-localisables. Nous dégageons ainsi le temps non-chronologique', Deleuze, *L'Image-temps*, pp. 161–162 / *Cinema 2: The Time-image*, p. 123.

52. Hebard, 'Disruptive Histories', p. 101.

53. 'Ce cri sans fin, substitué à l'incantatoire « plus jamais ça » des monuments aux morts, donne son sens à la définition flottante des victimes et des bourreaux', Lindeperg, '*Nuit et brouillard*', *un film dans l'histoire*, p. 128.

54. 'un glissement sémantique', Lindeperg, '*Nuit et brouillard*', *un film dans l'histoire*, p. 123. This suggests that testimony (like vision and memory) is also de-psychologized and de-invidualized to be a witnessing of the 'in-between'. I discuss this further in chapter 5.

55. 'D'un bout à l'autre de l'œuvre de Resnais on s'enfonce dans une mémoire qui déborde les conditions de la psychologie, mémoire à deux, mémoire à plusieurs, mémoire-monde, mémoire-âges du monde', Deleuze, *Cinema 2: L'Image-temps*, p. 155 / *Cinema 2: The Time-image*, p. 119. Jean-Pierre Salgas talks of the construction in the film of an 'a-temporal present' thirty years before Claude Lanzmann's *Shoah* ('Shoah, ou la disparition' in Denis Hollier (ed.), *De la littérature française* (Bordas, 1993), p. 1007).

56. In their discussion of the overlapping but different evolution of, on the one hand, the concentrationary universe and, on the other, genocide, Sylvie Lindeperg and Annette Wieviorka suggest that it is only 'in 1942 [that] the concentrationary universe and genocide, unconnected until then, come together in the same place, that of the mixed camp of Auschwitz-Birkenau' ('en 1942 [que l']univers concentrationnaire et génocide, jusque là disjoints, se rencontrent en un même lieu, celui du camp mixte d'Auschwitz-Birkenau'). This is shown in *Nuit et brouillard* in the footage of Himmler visiting the camp in July 1942 (*Univers Concentrationnaire et génocide: Voir, savoir, comprendre* (Mille et une nuits/Arthème Fayard, 2008), p. 59). Griselda Pollock and I make a case for seeing *Nuit et brouillard* in the context of the concentrationary universe rather than the genocide that came to be known as the Holocaust in 'Introduction: Concentrationary Cinema' in Pollock and Silverman (eds), *Concentrationary Cinema*, pp. 1–54.

57. See for example Robert Michael, 'Night and Fog', *Cineaste* 13, 4 (1984), 36–37. Although it is true that the word *juif* is only mentioned once in the film ('Stern, a Jewish student from Amsterdam' / 'Stern, étudiant juif d'Amsterdam', Cayrol, 'Nuit et brouillard (commentaire)', p. 19), the Jewish presence is clearly implicit in 'Schmulski, a merchant from Krakow' ('Schmulski, marchand de Cracovie') and 'rounded up in Warsaw … rounded up in the Vel' d'Hiv' ('[r]aflés de Varsovie … raflés du Vel' d'Hiv'), (Cayrol, 'Nuit et brouillard (commentaire)', pp. 19 and 20 respectively) and in the images of deportees with yellow stars. Lindeperg explains that 'the marginal but very real place given in the screenplay to the account of the genocide of the Jews' and 'the research done in Poland [which] considerably reinforced the presence in the film of shots and photographs referring to the extermination of European Jewry' were heavily excised in Cayrol's own commentary (Lindeperg, '*Night and Fog*: A History of Gazes', p. 60).

58. Resnais's use of montage is a crucial part of this political aesthetic. This is not to say that the painstaking effort involved in re-historicizing Resnais's promiscuous collage of places and times is not of the utmost importance (for example, distinguishing between those images relating to the concentration camps and those of the extermination camps, or recognizing that the young girl framed in the doorway of the cattle-truck (shot number 61) was not a Jew but, most probably, a Romany). However, we should recognize that montage serves the purpose of overlaying 'different' sites to arrive at a more Benjaminian concept of history.

59. For excellent discussions of the allegorical connections in *Nuit et brouillard* linking the camps with other moments of racialized violence, see Debarati Sanyal, 'Auschwitz as Allegory in *Night and Fog*' and Joshua Hirsch, '*Night and Fog* and Posttraumatic Cinema' in Pollock and Silverman (eds), *Concentrationary Cinema*, pp. 152–182 and pp. 183–198 respectively.

60. 'la bouche sera toujours ouverte, non pour la parole mais pour le cri', Cayrol, 'De la vie à la mort', p. 84. Cayrol made the following observation in 1956 about the relevance of

Nuit et brouillard in the present: 'Memory only remains when the present illuminates it. If the crematoria are nothing more than derisory skeletons, if silence falls like a shroud over the former camps, now overgrown with grass, we should not forget that our country is not exempt from the scandal of racism. It is then that *Nuit et brouillard* becomes not simply an example on which to reflect, but a call, a warning against every night and every fog that descends on ground that first emerged, nevertheless, in sun-lit and peaceful times' ('Le souvenir ne demeure que lorsque le présent l'éclaire. Si les crématoires ne sont plus que des squelettes dérisoires, si le silence tombe comme un suaire sur les terrains mangés d'herbe des anciens camps, n'oublions pas que notre pays n'est pas exempt du scandale raciste. Et c'est alors que *Nuit et brouillard* devient non seulement un exemple sur lequel méditer, mais un appel, « un dispositif d'alerte » contre toutes les nuits et tous les brouillards qui tombent sur une terre qui naquit pourtant dans le soleil et pour la paix'), Jean Cayrol, 'Nous avons conçu *Nuit et Brouillard* comme un dispositif d'alerte', *Lettres françaises*, 15 February 1956, reprinted in Jacques Gerber, *Anatole Dauman, Argos Films: Souvenir d'écran* (Centre Georges Pompidou, 1989), p. 101.

61. 'un temps "intemporel"', Cayrol, 'Préambule', p. 771.
62. 'là où Langlois pendant la guerre a sauvé bien des films proscrits par les nazis, et où la Cinémathèque française venait en 1963 … d'ouvrir ses portes', Raymond Bellour, *L'Entre-images 2: Mots, images* (P.O.L., 1999), p. 76.
63. 'After successive shots of the protagonist biting on the strings of the hammock in which he lies, with his head thrown back in agony, we are told that memories begin to surge forth "comme des aveux", forced out of him despite himself, as we see a succession of images of peacetime. There is a chilling recognition here of recent tortures in Algeria, which connects with *Le Joli Mai*'s preoccupations', Sarah Cooper, *Chris Marker* (Manchester: Manchester University Press, 2008), p. 50.
64. 'cet homme fut choisi entre mille, pour sa fixation sur une image du passé'.
65. These themes were explored in more detail in Marker's 1983 film *Sans Soleil* and in his 1997 CD-ROM *Immemory*. Bellour notes that Marker's use of Hitchcock's famous spiral from *Vertigo* is his way of marking 'the emblem of the new era' ('l'emblème du nouveau temps'), *L'Entre-images 2*, p. 32.
66. This recalls a similar play with the temporal indicators of chronological time in Luis Buñuel's surrealist masterpiece *Un Chien andalou*. In *La Jetée* it is not only time which is disturbed in this way; the narrator is not even sure whether he really saw this scene or whether it was a figment of his imagination; 'for a long time he wondered whether he had really seen or if he had created this sweet moment as a support against the moment of madness to come' ('il se demanda longtemps s'il avait vraiment vu, ou s'il avait créé ce moment de douceur pour étayer le moment de folie qui allait venir'). (See also, for example, 'He never knows whether he is moving towards her, whether his movement is controlled by others, whether he is inventing or whether he is dreaming' / 'Lui ne sait jamais s'il se dirige vers elle, s'il est dirigé, s'il invente ou s'il rêve'.)
67. Griselda Pollock, 'Dreaming the Face, Screening the Death: Reflections for Jean Louis Schefer on *La Jetée*', *Journal of Visual Culture* 4, 3 (2005), 292. Janet Harbord also likens the moment of the woman's awakening to 'a plane rushing along a runway, towards that moment of flight', *La Jetée* (London: Afterall Books, 2009), p. 32.
68. It is also the moment of the birth of cinema. For a fuller discussion of this interpretation of the sequence, see Saxton, *Haunted Images*, p. 110.
69. 'ce bruit soudain, le geste de la femme, ce corps qui bascule, les clameurs des gens sur la jetée, brouillés par la peur'.
70. 'Marker takes photographs and uses what is within them to create a fictional frame in which each photograph comes to signify anew' (Harbord, *La Jetée*, p. 24).

71. Harbord, *La Jetée*, pp. 3 and 9 respectively. Harbord describes Marker's technique of memory as follows: 'the dissolves work to bring one world into another, a layering that speaks of time frames as simultaneously occurring, or co-existing. An image bleeds through the surface of another, suggesting an uncanny co-presence that won't fade, like the man whose face we see several times in the underground camp' (*La Jetée*, p. 37).

72. Patrick Ffrench, 'The Memory of the Image in Chris Marker's *La Jetée*', *French Studies* 59, 1 (2005), 36.

73. Lucien Dallenbach describes the spatialized narrative structure of Claude Simon's novel *La Route des Flandres* (1960) in terms of '*l'art du chevauchement*' or straddling of sequences, and also compares this process to Freud's description of condensation in dreams (*Le Récit spéculaire* (Seuil, 1977), pp. 158–161). The understanding of the *nouveau roman* in terms of a Cayrolean notion of concentrationary art is an under-researched area of post-war French culture, as is the political aesthetic in general of the '*nouveau roman*' and the *nouvelle vague*. See, however, Lynn Higgins's *New Novel, New Wave, New Politics: Fiction in the Representation of History in Postwar France* (Lincoln and London: University of Nebraska Press, 1996) which challenges the critical orthodoxy of a dichotomy between the formal aesthetics of the *nouveau roman* and the *nouvelle vague* and the realism of politically committed literature.

74. Cooper, *Chris Marker*, p. 51.

75. 'Le souvenir imparfait mais inducteur d'une grande partie de notre sensibilité, ou l'espèce de mutilation mnésique de la guerre dans l'enfance : la première conscience d'une ère de destruction planétaire qui a logé en nous une âme, comme s'il s'était agi d'une balle de plomb ou d'un éclat d'obus qui nous atteignait, trouvait là, par hasard, un centre où il pouvait vivre encore après avoir seulement percé une ville ou fait mourir quelqu'un d'autre que nous', Jean Louis Schefer, 'À propos de *La Jetée*' in *Images mobiles: Récits, visages, flocons* (P.O.L., 1999), p. 133.

76. Pollock, 'Dreaming the Face, Screening the Death', p. 292.

77. Schefer, 'À propos de *La Jetée*', p. 133. Even his own death is not 'his' as the image of his fall, his body arched backwards with arms outstretched, recalls (intra-diegetically) the wings of the planes and the bird in flight and (extra-diegetically) the famous photo by Robert Capa of the falling soldier of the Spanish Civil War and Christ on the cross. Sarah Cooper cites Kaja Silverman's similar observation in relation to Marker's *Sans Soleil*: 'Silverman argues that *Sans Soleil* is penetrated by other people's memories to the extent that it remembers in the voice of the other and encourages spectators to do the same' (*Chris Marker*, p. 118).

78. Ffrench, 'The Memory of the Image in Chris Marker's *La Jetée*', p. 37.

79. 'Le montage est l'invention d'une réalité différente du monde', Jean Cayrol and Claude Durand, *Le Droit de regard* (Seuil, 1963), p. 57.

80. This observation is not entirely accurate as some of the affective charge of the objects at the beginning is also present in the images of the French army in Algeria – guns emitting smoke, a soldier smoking a cigarette, another soldier diving into a swimming pool.

81. Celia Britton, 'Broken Images in Resnais's *Muriel*', *French Cultural Studies* 1 (1990), 37–46; Emma Wilson, *Alain Resnais* (Manchester: Manchester University Press, 2006), pp. 100–101.

82. The only major character in the film who is not seen constantly smoking is Bernard (although there is an ashtray full of stubbed out cigarettes on the table in his bedroom). At one point, however, he takes out a packet of Marlboro cigarettes and, instead of producing a cigarette from the box, pulls out a scorpion. The image is a close-up of his hand holding the creature (reminiscent of images in Buñuel's classic surrealist masterpieces *Un Chien andalou* and *L'Age d'or*). The relationship between hands, cigarettes, violence and death that will be made explicit in the description of

Muriel's torture is thus prefigured metaphorically in this image, which reinforces the connections between everyday objects and weapons of torture.

83. Bersani and Dutoit, *Arts of Impoverishment*, p. 199.

84. 'le principal, c'est que tu sens chez toi ici, à ton aise'.

85. Naomi Greene, *Landscapes of Loss: The National Past in Postwar French Cinema* (Princeton, New Jersey: Princeton University Press, 1999), p. 49.

86. In fact, the major thrust of Britton's argument does go in this direction, with constant reference to echoes, connections and links: 'A series of parallels and contrasts is constructed between [torture and bombing]; just as torture is the legacy of the Algerian war, the bombing of Boulogne is the legacy of 1940. But the theme of bombing also continues into the present in the form of an OAS plastic bomb which destroys Bernard's studio' ('Broken Images in Resnais's *Muriel*', p. 40). Her later discussion of the intrusion of the outside world into interiors to shatter the safety and self-contained nature of that space, and 'the violent penetration of a woman's body' (p. 45) which connects Muriel and Hélène, also suggests the recomposition of fragments in new constellations. As Britton remarks in relation to the connection between Muriel and Hélène, '[i]t is as though Muriel's mutilation, itself unrepresentable, can only be represented metonymically in its displacement onto Hélène' (p. 41).

87. Bersani and Dutoit, *Arts of Impoverishment*, p. 198.

88. As in his own films, Hitchcock also makes a brief appearance as a cut-out figure outside a restaurant.

89. Wilson, *Alain Resnais*, p. 101. Marie-Claire Ropars lists the extraordinary number of places – including not only Algeria but also Paris, Italy, Indochina, Australia, New Caledonia and Montevideo – which 'contribute to opening up around Boulogne other geographical horizons' ('contribuent à ouvrir autour de Boulogne d'autres horizons géographiques'), Claude Bailbé, Michel Marie and Marie-Claire Ropars, *Muriel: Histoire d'une recherché* (Galilée, 1974), p. 19.

90. Françoise is an actress but, more generally, the staging of many scenes lends an air of theatricality to proceedings which removes them from a 'realistic' setting.

91. 'ce que je voulais montrer, c'est … comment on peut devenir un être éclaté qui survit', cited in Prédal, *L'Itinéraire d'Alain Resnais*, p. 139.

92. When Ernest enters Hélène's flat looking for Alphonse, there is a flash of recognition between Hélène and Ernest. Was Ernest Hélène's real lover? Is he the interchangeable double of Alphonse? He is, after all, introduced by Hélène as '*un revenant*' ('a ghost') and then claims that it was he, not Alphonse, who was due to meet Hélène in 1940 at the Club d'Or (contradicting the story as it was previously recounted by Alphonse). Is de Smoke Hélène's double? Not only is Hélène usually enveloped in a cloud of cigarette smoke; her flat occupies (palimpsestically) the same site as de Smoke's former attic. The interconnections between supposedly different 'lives' can also be seen in the technique of showing images of certain characters while the soundtrack continues the dialogue of others, as, for example, when images of Bernard and Françoise looking into restaurants in the streets of Boulogne are accompanied by the voices of Hélène and Alphonse in Hélène's apartment. As in *Nuit et brouillard*, disjunctions of this kind between image and sound reference the 'elsewhere' to both fragment and connect disparate sites. Hence, the inversion in image and sound-track that we noted above in relation to the first scene in Hélène's apartment and the torture of Muriel in Algeria emphasizes the inability of either to relate the whole truth. (See my later discussion of the image in Michael Haneke's *Caché* in chapter 5.)

93. Wilson, *Alain Resnais*, p. 105.

94. Deleuze, *L'Image-temps*, pp. 269–270 / *The Time-image*, p. 207. Following René Prédal's analysis of Resnais, Deleuze relates this version of '*mémoire-monde*' explicitly to the Lazarean optic of Resnais's work: 'René Prédal has shown the extent to which

Auschwitz and Hiroshima remained the horizon of all Resnais's work, how close the hero in Resnais is to the "Lazarean hero" which Cayrol made the soul of the new novel, in a fundamental relation with the extermination camps. The character in Resnais's cinema is Lazarean precisely because he returns from death, from the land of the dead; he has passed through death and is born from death, whose sensory-motor disturbances he retains. Even if he was not personally in Hiroshima …[, h]e passed through a clinical death, he was born from an apparent death, he returns from the dead, Auschwitz or Hiroshima, Guernica or the Algerian War.' ('René Prédal a montré combien Auschwitz et Hiroshima restaient l'horizon de toute l'oeuvre de Resnais, combien le héros chez Resnais est proche du "héros lazaréen" dont Cayrol faisait l'âme du nouveau roman, dans un rapport essentiel avec les camps d'extermination. Le personnage dans le cinéma de Resnais est précisément lazaréen parce qu'il revient de la mort, du pays des morts ; il est passé par la mort et il naît de la mort, dont il garde les troubles sensori-moteurs. Même s'il n'était pas en personne à Auschwitz, même s'il n'était pas en personne à Hiroshima … Il est passé par une mort clinique, il est né d'une mort apparente, il revient des morts, Auschwitz ou Hiroshima, Guernica ou guerre d'Algérie'), Deleuze, *L'Image-temps*, p. 270 / *The Time-image*, pp. 207–208.

95. Roland Barthes, *La Chambre claire: Note sur la photographie* (Seuil, 1980).
96. Bersani and Dutoit, *Arts of Impoverishment*, p. 196. The object as a trigger for the return of the past in *Muriel* is far more ambivalent than the Proustian epiphany. Even though Muriel (and, accompanying her story, the censored episode in French history that was torture in Algeria) returns, this return is not a full reinstatement of the past but a recognition of the impossibility of a total return as the trauma will continue to be displaced onto different objects and there will always be an absence at the centre. Lynn Higgins is surely right when she says, '[t]he "return" of the title is multidirectional, an unstable, reversible movement' (*New Novel, New Wave, New Politics*, p. 111). The 'time of a return' is the spiral with no closure.

Chapter 3

ANTI-COLONIALISM REVISITED

In the post-war period there were impassioned debates about new directions for humanity in the wake of disaster (the concentration camps and the atom bomb) and the collapse of Western ideas of progress and civilization. The elaboration of an anti-colonial discourse and politics signalling the end of empire thus took place at a time of intercultural and transnational dialogue and practice. Winifred Woodhull observes that the journal *Présence Africaine*, founded in 1947, and its accompanying publishing house 'not only bring together various dissident currents in Paris and the black world [but] self-consciously inscribe themselves in a global frame', and that the intellectual crucible that was Paris at this time, bringing together writers like Richard Wright, James Baldwin, Mohammed Dib, Kateb Yacine and Albert Memmi, was characterized by 'a concern to explore the intersections of cultures: the colonial scourges of unemployment and hunger in the Maghreb; the new United States military bases in Morocco and the "occupation of North Africa"; United States racism; black writing from Cuba to Sudan; and Jewish cultures around the world'.[1] Even the separatist and essentialist concept of Negritude may hide a more complex story in which, as David Macey observes in relation to the work of Léopold Senghor, 'a celebration and endorsement of specifically black-African culture and values' is in tension with 'the cry of revolt voiced by the wretched of the earth'.[2] Recognition of the challenges to Western concepts of civilization and humanity posed by the concentration camps and colonialism prompted UNESCO to ask prominent thinkers in different disciplines to reflect on the reasons for the devastation of recent years (Claude Lévi-Strauss's *Race et histoire* was a product of this project), and led to a broadening of the scope of the French anti-racist organization, the Mouvement contre le racisme et pour l'amitié entre les peuples (MRAP), from opposition to anti-semitism to opposition to anti-semitism and colonialism. Rothberg calls this period 'a moment of transition and a laboratory for thinking about the relationship between different legacies of violence', while Gilroy names it 'the UNESCO or human rights moment'.[3]

Yet our understanding of anti-colonialism rarely embraces the complexity of this context, or, if it does, tends to view links made with the Second World War and the Holocaust either as a historical confusion of distinct events or as a cynical attempt to deflect attention from the specificity of colonialism. Despite the clear pronouncements of Césaire and Fanon on the intersections between the histories of genocide and colonialism, much of the post-war approach to extreme violence has, more recently, been lost from view. The rise of post-colonial studies in the American and British academies (though notably not in a comparable way in France), while undoubtedly transforming our understanding of the relationships between metropolitan 'centres' and colonial 'peripheries' and challenging the power relations between them, has nevertheless established a new orthodoxy which still ties 'centre' to 'periphery' in restrictive ways. Dominic Thomas is surely right when he says 'francophone and postcolonial studies could considerably enhance their validity and authenticity by continuing to insist on the need for a model that is as democratic and inclusive as possible with regard to the various geographic zones in which thinking is generated'.[4] This has certainly happened in recent years, in which there has been an expansion of the notion of the post-colonial from its origins in Anglophone literary criticism and critical theory to embrace 'the relationships between the different European imperial projects and their various aftermaths'.[5] Yet, pushed to its logical limits, Thomas's approach must eventually reflect self-consciously on the very limitations of *any* post-colonial framing.[6] In her discussion of French Caribbean writing, Jeannie Suk's acute perception that 'allegory offers the possibility of liberation from determinate narratives of history' also provides a base to adopt a genuinely 'interstitial perspective'; yet this rarely strays outside the lines drawn between France and the Antilles.[7] Ironically, the newly valued terms of hybridity, diaspora, *métissage, créolisation*, relationality and the mosaic (originally associated predominantly with the critical work of Homi Bhabha and the writing of Edouard Glissant), which should provide the vocabulary to realize a genuinely 'travelling' model, rarely go beyond the space demarcated by colonial histories. Even Peter Hallward's stimulating critique of the 'non-relationality' of the post-colonial paradigm (what he calls its 'singularity') fails to extend the relational 'specificity' of post-colonial literature beyond a fairly circumscribed field.[8] The work of Edward Said is a notable exception in that he invariably viewed histories of culture, violence and power in the broadest possible terms. In the first chapter of *Culture and Imperialism*, entitled 'Overlapping Territories, Intertwined Histories', Said encourages us to study 'the map of interactions, the actual and often productive traffic occurring on a day-by-day, and even minute-by-minute basis among states, societies, groups, and identities'.[9] Yet elsewhere in post-colonial critical thought it is often the case that walls are pulled down only to erect new ones. 'Travelling theory' seems to stop when the colonial connection can no longer be located; yet, as Said points out, the circulation of ideas and practices does not respect this red light.

Hence, a limited framework may efface significant interconnections and fail to recognize the complexity of unconscious processes at work in acts of memory. Can we understand, for example, the censorship of Resnais's image of the French gendarme at the camp of Pithiviers in *Nuit et brouillard* without situating this decision by the French censor within the context of events in Algeria at the time and Resnais's earlier anti-colonial work with Chris Marker *Les Statues meurent aussi* (1953), which had itself incurred the wrath of the French 'commission de contrôle'?[10] Why does the Moroccan writer Abdelkebir Khatibi open his novel *La Mémoire tatouée* with the words 'I was born with the second war' and go on to say 'Radio-Berlin captured the attention of our fathers; international history entered my childhood through the voice of the sinister dictator' when the text is, according to its sub-title, the 'autobiography of a decolonized man'?[11] We can only attempt to answer these and other similar questions if we take Paul Gilroy's comment on 'the knotted intersection of histories' seriously. In this chapter I will consider three texts that are normally read as anti-colonial works to demonstrate how, in fact, anti-colonial themes do not constitute a unified and homogeneous discourse but are profoundly interconnected with other sites of suffering and racialized violence.

Frantz Fanon: *Peau noire masques blancs / Black Skin White Masks*

I belong irreducibly to my time.[12]

In the vast body of literature on Frantz Fanon in recent years, there has been very little serious analysis of Fanon's discussion of the links between anti-Black colonial racism and other forms of racism, especially anti-semitism. Two important exceptions to this are the work of Paul Gilroy and Bryan Cheyette. Gilroy brackets Fanon with other post-war thinkers, like Arendt and Césaire, who approached the iniquities of modern raciological thinking by grappling with the intersections between histories. Cheyette points up the dangers of a reductive post-colonial critique of Europe which rules out the history of anti-semitism for, 'by excluding this historical formation from within imperial culture, many post-colonial theorists help to replicate the very oppositions that they are working against'.[13] With this in mind, it is worth returning to Fanon to remind ourselves of an approach which, both consciously and unconsciously, stages multiple encounters with other histories of violence.

Fanon's famous attack on Octave Mannoni's *Psychologie de la colonisation* in Chapter 4 of *Peau noire masques blancs* ('The so-called dependency complex of colonized peoples' / 'Du prétendu complexe de dépendance du colonisé') stages one such encounter between different sites of violence. Fanon challenges Mannoni's statements on South Africa not directly but via Sartre's discussion of anti-semitism in *Réflexions sur la question juive*. He counters Mannoni's desire to differentiate colonial racism from other forms of racism ('colonial racialism is different from other kinds of racialism', says Mannoni) by positing a universalist approach which refuses such distinctions ('Colonial racism is no different from any other racism', says Fanon).[14] Fanon's evidence to back up this claim consists of quotations taken from the writings of Césaire (political speeches and his text *Discours sur le colonialisme*) on the persistence of a Hitlerian presence in all forms of racism, and Karl Jaspers's discussion of collective guilt and responsibility for the barbarism of the Second World War. He also invokes Césaire's similar indictment of Western civilization to refute Mannoni's claim that 'European civilization and its best representatives are not, for instance, responsible for colonial racialism'.[15] Fanon then cites an imaginary example of a Martinican being mistaken for an Arab by French police before quoting Francis Jeanson on collective guilt in relation to events in Algeria. He returns to Sartre's *Réflexions sur la question juive* to apply Sartre's famous formula concerning the construction of the Jew by the anti-semite ('the Jew is one whom other men consider a Jew .... It is the anti-semite who *makes* the Jew') to colonial racism ('*it is the racist who creates his inferior*').[16] This argumentation, it should be remembered, is by way of disproving Mannoni's thesis on the nature of the Malagasy ('le Malgache').[17]

It could be said that Fanon mixes different histories in an entirely ahistorical way and juxtaposes different theoretical models to produce a fairly crude universalist form of anti-racism. It could also be said that there is no consistency to Fanon's ideas; there is no recognition here, for example, of the distinctions between different levels of Blackness that he has mentioned in his earlier discussion of the hierarchical ordering of race thinking.[18] Furthermore, the universalism expressed in his critique of Mannoni, in which there is no difference between the plight of the Jew and that of the Black, is contradicted later when he discusses the differences between Jews and Blacks in the racist imaginary. Cheyette does an excellent job of finessing the slippages and contradictions of Fanon's text regarding the relationship between Blacks and Jews:

> There are ... two incommensurable narratives in *Peau noire* concerning Blacks and Jews that revolve around the uncertainty of whether Jews should be regarded as 'black' or 'white' .... In other words, the references to Jews and anti-Semitism in *Peau noire* are part of a wider tension concerning the relationship between a particularist anti-colonial nationalism (which excludes 'the Jew') and more universalist or transnational theories of racial oppression (which include 'the Jew').[19]

A later reference to Mannoni, in which Fanon highlights not the similarities but the differences between anti-semitism and anti-Black racism, corroborates this point.[20]

However, I would like to draw attention not so much to the inconsistencies and contradictions of Fanon's argument as to the interconnections at the heart of his approach. Fanon is looking across the fault lines of race and searching for similarities and differences. In this sense, he is trying to map different models and different events on to each other in his attempt to subvert the invidious codes of race-thinking at the heart of Western thought and practice. The result is not unproblematic but the method, intention and strategy are perhaps more interesting than the outcome for they show a hybrid consciousness at work struggling to redefine the human in the wake of the crisis of Western notions of civilization, one which is part of a broader ongoing dialogue in the post-war period in which different racisms are drawn into contact with each other. In this sense, he is (like Césaire) concerned with the broader picture of the spread of Western ideas and practice across the globe in which barbarity masquerades as civilization and Enlightened thought. Robert Bernasconi takes Hannah Arendt to task for acknowledging, in *The Origins of Totalitarianism*, the connections between imperialism and genocide but wanting, nevertheless, to preserve the tradition of Enlightenment thought (especially that of Kant) from complicity with barbarity.[21] Fanon, on the other hand, challenges Mannoni and others precisely because he recognizes the subtle ways in which race-thinking inhabits even the most 'enlightened' arguments on humanity.

Fanon's discussion of the relationship between Jew and Black is therefore significant in terms of a radical investigation of the general malaise of a Western racialized imaginary. In his conclusion to *Réflexions sur la question juive* Sartre cites the view of the Black American writer Richard Wright on anti-Black racism to confirm his own view on anti-semitism: '"There is no Negro problem in the United States, there's only a White problem." In the same way, we must say that anti-Semitism is not a Jewish problem; it is *our* problem'.[22] When Fanon echoes Wright's claim, 'there is no black problem' ('il n'y a pas de problème noir'), and when he mentions Wright again during his discussion of the racist's need for a scapegoat (be it Jew or Black),[23] his description of 'a manicheism delirium' ('un manichéisme délirant')[24] is already founded on a hybrid model of the Western racial imaginary composed of an intertextual dialogue between (at least) Sartre and Wright and comprising (at least) the three figures of the American 'Negro', the Jew and the Antillean Black. I say 'at least' because others were part of this post-war dialogue. Rothberg discusses how the thinking of the African-American intellectual and activist W. E. B. Du Bois on 'double consciousness' and the 'colour line' was transformed after his visit to Warsaw in 1949. He cites an extract from an article entitled 'The Negro and the Warsaw Ghetto' written by Du Bois and published in the magazine *Jewish Life* in 1952, the same year as the publication of Fanon's text: 'the race problem in which I was interested cut across lines of color and physique and belief and status and was a matter of cultural patterns, perverted teaching and human hate and prejudice, which reached all sorts of people and caused endless evil to all men'. Du Bois, like Césaire, Fanon, Wright and Sartre, was looking across the 'colour line' to reformulate racial thinking and rights between universalist and particularist claims.[25]

Yet even this post-war dialogue across the 'colour line' should be placed in a wider historical context of the development of racial thinking underpinning Enlightenment thought,[26] for the articulation of the 'Black' and the Jew (and, ultimately, colonial and genocidal inferiorization), has a lineage which stretches back to nineteenth century racial science and beyond. Sander Gilman has observed how the racialization of the Jew in the second half of the nineteenth century was often in terms of Blackness: 'The black and the Jew were associated not merely because they were both "outsiders" but because qualities ascribed to one became the means of defining the difference of the other. The categories of "black" and "Jew" thus became interchangeable at one point in history.'[27] Neil Macmaster (following Albert Lindeman's work on modern anti-semitism) illustrates this clearly by quoting an attack by Karl Marx in 1862 on the socialist and 'Jewish nigger' Ferdinand Lassalle:

> It is clear to me that, as both the shape of his head and his hair texture shows, he descends from the Negroes who joined Moses' flight from Egypt (unless his mother or grandmother on the paternal side hybridized with a nigger). Now this combination of Germanness and Jewishness with a primarily Negro substance creates a strange product. The pushiness of the fellow is also nigger-like.[28]

Macmaster, like Gilman, places articulations of this kind 'within a specific historical context, the point at which a crucial transition took place towards more radical forms of both colonial racism and anti-Semitism after 1860'.[29] During this period, the medicalization of the other played a significant role in the process of racialization. Fanon's critique of Western psychiatry throughout his work (see especially the chapter on the imposition of Western medical science in Algeria in *L'An V de la révolution algérienne / A Dying Colonialism* and the chapter 'Colonial War and Mental Disorders' in *Les Damnés de la terre / The Wretched of the Earth*) relates to the pathologizing since the nineteenth century not only of the Black body but of other bodies too, and the interchangeability of 'complexes' from one group to another that this process entailed. Richard Keller notes that, although psychiatric studies at the end of the nineteenth century and beginning of the twentieth century showed that Muslims in French North Africa were least capable of all groups of making good soldiers because of their psychological make-up, they also revealed that 'Jews were hypersensitive and showed depressive and nervous tendencies when pressed into service'.[30] In his essay on Raymond Schwab, Said writes the following:

> Read Schwab and you will not remember that Conrad's Kurtz is one of the chief products of Orientalism, or that race theory, scholarly anti-Semitism, and proto-Fascism are literal products of nineteenth-century Oriental philology. At the same time that Friedrich Schlegel, Wilhelm von Humboldt, and Ernest Renan were making their distinction between organic, lively, wonderful Indo-European and inorganic, agglutinative, uninteresting Semitic, they were also constructing the doxology of twentieth-century anti-Arab and anti-Jewish Orientalist scholarship.[31]

Gilroy, as we have noted, believes that one cannot properly understand the development of modern race theory without exploring articulations of this kind in the development of the modern nation-state and empire. In a fascinating study of 'the Jewish question and the crisis of post-colonial culture', Aamir Mufti (like Gilroy) adopts an Arendtian perspective to understand the connections between the 'Jewish question' in the nineteenth century and the production of colonial 'minorities' in Enlightenment thought.[32] Although Michel Foucault spent very little of his time considering the relationship between race and disciplinary society, his work nevertheless provides an overarching framework for analyses that explore the broad parameters of the construction of different minorities in modern society. As Mark Mazower says in a comparative study of Foucault and Agamben, '[t]he nineteenth-century injection of state racism transforms and radicalizes definitions of "what must live" and "what must die"'.[33]

Fanon's intervention in 1952 is therefore a point of intersection of different but overlapping strands of racializing ideology that gained currency in scientific thought and in the popular imagination long before. The inconsistencies of his approach, which slips between a conflation of Jew and Black and a separation of them – '[s]eeing only one type of Negro, assimilating anti-Semitism to Negrophobia, these seem to be the errors of analysis being committed here',[34] – should not obscure the fact that the text is profoundly marked by this wider dialogue on the relationship between the Jew and other minorities in Enlightenment thought. It is indebted to the trans- and intercultural debates of the period but also reveals the conscious and unconscious peripetias of race thinking and its critique underpinning these debates.

Moreover, *Peau noire masques blancs* is a very self-consciously composite text. Fanon's strange blend of polemical argument, scientific discussion, literary criticism and poetic musing and his eclectic references and influences have often been seen as a shortcoming as they detract from the text's coherence. However, looked at differently, the very fragmented narrative structure and formal composition accentuates the hybrid and intertextual character of the text. It reinforces the splintering of the self central to the argument and displays graphically the disjointed pieces that make up the psychic and historical character of the work. The intertextual poetics of *Peau noire masques blancs* is thus in keeping with a spatialized politics of interlocking and overlapping contexts.

Mohammed Dib: *Qui se souvient de la mer*

Qui se souvient de la mer has often been described as a dream-like depiction of the Algerian War of Independence, even 'as a symbol of the destruction of the colonial system' (although there is no mention of the war or colonialism in the text).[35] This is only half true, in the same way, perhaps, that the depiction of Resnais's *Nuit et brouillard* as a film about the Holocaust only tells half the story.[36] In fact, the work is a broader depiction of horror in the post-war period which unsettles the dividing line between the specificity of the Algerian War and the general nature of apocalypse.

In the brief postscript to the novel, Dib puts the Algerian War in the context of other moments and sites of extreme violence and describes the work as an attempt to find a medium capable of capturing the horrors of recent years:

> The exterminations of the last war, the monstrous nature of the concentration camps, the abomination of the atomic bomb still haunt our lives. How should we speak about Algeria after Auschwitz, the Warsaw ghetto and Hiroshima? How can we guarantee that what needs to be said can still be heard and not simply swallowed up by this immense and demoniacal cloud which has been hanging over the world for so many years, nor simply dissolved into the hell of banality in which horror has been able to cloak itself and cloak us?[37]

The example that he offers as a way of addressing this task is Picasso's *Guernica*, a work that breaks through the stock images of horror by creating a language capable of expressing the collective unconscious of apocalypse that haunts our waking lives. Dib's work, similarly, uses a fragmented and expressionistic poetic language to capture trauma. Resnais had already made a short film about Picasso's *Guernica* before *Nuit et brouillard* (*Guernica*, 1950, with a text by the surrealist poet Paul Éluard), and Dib's effort to read horror through the banal also echoes Cayrol's vision of concentrationary art. More surprising still (although indicative of the intercultural dialogue at play) are the similarities between Dib's text and Marker's *La Jetée*, which appeared in the same year. In both works the city, after catastrophe, has become a dehumanizing space of enclosure in which an Orphic quest for liberation and wholeness is undertaken by a nameless narrator through the memory/imagination of lost objects of desire; in both, a blend of science fiction and dream-like sequences creates a new post-apocalyptic language of trauma and desire.[38]

Let us focus in particular on the palimpsestic nature of Dib's post-apocalyptic language. The presence of the mother, like the sea (*mère/mer*),[39] is the constant murmur and wordless song which acts as a backdrop to the petrified words of the city. In one instance the narrator describes his memory of her as follows:

> Thus, recently, I have often seen my mother in my dreams... My mother who had so little presence in her own home and of whom I have retained only a vague impression. Her features, which float in the depths of my memory beneath a light fog, her image drowned in layers of shadow, return from so far away that the other mother, the real one, seems lost forever. Two huge dark eyes illuminate my nights, the rest is obscure. In the morning I look again at the photos of her: not one remotely resembles the image I retain of her. I cannot see those open eyes in my imagination, like windows on a horizon which surely belongs to another world.[40]

The ghost-like presence of the mother is evoked through a language which recalls other ghosts from another site of disaster. Expressions such as 'un fin brouillard', 'son image noyée par des nappes d'ombre', 'deux yeux noirs immenses éclairent mes nuits, et le reste est brouillé' and 'ces yeux ouverts dans mon imagination' conjure up (even unconsciously) the ghosts of *Nuit et brouillard* which haunt the ruins of Auschwitz. Numerous descriptions of the horror of the city and its petrified inhabitants use a language of disaster which goes beyond the specificity of the Algerian War of Independence to speak more generally: 'Sometimes explosions shake the very foundations of the city; History provides no examples, not even approximate, for what is taking place before my eyes. The bombardments, the shots, the screeching and hooting sounds, the flashes which envelop the new city, if by chance they ease up it is never for long'; 'So we wander, circling between the walls which knot and coil inexplicably around us, and a horror which nobody can shake off deadens us'; 'I saw them burn the inhabitants'; 'Cymbals, a chorus of dogs, an orchestra, explosions: nothing was missing that night'; 'On the road, piled up, were as many inert statues as mutilated torsos, arms, legs, in incomplete postures and movements'.[41] The image of the *musulman* in the concentration camps is captured convincingly by Dib in the following passage:

> Around me, myself a pitiful being, all these statues resembled the dead, proud in their strength and their strangeness. I was incapable of detaching my look from theirs, hypnotized, or of escaping from their silence. The familiar expression lighting up their features, extinguished, clearly extinguished.[42]

Like Picasso's painting, which incorporates Guernica into a new poetics of horror, Dib finds a language which embraces the specificity of the Algerian War and the general character of a post apocalyptic imagination.

Furthermore, the novel's structure of 'doubling' (*dédoublement*), in which the visible present is always shadowed by an invisible past, corresponds to the 'strangeness' of self and the world central to Cayrol's Lazarean art. 'An ancient and silent cataclysm having torn us from ourselves and from the world'[43] means that the present has been ripped apart and is constantly doubled by the ghosts of elsewhere: the ruined *chateau* associated with the narrator's childhood haunts the 'new constructions' ('nouvelles constructions') of the present; the mother is a double for the narrator's wife Nafissa (and both are associated with the Orphic quest for *'la mer'*); the subterranean city is the counter-culture of the city above ground; the fluidity of the sea is the constant backdrop to stone-like words and the city of *'le basalte'*;[44] the narration of the present is doubled by the narration of the past. The sea (like the image of the woman in *La Jetée*) is always an absent presence, a memory or a dream which haunts the narrator and whose ghost-like existence signals a dim, distant but profound longing for a return and for unity after the 'ancient and silent cataclysm'. The novel ends on an ambiguous note with the persistence of the deep memory of the sea: 'Sometimes I am conscious again of a deep pain, a muted song, and I dream, I remember the sea'.[45]

The memory of the sea in a world in which humanity has been transformed into petrified stone is Dib's metaphorical equivalent of Césaire's famous statement in *Discours sur le colonialisme*, 'colonization = objectification' ('*colonisation* = *chosification*'),[46] Cayrol's defamiliarization of the modern world of objects, Resnais's and Marker's subversion of the Western gaze which turns others into statues (in *Les Statues meurent aussi*), Arendt's plea for spontaneity, and Fanon's de-objectification of the racialized self. In his critique of the anti-semite's failure to face up to freedom in *Réflexions sur la question juive*, Sartre states 'there are people who are attracted by the durability of a stone', and 'the anti-Semite is a man who wishes to be pitiless stone'.[47] Debarati Sanyal observes how Sartre uses a similar imagery to describe colonialism in his preface to Fanon's *Les Damnés de la terre*, and demonstrates how, in Sartre's allegorical play *Les Séquestrés d'Altona*, his 'figures of petrification draw analogies between distinct sites and regimes of violence'.[48] The imagery of the culture and counter-culture of violence in *Qui se souvient de la mer* in terms of petrification and fluidity thus cuts across different sites of racialized violence. In a different context, but of relevance here, Iain Chambers and Lydia Curti comment on how the sea subverts 'petrified' boundaries and creates connections between different sites:

> The sea itself confronts meaning. Its winds, currents, flotsam, varying depths and multiple shorelines induce a provocative contrast with the seemingly

stable homelands proposed by the inherited archive of cultural, historical and disciplinary identities. Opposed to the geometrical (and geopolitical) logic of barriers to overcome and differences to integrate, the sea both reflects and absorbs maps that suggest an altogether more fluid understanding. It permits the possibility of an open-ended comprehension of the continual composition of a multiple Mediterranean, where West and East, North and South, Europe, Asia and Africa are caught up in a historical and cultural net that stretches over centuries, even millennia. Here the 'Mediterranean' is interrupted continually by a vulnerability that accompanies the encounter with other voices, other bodies, other histories.[49]

Charles Bonn talks of the play in *Qui se souvient de la mer* between the themes of 'dispersal' and 'closure' ('éclatement' and 'clôture').[50] The ambiguous ending of the novel highlights the otherness which haunts all attempts at 'nouvelles constructions'. In Dib, the poetics of surrealism and the *nouveau roman* find their political voice, as the subversion of the fixity of the object reveals both the re-enchanted world beyond the word and the actuality of horror. A passage on the ability of the ashtray to 'overflow' its social function and become 'the instrument of some fatality, the seat of a deadly power' is reminiscent of the link between objects, anxiety and torture that we noticed in *Muriel*: 'The tortures, the inquisitions, the *poire d'angoisse* instruments, the wheel, the stake, have only ever served the enemy; one glimpses the traps that they conceal'.[51] Dib shows how the heated debate in France in the 1960s, in which Sartre's model of committed literature (*littérature engagée*) was seen as the antithesis of the avant-garde *nouveau roman* was founded on a false dichotomy as many of the formal techniques of the latter are ways of expressing the concerns of the former.[52] Cayrol himself demonstrates the wrong-headed nature of this opposition: he brings a new surrealist poetics to bear on existential questions in a post-apocalyptic age and, in the process, reveals the dangers to humanity of 'petrification' across the sites of the Holocaust and colonialism. Dib's work is clearly part of this post-war dialogue.

Assia Djebar: *Femmes d'Alger dans leur appartement*

In her collection of stories *Femmes d'Alger dans leur appartement*, Assia Djebar also looks to Picasso for a new language capable of resisting the violence of 'petrification'. 'Petrification' in the work of Djebar takes numerous forms: a rigidified language which 'fixes' the world, a narrow sense of history which effaces the plurality of memories, and, especially, the 'imprisonment' of women in patriarchal society. In the postscript to the collection of stories, 'Forbidden Gaze, Severed Sound' ('Regard interdit, son coupé'), Djebar contrasts the voyeuristic and objectifying look of Delacroix in his famous painting 'Femmes d'Alger dans leur appartement' (1834) with the liberating technique employed by Picasso in his 'counter-narrative' paintings 'Femmes d'Alger' (1954). In her story *Femmes d'Alger dans leur appartement*, Djebar, like Picasso, releases the women Delacroix has imprisoned from their harem by fragmenting the linear narrative and transforming it into a collage of laments, or songs of suffering, by women whose voices normally go unheard. By opening out the cloistered world of Algerian women, Djebar subverts not only patriarchal order but also the imprisoning categories of nation and culture. Songs from the past recounting the different but interconnecting memories of various women 'tear' the rigidified present and transform the city of Algiers (the new harem in which women are confined twenty years after Algerian independence) into a hybrid space which cuts across cultures and nations.

The poetics and politics of confinement and liberation are presented at the beginning of Djebar's story. It opens with the dream (or nightmare) of Ali who was in the FLN (Algerian National Liberation Front) at the time of the war of independence and is now a surgeon by profession. In a scene reminiscent of the experiment with the man in *La Jetée*, Ali dreams of a woman in a blindfold (or mask) whom he thinks is his wife Sarah. The woman is about to be sacrificed in an operation that he is about to perform. Yet he is neither fully in control of what is going on in his operating theatre ('I am not operating for I am not there, inside')[53] nor fully aware of what Sarah's affliction is. On one level, Djebar transposes Delacroix's orientalist painting onto the unconscious of a post-independence Algerian man. Like Delacroix, Ali can only 'picture' this scene through aestheticizing it. His description is that of a painter defining the colour of the woman's hair, the features of the face, the background ('a pure white sky, as if painted')[54] and so on, yet failing to get beyond the layer of paint (words) and remaining resolutely on the outside looking in, capable only of objectifying the woman, who herself cannot see or speak.[55] The analogy not only depicts orientalist painting as a surgical operation – drawing also on the link between surgery and torture,[56] hence Western art as violence on the woman's body — but also, as Rita Faulkner observes, challenges the view posited by Fanon (and others) that the 'violation' of the Algerian woman is at the hands of the colonizer alone by suggesting, instead, that Algerian patriarchy is also complicit in the same violence.

However, like all dreams, other stories overlay these links between orientalist painting, colonial torture and Algerian patriarchy to create not only a more condensed site of superimposition but also a transcultural collage which broadens out the picture of violence from the colonial setting. It is often thought that the biblical Sarah was in Pharaoh's harem prior to becoming Abraham's wife. In the accounts of the three Abrahamic faiths (Judaism, Christianity and Islam), Sarah thus transfers her allegiance from one male ruler (Pharaoh) to another (Abraham), which (in Djebar's text) could be read as the transference of power from the male colonizer to Algerian patriarchy. In the biblical story it is, of course, Isaac who is to be sacrificed by his father Abraham at God's request, only to be substituted at the last moment for a ram. In Ali's dream it is Sarah who is the voiceless victim of male power, her 'neck thrown backward' transforming, in Ali's mind, into 'a white goat with a neck stretched out'.[57] Djebar extends her critique of patriarchy beyond the colonial and Algerian national context to embrace the three Abrahamic faiths which immure women in one harem or another.[58]

While the overlaying of different stories of patriarchy reinforces the picture of a long history of violence against women, the composite, fragmented and poetic nature of the dream itself announces the possibility of a very different space. At the very outset, then, Djebar both presents the reader with a written version of Delacroix's poetics and politics and, at the same time, subverts that poetics and politics from within, just as Picasso's paintings take Delacroix's original and transform it into a different space. Indeed, in Ali's unconscious there is already a vague premonition of this other space. Although Sarah is voiceless and blindfolded, Ali thinks 'she's going to rip it off, she's going to burst out laughing, explode with life in front of me';[59] although the clinical operation is about to take place – 'the head nurse is fiddling with a motor, gets it to start' – nevertheless, 'the water of the fountain submerges everything in floods nourished by deliverance';[60] although Ali is in the process of sacrificing his wife, he is (as mentioned above) not fully in control of the situation. Ali's unconscious announces the otherness of woman (in the form, especially, of music and water, two powerful motifs in the story), which his conscious mind could never entertain. Sarah's journey in the story, from voiceless victim to be sacrificed in a drama written by men, to the embodiment of a pluralized memory, a hybridized present and a collective destiny, is therefore already prefigured in the opening scene. At the end of the story, it is no longer Sarah or the other women who are confined to the harem by men, but the other way round. 'This is the moment', thinks Sarah, 'that Ishmael will really wail in the desert: the walls torn down by us will continue to surround him alone'. (Ismael, Abraham's eldest son by Sarah's servant Hagar, is often thought to be the ancestor of Arabs.)[61]

The experience of Sarah, the central character in the story, demonstrates how the walls which must be broken for liberation are not only those of language and social space but also those of memory, culture and nation. Imprisoned and tortured during the war of independence and now profoundly conscious of the continued 'imprisonment' of Algerian women in independent Algeria, Sarah is closely linked to Leila, herself imprisoned for her acts of resistance against the French colonizer only to be 'imprisoned' once again in the present for having become delirious. Sarah has kept her own past experience secret, but contact with Leila and with the pasts of the women whose voices Sarah records for her research project and those with whom she converses in the baths, reawakens her repressed memory and allows her to confess her own past (especially concerning the death of her mother while Sarah was in prison) to her French friend Anne. The unlocking of personal memory is therefore realized not through normal speech ('I've always had problems with words', Sarah says to Anne)[62] but through a collective lament mediated through the many songs of the past ('A world of tenderness, with which these voices were filled, was coming to the surface again, like a water lily from oblivion').[63]

Leila's own story shows how the collective lament of subjected women is composed of an overlaying of different songs. In her state of delirium, Leila listens endlessly to an old record by the Algerian Jewish singer of the 1930s, Meriem Fekkai. While she listens to her nostalgic voice singing 'What has become of my friend, the one who was with me?', Leila is reminded of her own childhood: 'the looks of women veiled in white or in black but their faces freed, who were weeping silently, as if behind a windowpane. And Leila was telling herself, her body in pain, that they, these disappeared aunts and grandmothers, were weeping over her, over her dismantled memory.'[64] The *'complainte'* of the *'chanteuse juive'* therefore triggers Leila's memory, which, in turn, triggers Sarah's. It reappears later sandwiched between the two *'diwans'*, the story of the tragic past of the *'masseuse'* Fatma and Leila's own story as a carrier of bombs in the war and as a victim of torture. Fekkai's song, rather like the endless cry which closes *Nuit et brouillard*, is the ancient lament of suffering which traverses time, space and culture and connects the individual stories of different women: 'In front of Fatma's prostrate body the surgeon is fully focused; Anne sits rooted in the waiting room. At that same moment, Sarah stands in front of Leila's bed; Leila is delirious. The Jewish songstress on the record has stopped her wailing song of the thirties ...'.[65] When Sarah confesses her secret to Anne about her torture and the death of her mother, she realizes (using the musical metaphor once again) that the voice which must be used to break the walls within which women are imprisoned is not 'the voice of female vocalists whom they imprison in their sugar-sweet melodies' but

> the voice they've never heard, because many unknown and new things will occur before she's able to sing: the voice of sighs, of malice, of the sorrows of all the women they've kept walled in... The voice that's searching in the opened tombs.[66]

This is precisely the voice of suffering of the *'chanteuse juive'* which, like the figure of Lazarus, returns from the open tomb to haunt the present. In the postscript, Djebar describes this voice as one which traverses culture and generation:

Ritual lament of the Jewish and Arabic women folksingers who sing at Algerian weddings, this outdated tenderness, this delicately loving nostalgia, barely allusive, is transmitted little by little from the women to the adolescent girls, future sacrificial victims, as if the song were closing in upon itself.[67]

This voice is both single and plural at the same time, of one time and many times, overspilling the restrictive teleology inscribed in a monolithic version of history. As Michelle Perrot says, 'Assia Djebar depicts Algerian time in terms of long duration, not with the intention of narrating its contemporary journey but rather to unearth the abundant wealth of a sedimented past to illuminate its cultural complexity'.[68] Djebar's narrating voice is the conversion of a fixed language into song, the transformation of the petrified world of male sense into the pluralized, collective and transcultural female voice of memory. Ali's dream at the beginning of the story showed this tension between fixity and freedom through the possibility of slippage, substitution and transformation. Music and water hover behind the sharp implements of surgery (or torture); Sarah's speechlessness seems about to give way to an explosion of sound; Sarah as 'sacrificial lamb' can be substituted for a goat. The opening up of the harem will be through an allusive (and elusive) language which will transform the fixed body of signifieds into the play of signifiers. Sarah declares at the end, 'What a new, offensive harem! ..., precisely without *haram*, without taboo. In the name of whom? In the name of what?'.[69] As suggested in the text, *haram* in Arabic (or *(c)herem* in Hebrew) means 'forbidden'; the stripping out of *haram* from the harem, though a simple substitution of one letter for another, has the far-reaching effect of transforming the harem from a cloistered space of confinement of women into a new and 'offensive' space of resistance, regulated by what Djebar refers to in the postscript as 'affective memory' ('la mémoire affective'). The shift in signifier is the means by which the written word of the law, which regulates women through prohibition, is challenged by the play of sound derived from the 'oral roots of history'.[70] Sonia's sister has already commented on the significance of a simple change of letter – chromosome X or Y – in the distinction between the sexes: '"Just change one letter," she'd sigh emphatically, "and for us everything here would change, really everything!"'[71] Djebar pursues this theme in the postscript when she describes the usurping of the female voice by a male substitute in marriage proceedings: 'A terrible substitution for the word of one by another, which, moreover, opens the way to the illegal practice of the forced marriage. Her word deflowered, violated, before the other deflowering, the other violation intervenes.'[72] To exchange one letter for another, or one voice for another, is not an innocent act; it can either consolidate violent power relations or, conversely, subvert them and transform the spaces they inhabit.

Djebar, herself, refuses to be the substitute for the silenced voices that she exhumes. Mireille Calle-Gruber highlights the care Djebar takes 'to work at a distance so as not to confuse solidarity (or sorority) with identity, or to fall into the trap of being a spokesperson, a substitute, an intellectual who has acquired the right to speak for and to discourse on'.[73] Instead, Djebar transforms substitution from a power relation to a force for liberation: it is more like metaphor and translation, allowing for new connections to be constructed which subvert normalized meaning. Djebar plays on substitution to convert a cloistered, patriarchal language into an open-ended, 'feminized' language (the prohibition of patriarchal law becoming the open-ended musicality of song). In so doing, she transforms a monologic and patriarchal version of history into the pluralized, transcultural and transgenerational voice of memory.[74] Ultimately, it is the marks of torture – violently inscribed on women's bodies (like the words that have disfigured them) – which can be re-appropriated and converted into signs of intergenerational and intercultural solidarity. When Sarah finally reveals the scar of torture that she has secretly carried on her body for twenty years, this trace of the past not only connects her with Leila and with Anne in a new way; like the lament of the Jewish Algerian singer, it is the mark of the open-ended cry of suffering and resistance across time.

Notes

1. Winifred Woodhull, 'Mohammed Dib and the French Question', *Yale French Studies* 98 (2000), 69 and 70–71 respectively.
2. David Macey, *Frantz Fanon: A Life* (London: Granta), 2000, p. 184. In a speech entitled *Discours sur la Négritude* delivered at a conference in 1987, Aimé Césaire slides between particularist and more universalist definitions of Negritude. Statements such as 'I believe in the value of everything that has been buried in the collective memory of our peoples and even in the collective unconscious' ('Je crois à la valeur de tout ce qui est enfoui dans la mémoire collective de nos peuples et même dans l'inconscient collectif'), and 'Negritude has been a revolt against what I will call European reductionism' ('la Négritude a été une révolte contre ce que j'appellerai le réductionnisme européen') show that Césaire's understanding of Negritude is always far more than a simple biological or cultural essentialism (in *Discours sur le colonialisme*, pp. 77–92, pp. 83 and 84 respectively).
3. Rothberg, *Multidirectional Memory*, p. 107; Gilroy, *Between Camps*, p. xv. For a detailed discussion of the MRAP's establishment of 'a series of connections between the treatment of Jews during the Occupation and that of Algerians by successive French regimes', see James House, 'Memory and the Creation of Solidarity during the Decolonization of Algeria' in Michael Rothberg, Debarati Sanyal and Max Silverman (eds), *'Noeuds de mémoire*: Multidirectional Memory in Post-war French and Francophone Culture', *Yale French Studies* 118/119 (2010), 15.
4. Dominic Thomas, 'Intersections and Trajectories: Francophone Studies and Postcolonial Theory' in H. Adlai Murdoch and Anne Donadey (eds), *Postcolonial Theory and Francophone Literary Studies* (Gainesville: University Press of Florida, 2005), p. 238.

5. Charles Forsdick and David Murphy, 'Introduction: Situating Francophone Postcolonial Thought' in Charles Forsdick and David Murphy (eds), *Postcolonial Thought in the French-speaking World* (Liverpool: Liverpool University Press, 2009), p. 10.

6. This is assuming that the 'post-colonial' is not simply a chronological term (that which comes after the colonial) but also a way of thinking critically about normalized relations (see Stuart Hall, '"When Was the Post-colonial?" Thinking at the Limit' in Iain Chambers and Lidia Curti (eds), *The Post-colonial Question: Common Skies, Divided Horizons* (London and New York: Routledge, 1996), pp. 242–260), as the term is invariably used only when the normalized relations in question are those between colonizing European nations and their others. Françoise Lionnet makes a good case for linking 'transnational feminisms' to post-colonial studies under the banner of 'the term *postcolonial* as a theoretical rather than as a temporal marker', but why stop there? (Françoise Lionnet, 'Afterword: *Francophonie*, Postcolonial Studies, and Transnational Feminisms' in Murdoch and Donadey (eds), *Postcolonial Theory and Francophone Literary Studies*, p. 258.) Indeed, Lionnet has not stopped there, hence her excellent article '"Dire *exactement*": Remembering the Interwoven Lives of Jewish Deportees and Coolie Descendants in 1940s Mauritius' in Rothberg et al., *'Noeuds de mémoire'*, 111–135.

7. Jeannie Suk, *Postcolonial Paradoxes in French Caribbean Writing: Césaire, Glissant, Condé* (Oxford: Oxford University Press, 2001), pp. 6 and 2 respectively.

8. Peter Hallward, *Absolutely Postcolonial: Writing between the Singular and the Specific* (Manchester and New York: Manchester University Press, 2001). Hallward's dichotomy between singular and specific turns out to be a rather crude way of distinguishing between different texts. Hallward places Mohammed Dib in the former category (which he critiques) and Assia Djebar in the latter (of which he approves). However, I will attempt to show in this chapter how both writers are 'specific' in Hallward's sense of establishing a relationality between 'different' positions, yet will extend his notion of relationality to include sites normally considered outside post-colonial configurations.

9. Edward Said, *Culture and Imperialism* (London: Chatto and Windus, 1993), p. 21.

10. See Sylvie Lindeperg, *Les Écrans de l'ombre: La Seconde guerre mondiale dans le cinéma français (1944–1969)* (CNRS Éditions, 1997), p. 316.

11. 'Je naquis avec la deuxième guerre', 'Radio-Berlin captait l'attention de nos pères ; l'histoire internationale entra dans ma petite enfance par la voix du sinistre dictateur', Abdelkebir Khatibi, *La Mémoire tatouée: Autobiographie d'un décolonisé* (Denoel, 1971), p. 9.

12. 'J'appartiens irréductiblement à mon époque', Frantz Fanon, *Peau noire masques blancs* (Seuil, 1952), p. 10 / *Black Skin, White Masks*, trans. Charles Lamm Markmann (London: Pluto, 2008), p. 6.

13. Bryan Cheyette, 'Jews and Jewishness in the Writings of George Eliot and Frantz Fanon', p. 17. See also Gilroy, *Between Camps* and Bryan Cheyette, 'Frantz Fanon and the Black Jewish Imaginary' in Max Silverman (ed.) *Frantz Fanon's Black Skin White Masks* (Manchester: Manchester University Press, 2005), pp. 74–99.

14. 'le racisme colonial diffère des autres racismes' (Mannoni); 'Le racisme colonial ne diffère pas des autres racismes', Fanon, *Peau noire masques blancs*, p. 71 / *Black Skin, White Masks*, p. 65.

15. 'La civilisation européenne et ses représentants les plus qualifiés ne sont pas responsables du racisme colonial', Mannoni quoted in Fanon, *Peau noire masques blancs*, p. 73 / *Black Skin, White Masks*, p. 66.

16. 'le Juif est un homme que les autres hommes tiennent pour Juif .... C'est l'antisémite qui *fait* le Juif' (Sartre); '*c'est le raciste qui crée l'infériorisé*', Fanon, *Peau noire masques blancs*, p. 75 / *Black Skin, White Masks*, p. 69, italics in original.

17. In *Discours sur le colonialisme* Césaire also situates his critique of Mannoni in the wider context of Western bourgeois thought and its links with Hitlerism.

18. In his discussion of 'why the Negro adopts such a position, peculiar to him, with respect to European languages' ('pourquoi le Noir se situe de façon caractéristique en face du langage européen') in chapter 1 of *Peau noire masques blancs* ('The Negro and Language' / 'Le Noir et le langage'), Fanon maintains that his comments cannot be considered to be universally valid as 'the conclusions I have reached pertain to the French Antilles; at the same time, I am not unaware that the same behavior patterns obtain in every race that has been subjected to colonization' ('les conclusions auxquelles nous aboutirons valent pour les Antilles françaises; nous n'ignorons pas toutefois que ces mêmes comportements se retrouvent au sein de toute race ayant été colonisé'), Fanon, *Peau noire masques blancs*, p. 20 / *Black Skin, White Masks*, p. 15. He states that, according to the Eurocentric hierarchy of race which regulates perception, the Antillean does not want to be associated with the Black African because he or she is 'more "civilized"' ('plus "évolué"'). However, the category of 'the Antillean' being employed here is immediately undermined by the idea that, even amongst Antilleans, there is a hierarchy at work which distinguishes Martinicans from Guadeloupians (the latter being, according to some Martinicans, 'more savage than we are' / 'plus sauvages que nous'), Fanon, *Peau noire masques blancs*, p. 21 / *Black Skin, White Masks*, p. 15. We have moved here from the general category of 'le Noir' to the specific category of 'the Antillean' which itself is shown to be an unstable term. The term 'Black' thus slides between a generic term in relation to 'White' (encompassing all darker skins) and a highly unstable term in itself, in that it comprises different levels of Blackness. The problem here, as elsewhere in the text, is the slippage between a universalist and a particularist framework (in which even the particular is an unstable term). However, the significant point to note, in relation to the present discussion, is that Fanon cannot help but make slippages of this kind as conflicted connections across cultures and nations are inevitable in a world divided according to race thinking.

19. Cheyette, 'Frantz Fanon and the Black Jewish Imaginary', pp. 81–82. Cheyette argues, quite rightly, that Fanon's slippages are an attempt to agree with and distance himself from Sartre's model in *Réflexions sur la question juive*. Sartre's view that the racialized Jew and Black will eventually disappear with the advent of a classless society disturbs Fanon because he realizes that this dialectical approach (that Sartre expressed in *Orphée noir*) fails to understand the specificity of Blackness in a White world. I have discussed this elsewhere in terms of Fanon's sliding perspective between universalism and particularism, which allows him to challenge an invidious binary opposition, which he perceives as a trap, and unconsciously subscribe to it at the same time (see Max Silverman, 'Reflections on the Human Question' in Max Silverman (ed.), *Frantz Fanon's Black Skin White Masks* (Manchester: Manchester University Press, 2005), pp. 112–127). In the space of two paragraphs, Fanon first agrees with Gabriel d'Arbousier's critique of Sartre for putting 'Antilleans, Guianans, Senegalese, and Malagasies on the same footing' ('sur le même pied Antillais, Guyannais, Sénégalais et Malgaches'), d'Arbusier quoted in Fanon, *Peau noire masques blancs*, p. 139 / *Black Skin, White Masks*, p. 132, then say that, nevertheless, 'the Antillean is first of all a Negro,' ('l'Antillais est avant tout un Noir'), Fanon, *Peau noire masques blancs*, p. 139 / *Black Skin, White Masks*, p. 133, whose concrete existence as such 'places him beside the Jew', ('il rejoint en quelque sorte le Juif'), Fanon, *Peau noire masques blancs*, p. 140 / *Black Skin, White Masks*, p. 133; hence, the validity of the (Sartreian?) universalist view, '[w]herever he goes, the Negro remains a Negro' ('où qu'il aille, un nègre demeure un nègre'), Fanon, *Peau noire masques blancs*, p. 140 / *Black Skin, White Masks*, p. 133.

20. Fanon, *Peau noire masques blancs*, p. 133 / *Black Skin, White Masks*, p. 126.

21. Robert Bernasconi, 'When the Real Crime Began: Hannah Arendt's *The Origins of Totalitarianism* and the Dignity of the Western Philosophical Tradition' in Richard H. King and Dan Stone (eds), *Hannah Arendt and the Uses of History: Imperialism, Nation, Race and Genocide* (Oxford and New York: Berghahn, 2007), pp. 54–67. For a critique of Kant from this perspective, see also Gilroy, *Between Camps*.

22. '"Il n'y a pas de problème noir aux États-Unis, il n'y a qu'un problème blanc." Nous dirons de la même façon que l'antisémitisme n'est pas un problème juif : c'est notre problème', Jean-Paul Sartre, *Réflexions sur la question juive* (Gallimard, 1954 [1946]), pp. 183–184 / *Anti-semite and Jew*, trans. George J. Becker (New York: Schocken Books, 1948), p. 152.

23. Fanon, *Peau noire masques blancs*, p. 23 and p. 148 respectively / *Black Skin, White Masks*, p. 18 and p. 141.

24. Fanon, *Peau noire masques blancs*, p. 148 / *Black Skin, White Masks*, p. 141.

25. Rothberg, *Multidirectional Memory*, p. 116. In contrast to the arguments of Arendt and Césaire who 'don't always elude the pitfalls of the universal/particular dichotomy' (and one could certainly say the same of Fanon too), Rothberg suggests that 'Du Bois can serve as a model of multidirectional memory because of the way his writings on Jews, race, and genocide hold together commonality and difference in a revised version of double consciousness' (p. 112).

26. In his book *The Anti-Enlightenment Tradition* (New Haven and London: Yale University Press, 2009), the historian Zeev Sternhell proposes the well worn opposition between Enlightenment rationality and the counter-Enlightenment tradition of romantic and racial thought, which progresses in a straight line from Burke and Herder to fascism. This dichotomy effaces the complex connections between rationality and racial thinking as part of Enlightenment modernity. (For a similar argument, see Alain Finkielkraut, *La Défaite de la pensée* (Gallimard, 1987). For a critique of this approach – and especially the ambivalent discourse of nation in Ernest Renan's 'Qu'est-ce qu'une nation?' – see Max Silverman, *Deconstructing the Nation: Immigration, Racism and Citizenship in Modern France* (London and New York: Routledge, 1992).

27. Sander Gilman, *Difference and Pathology: Stereotypes of Sexuality, Race and Madness* (Ithaca: Cornell University Press, 1985), p. 35.

28. Neil Macmaster, '"Black Jew: White Negro": Antisemitism and the Construction of Cross-racial Stereotypes', *Nationalism and Ethnic Politics* 6, 4 (2000), 66–67.

29. Macmaster, '"Black Jew: White Negro"', p. 67.

30. Richard C. Keller, *Colonial Madness: Psychiatry in French North Africa* (Chicago and London: University of Chicago Press, 2007), p. 131. See also Sander Gilman's description of the 'weakness' of the 'Jewish foot' taken as a sign of Jewish cowardice in war in *Inscribing the Other* (Lincoln: University of Nebraska Press, 1991).

31. Edward Said, 'Raymond Schwab and the Romance of Ideas' in *The World, the Text, and the Critic* (London: Faber and Faber, 1984 [1983]), p. 264.

32. Aamir R. Mufti, *Enlightenment in the Colony: The Jewish Question and the Crisis of Postcolonial Culture* (Princeton and Oxford: Princeton University Press, 2007). See also Zygmunt Bauman, *Modernity and Ambivalence* (Cambridge: Polity, 1991) and my discussion of Sartre's *Réflexions sur la question juive* in the context of modern constructions of race in '"Killing me softly": Racial Ambivalence in Jean-Paul Sartre's *Réflexions sur la question juive*' in Phyllis Lassner and Lara Trubowitz (eds), *Antisemitism and Philosemitism in the Twentieth and Twenty-first Centuries: Representing Jews, Jewishness and Modern Culture* (Newark: University of Delaware Press, 2008), pp. 47–62.

33. Mark Mazower, 'Foucault, Agamben: Theory and the Nazis', *Boundary 2* 35, 1 (2008), 26.

34. 'Ne voir qu'un type de nègre, assimiler l'antisémitisme à la négrophobie, telles semblent être les erreurs d'analyse commises ici', Fanon, *Peau noire masques blancs*, p. 148 / *Black Skin, White Masks*, p. 141. One of Fanon's main arguments against the conflation of anti-

semitism and anti-Black racism is that 'the Negro symbolizes the biological danger; the Jew, the intellectual danger', p. 127 / '[l]e nègre représente le danger biologique. Le Juif, le danger intellectuel' (p. 134). Here, Fanon shows no knowledge whatsoever of the role of sexual myths in the racialization of the Jew. Popular and political forms of anti-semitism in France, from the late nineteenth century onwards and especially in the 1930s, were very often founded on a blend of fears, including the sexual potency, degeneracy and ambiguity of the Jew. Fanon's comment 'the Jewish menace is replaced by the fear of the sexual potency of the Negro' / '[l]e péril juif est remplacé par la peur de la puissance sexuelle du nègre' (Fanon, *Peau noire masques blancs*, p. 133 / *Black Skin, White Masks*, p. 126) is therefore completely inaccurate; on the level of sexual myth alone, he would have had good reason to propose the similarity between the two forms of racism rather than their difference. As Macmaster says, the construction of the hybrid figure of the 'Negro-Jew' in the latter part of the nineteenth century 'carried all the threat (and fascination) of the dangerous libidinal forces at work under the veneer of white civilization' ('"Black Jew: White Negro"', p. 74).

35. 'comme le symbole de la destruction du système colonial', Charles Bonn, 'Les Pouvoirs du langage' in *Mohammed Dib, Itinéraires et Contacts de Culture*, vols 21–22 (L'Harmattan, 1996), p. 152. (Bonn adds, 'And if one takes the Algerian revolution to be the historical referent of the text … it is not named' / 'Et si l'on comprend que la Révolution algérienne est le référent historique du texte, elle … n'est pas nommée'.)

36. 'Algerian War, but also any war: "This game was being played out at the same moment in the metabkha with its low, smoke-blackened ceiling and its grease-stained walls, and across the whole world; the place was not important"' ('Guerre d'Algérie, mais aussi bien n'importe quelle guerre : "Ce jeu se jouait au même moment dans la metabkha au plafond bas et enfumé, aux murs tachés de graisse, et à travers le monde, l'endroit était sans importance"'), Naget Khadda, *Mohammed Dib: Cette impestive voix recluse* (Aix-en-Provence: Édisud, 2003), p. 52. See also Aouicha Hilliard, 'Discourse and Language of the Mother in Mohammed Dib's *Qui se souvient de la mer*' in Kamal Sahli (ed.), *Francophone Studies: Discourse and Identity* (Exeter: Elm Bank Publications), pp. 173–188.

37. 'les exterminations de la dernière guerre, la monstruosité des camps de concentration, l'abomination de la bombe atomique, n'ont pas fini de hanter les nuits des hommes. Comment parler de l'Algérie après Auschwitz, le ghetto de Varsovie et Hiroshima ? Comment faire afin que tout ce qu'il y a pourtant à dire puisse être encore entendu et ne soit pas absorbé par cette immense nuée démoniaque qui plane au-dessus du monde tant d'années, ne se dissolve pas dans l'enfer de banalité dont l'horreur a su s'entourer et nous entourer ?', Dib, 'Postface' in *Qui se souvient de la mer*, p. 218.

38. In the postscript, Dib describes the proximity of his technique to that of novels of science fiction (none of which he had ever even read before) as follows: 'In the best of these, as in the transparent and mysterious language of dreams, can one not see the hauntings, the desires, the terrors, and the most powerful ancient and modern myths, mirroring the most profound aspirations of the human spirit, rise to the surface and present themselves to us with greater clarity than in so-called "realist" literature?', ('Dans les meilleurs de ceux-ci, tout comme à travers le langage transparent et sibyllin des rêves, ne voit-on pas les hantises, les désirs, les terreurs, les mythes anciens et modernes les plus actifs comme les aspirations les plus profondes de l'âme humaine, faire surface et se montrer à nous mieux que dans la littérature dite « réaliste » ?'), Dib, *Qui se souvient de la mer*, p. 220.

39. Both the mother and the sea have the power to relieve the suffering of the present: 'I can hear, at this moment, near me, a gentle, regular breathing, alternating with long silences. The sea. It rises. Its peace covers the night, fills space. My fears subside, my old resentments against the world fade away, and the fire – escaped from the new

constructions? – which has for long lacerated my body with its claws disappears into the shadows' ('J'entends à ce moment, près de moi, un halètement doux, régulier, alternant avec de longs silences. La mer. Elle monte. Sa paix s'étend à travers la nuit, remplit l'espace. Mes frayeurs s'assoupissent, mes vieilles rancunes contre le monde, elles-mêmes, tombent, et le feu – échappé des nouvelles constructions ? – qui m'a longtemps lacéré de ses griffes s'enfuit dans les ténèbres'); 'I was conscious of how beneficial the presence of my mother could be, how her gentle, slightly monotonous voice soothed my suffering' ('je m'apercevais combien la présence de ma mère pouvait m'être bienfaisante, combien sa voix, douce, un peu monotone, allégeait ma souffrance'), Dib, *Qui se souvient de la mer*, pp. 104 and 112–113 respectively.

40. 'Ainsi, depuis peu, revois-je souvent ma mère en rêve… Ma mère qui n'avait jamais su tenir une place considérable dans sa propre maison et dont je ne garde qu'une impression à demi effacée. Ses traits qui flottent au fond de ma mémoire sous un fin brouillard, son image noyée par des nappes d'ombre, me parviennent de si loin, que l'autre, la vraie, me semble perdue à jamais. Deux yeux noirs immenses éclairent mes nuits, et le reste est brouillé. Le matin, je reprends ses photos : aucune n'a le moindre air de ressemblance avec l'image qui dort en moi. Je ne retrouve pas ces yeux ouverts dans mon imagination comme des fenêtres sur un horizon qui n'appartient assurément pas à ce monde', Dib, *Qui se souvient de la mer*, p. 68.

41. 'Parfois des explosions en partent qui tordent les bases de la ville ; l'Histoire ne donne pas d'exemple, même approximatif, de ce qui se passe là, sous mes yeux. Les bombardements, les tirs, les stridulations, les huées et les éclairs qui entourent la nouvelle cité, s'il leur arrive par hasard de s'interrompre, ce n'est jamais pour bien longtemps'; 'Nous errons, alors, tournons en rond entre les murs qui se nouent, s'entortillent inexplicablement autour de nous, et une horreur que personne ne parvient plus à secouer nous engourdit'; 'Je les ai vus brûler des habitants'; 'Cymbales, chœur de chiens, orchestre, explosions : rien n'a manqué à cette nuit'; 'Sur la chaussée s'amoncelaient autant de statues inertes que de bustes mutilés, de bras, de jambes, dans des poses et des mouvements inachevés', Dib, *Qui se souvient de la mer*, pp. 97, 98, 99, 104 and 121 respectively.

42. 'Autour de moi, qui figurais un vivant pitoyable, toutes ces statues ressemblaient à des morts orgueilleux de leur force et de leur étrangeté. J'étais incapable de détacher mes regards des leurs, hypnotisé, ou de me délivrer de leur silence. Éteinte, l'expression familière qui flottait sur leurs traits, éteinte, évidemment', Dib, *Qui se souvient de la mer*, p. 122.

43. 'Un ancien et silencieux cataclysme nous ayant arrachés à nous-mêmes et au monde', Dib, *Qui se souvient de la mer*, p. 96. The terror that follows being parted from Nafissa is described in similar terms: 'I was not aware of the suffering of being torn away, but as soon as I was parted from you I lived in a world of permanent terror' ('Je ne soupçonnais pas la souffrance de l'arrachement, mais dès que de toi je fus privé, je vécus sur une terre de terreur permanente'), p. 151.

44. For example, 'People hobble about in silence, stepping carefully. I sensed what they lacked; the presence of the sea. Now all we had was the dry and deathly expectation of a world of stone' ('Les gens clopinent en silence, à pas prudent. Je sentais ce qui leur manquait ; la présence de la mer. Nous ne connaissons plus que la sèche, la mortelle attente d'un monde de pierre'), Dib, *Qui se souvient de la mer*, pp. 135–136.

45. 'Quelquefois me parvient encore un brisement, un chant sourd, et je songe, je me souviens de la mer', Dib, *Qui se souvient de la mer*, p. 216.

46. Césaire, *Discours sur le colonialisme*, p. 23 / *Discourse on Colonialism*, p. 42 (trans. modified). For a comparison of de-objectification in *Nuit et brouillard* and *Les Statues meurent aussi*, see Raymond, *Poétique du témoignage*, pp. 22–25.

47. 'Il y a des gens qui sont attirés par la permanence de la pierre'; '[l]'antisémite est l'homme qui veut être roc impitoyable', Sartre, *Réflexions sur la question juive*, pp. 21 and 64 / *Anti-semite and Jew*, pp. 18 and 54 respectively.

48. Debarati Sanyal, 'Crabwalk History: Torture, Allegory and Memory in Sartre' in Rothberg et al. (eds), *'Noeuds de mémoire'*, p. 62. In his novel *La Statue de sel* (1953) Albert Memmi also plays with images of fixity and fluidity. In this story of a Tunisian Jewish boy growing up between the ravages of the Second World War and French colonialism, Memmi uses the biblical story of Lot's wife being turned into a statue of salt when looking back at Sodom as a metaphor for the dangers of memory and the illusory fixity of identity.

49. Iain Chambers and Lidia Curti, 'Migrating Modernities in the Mediterranean', *Postcolonial Studies* 11, 4 (2008), 387–388. Dib's metaphorical use of the sea prefigures Édouard Glissant's description of the archipelago as a hybrid space with incalculable frontiers in relation to the fixity of the continent.

50. Charles Bonn, *Lecture présente de Mohammed Dib* (Alger: ENAL, 1988); (see chapter 1, 'Le dépassement du réalisme dans L'Incendie (1954) et Qui se souvient de la mer (1962)').

51. 'l'instrument de quelque fatalité, le siège d'une funeste puissance'; 'Les tortures, les inquisitions, les poires d'angoisse, la roue, le bûcher, n'ont jamais su servir que l'ennemi ; l'on entrevoit les pièges qu'ils recèlent', Dib, *Qui se souvient de la mer*, p. 105. This is also a reference, of course, to Sartre's frequent use (from *La Nausée* onwards) of the ashtray (*le cendrier*) as the fixed object (*en-soi*) which we misguidedly (through bad faith/*mauvaise foi*) proclaim as the status of Man.

52. See Higgins, *New Novel, New Wave, New Politics*.

53. 'je n'opère pas car je ne suis pas là, à l'intérieur', Assia Djebar, *Femmes d'Alger dans leur appartement* (Des Femmes, 1980), p. 12 / *Women of Algiers in their Apartment*, trans. Marjolijn de Jager (Charlottesville and London: University Press of Virginia, 1992), p. 6.

54. 'un ciel tout blanc, comme peint', Djebar, *Femmes d'Alger*, p. 12 / *Women of Algiers*, p. 6.

55. It is no coincidence that the only other significant male in the story is Ali's friend, known to us only as *'le peintre'*. Like Ali, 'le peintre' was also formerly in the FLN. He rescues Leila from the asylum in order to protect her, yet it is clear that he has as little understanding of her real suffering as Ali has of Sarah's.

56. The dream ends with the words 'The motor begins to run dangerously, the "gene" – generator – is wired, place of torture…' ('Le moteur se met en marche dangereusement, la "gégène" …'), Djebar, *Femmes d'Alger*, p. 12 / *Women of Algiers*, p. 6. The *gégène* was used as an instrument of torture in the Algerian War.

57. 'cou renversé'; 'une chèvre blanche avec un cou tendu', Djebar, *Femmes d'Alger*, pp. 11 and 12 / *Women of Algiers*, pp. 5 and 6 respectively.

58. Jane Hiddleston suggests that 'Islam is subject to the same intricate processes of self-questioning as both Judaism and European philosophy' as part of her understanding of 'Derridean notions of singularisation and its partial trace within Djebar's texts', *Assia Djebar: Out of Algeria* (Liverpool: Liverpool University Press, 2006), p. 110. In chapter 6 I adopt Derrida's use of the trace to explore similar interconnections.

59. 'elle va l'arracher, elle va pouffer de rire et éclater de vie devant moi', Djebar, *Femmes d'Alger*, p. 11 / *Women of Algiers*, p. 5.

60. 'l'infirmier-chef manipule, il met en marche un moteur'; 'l'eau de la fontaine submerge tout en flots nourris de délivrance', Djebar, *Femmes d'Alger*, p. 12 / *Women of Algiers*, p. 6.

61. 'C'est maintenant … qu'Ismael hurlera vraiment dans son désert : les murs abattus par nous continueront à le cerner seul !', Djebar, *Femmes d'Alger*, p. 61 / *Women of Algiers*, p. 51. In Djebar's story, Sarah is step-mother to Ali's son Nazim, just as the biblical Sarah is step-mother to Ismael. Like Ismael – cast out from the home by Abraham with his

mother Hagar – Nazim also leaves home and is cut off from his father. The breakdown in relations between father and son is contrasted to the binding together of women of different generations.

62. 'J'ai toujours eu des problèmes avec les mots', Djebar, *Femmes d'Alger*, p. 55 / *Women of Algiers*, p. 45 (trans. modified).

63. 'Toute une tendresse dont ces voix étaient pleines, remontait en nénuphar de l'oubli', Djebar, *Femmes d'Alger*, p. 24 / *Women of Algiers*, p. 18 (trans. modified).

64. 'Qu'est devenu mon ami, lui qui était avec moi ? '; 'regards de femmes voilées en blanc ou en noir mais le visage libre, qui pleuraient silencieusement, comme derrière une vitre. Et Leila se disait, le corps endolori, qu'elles pleuraient, ces tantes et ces aïeules disparues, sur elle, sur sa mémoire défaite', Djebar, *Femmes d'Alger*, p. 29 / *Women of Algiers*, p. 22. Sarah is also reminded of her childhood while listening to the tapes of the 'women's songs of times gone by' ('chants des femmes d'autrefois'), Djebar, *Femmes d'Alger*, p. 23 / *Women of Algiers*, p. 16.

65. 'Devant le corps étendu de Fatma, la chirurgienne se concentre en pleine action ; Anne figée dans la salle d'attente. Au même moment, Sarah se dresse devant le lit de Leila qui délire. La chanteuse juive du microsillon s'est arrêtée dans sa complainte des années 30…', Djebar, *Femmes d'Alger*, p. 53 / *Women of Algiers*, p. 43.

66. 'la voix des cantatrices qu'ils emprisonnent dans leurs melodies sucrées'; '[l]a voix qu'ils n'ont jamais entendue, parce qu'il se passera bien des choses inconnues et nouvelles savant qu'elle puisse chanter : la voix des soupirs, des rancunes, des douleurs de toutes celles qu'ils ont emmurées… La voix qui cherche dans les tombeaux ouverts !', Djebar, *Femmes d'Alger*, p. 61 / *Women of Algiers*, p. 50.

67. '*Lamento* du folklore des chanteuses juives et arabes des noces algéroises, peu a peu, cette douceur surannée, cette nostalgie amoureuse, à peine allusive, se transmet des femmes à des adolescentes, futures sacrifiées, comme si le chant se refermait sur lui-même', Djebar, *Femmes d'Alger*, p. 161 / *Women of Algiers*, pp. 147–148.

68. 'Assia Djebar a le désir d'embrasser le temps de l'Algérie dans sa plus longue durée, accompagnant son devenir contemporain, moins pour le narrer, que pour en sonder la foisonnante richesse sédimentaire, susceptible d'expliquer sa complexité culturelle', Michelle Perrot, 'Histoire et mémoire des femmes dans l'œuvre d'Assia Djebar' in Mireille Calle-Gruber (ed.), *Assia Djebar, Nomade entre les murs…: Pour une poétique transfrontalière* (Maisonneuve et Larose, 2005), p. 36. Hiddleston also talks of Djebar's narrative voice in terms of a 'singularity (which) is plural in that it is composed … of a proliferation of different voices, dialects and influences' (*Assia Djebar: Out of Algeria*, pp. 58–59).

69. 'Quel nouveau, quel offensif harem … justement sans *haram* sans interdit ! Au nom de qui ? Au nom de quoi ?', Djebar, *Femmes d'Alger*, p. 61 / *Women of Algiers*, p. 50.

70. 'racines orales de l'histoire', Djebar, *Femmes d'Alger*, p. 160 / *Women of Algiers*, p. 146.

71. '"Une lettre à changer", soupirait-elle emphatiquement, "et tout, vraiment tout ici, serait changé pour nous !"', Djebar, *Femmes d'Alger*, p. 33 / *Women of Algiers*, p. 26.

72. 'Terrible substitution d'une parole à une autre, et qui, de plus, ouvre la voie à la pratique illégale du mariage forcé. Parole déflorée, violentée avant que n'intervienne l'autre défloration, l'autre violence', Djebar, *Femmes d'Alger*, p. 158 / *Women of Algiers*, p. 145. The discussion of substitution and its relation to interconnected memory will be pursued in chapter 4 in relation to Georges Perec's *W ou le souvenir d'enfance*.

73. 'd'œuvrer dans la distance, de ne pas confondre solidarité (ou sororité) avec identité, de ne pas tomber dans le piège du porte-parole, du substitut, de l'intellectuel à qui est dévolu le droit de parler pour et de discourir sur', Mireille Calle-Gruber, *Assia Djebar ou la résistance de l'écriture* (Maisonneuve et Larose, 2001), p. 26.

74. Mireille Calle-Gruber talks of Djebar's work in terms of 'a poetics across frontiers' ('une poétique transfrontalière'), (Calle-Gruber (ed.), *Assia Djebar, Nomade entre les*

murs). Nicholas Harrison observes, 'Djebar ... is interested in communities beneath and beyond national categories and the colonizer/colonized opposition, especially those that may arise from a transnational and translinguistic feminine or feminist solidarity' ('Assia Djebar: Fiction as a Way of "Thinking"' in Forsdick and Murphy (eds), *Postcolonial Thought in the French-speaking World*, p. 71). The translation of songs from Arabic into French, which is part of Sarah's research project, is an example of 'translinguistic solidarity' in that it allows for interconnections to be made across language and culture. In this sense, substitution of one language for another is not the obliteration of one in favour of the other but the opening up of one to the traces of the other.

Chapter 4

COLONIAL HAUNTINGS OF THE
HOLOCAUST IMAGINARY

History is precisely the way we are implicated in each other's traumas.[1]

The way in which we have come to perceive the Holocaust in recent decades, with its specific focus on the (racial and genocidal) extermination of the Jews, has tended to obscure the broader post-war approach to memory that I discussed in chapter 2. What I am calling the 'concentrationary memory' of that period, with its examples in the work of Cayrol, Resnais, Marker and others, registers the totalitarian and dehumanizing potential of modernity and the shadow that the legacies of the concentration camps, the gulag and colonialism cast over modern consumer society. Yet just as screen memory in general does not mean that one memory completely effaces another for which it is a substitute but, instead, enters into a complex relationship with it, so we could argue that 'concentrationary memory', though obscured by 'Holocaust memory', can still be located in the interstices, so to speak, of contemporary formulations.

Let us take, for example, questions of trauma, testimony and representation which have been central to the debates of recent years on Holocaust memory. The gap between trauma and cultural memory is often seen in terms of the incommensurable distance between event and representation and, hence, the limitations of culture to carry the affective weight of the traumatic moment. The anti-representational stance that characterizes Claude Lanzmann's justification of the absence of archive footage in his film *Shoah*, and the central importance given to Lanzmann's approach in the work of Shoshana Felman and Dori Laub on trauma and testimony, reconfirmed the notion established by Elie Wiesel of the radical singularity of the Holocaust, that is, that the Holocaust occupies a sacred space beyond all human comprehension (and outside history?) as a sort of 'negative sublime'. In this scenario, any form of relational contextualization of the Holocaust is not only a denigration of its singularity but also a blasphemy. However, while supporting the refusal contained in this approach to clothe the Holocaust in a banalizing or sentimentalizing aesthetic, and hence devalue its import, we could nevertheless focus not so much on the limitations of culture in the face of extreme horror but rather on the inevitable cultural mediation of trauma once it returns belatedly in testimony and other memorial works. The critical engagement by Jacques Rancière, Georges Didi-Huberman, Gillian Rose and others with Lanzmann's effective prohibition on representation of the Holocaust (what Rancière calls Lanzmann's imposition of an 'aura of holy terror' and Rose his 'Holocaust piety') is illuminating in this regard.[2]

In his essay 'Are Some Things Unrepresentable?' ('S'il y a de l'irreprésentable?'), Rancière strips away the erroneous premises of the anti-representational argument to suggest that nothing is unrepresentable in the light of 'the *aesthetic* regime' ('le régime *esthétique*') which regulates all art forms in the modern era.[3] Rancière shows how a description in Robert Antelme's *L'Espèce humaine*, which conjoins human pathos with a detail of material existence, employs the same paratactic device as that employed by Flaubert in *Madame Bovary*. The effect is the same in both works. Lanzmann's *Shoah* itself does not exist outside the aesthetic regime but is as much a part of it as all modern art. In *Mourning Becomes the Law*, Rose talks in terms of 'the fascism of representation' by which we are implicated (inevitably) in the regime of representation which constitutes the limits within which we struggle to make sense of our selves and our world. In *Images malgré tout*, Didi-Huberman responds to Lanzmann's prohibition on representation to argue for the link between the image and the real once we remove the image from the regime of resemblance. Between Rancière's aesthetic regime, Rose's 'fascism of representation' and Didi-Huberman's *'images malgré tout'*, we are always within the field of representation.

I mention briefly these critiques of the anti-representational position (but will return to all three writers in later chapters) to suggest that viewing testimony not as bearing witness to the failure of language but as the belated cultural configuration of trauma obliges us to see it as regulated by the same aesthetic choices as other writing: the same use of figures of speech and the same substitutions and displacements of meaning, and occupying the same intertextual space. The passage from trauma to cultural memory of any sort leads to an impure form of representation (can any form of representation be pure?) because trauma is inevitably refracted through an imagined and hybrid symbolic order. This perspective displaces the problem of whether representation facilitates or denies access to the real to focus instead on the imaginary channels which inform representation and which representation, in turn, refracts.[4] Second order memory (the memory of the second generation that Marianne Hirsch has named 'postmemory') is more clearly mediated in this way, as the trauma described is 'second-hand' rather than 'first-hand' experience.[5] Yet even first order memory (the testimony of the survivor) is subject to the same 'aesthetic regime', as Rancière demonstrates in the case of Antelme.[6] Paul Ricœur says, 'to remember, even in a solitary and private way, one has to have access to the medium of language …. There is no memory without language. And the mediation of language is immediately a social question'.[7] In this sense, the most personal Holocaust memory can never be unequivocally related to a specific and singular event but is always indirectly implicated in (or contaminated by) other regimes of sense.

Cathy Caruth's ground-breaking work on trauma, *Unclaimed Experience*, is therefore particularly significant in this regard. It seems strange that trauma theorists have not engaged more seriously with the ideas of cultural intersection and interconnection that Caruth proposes in this work. It is no coincidence that one of her chapters is on Resnais's *Hiroshima mon amour* (1959), one of whose central features is the emergence of a hybrid or pluralized memory between different traumatic experiences connected with occupied France and Hiroshima during the Second World War. Caruth proposes that one traumatic event cannot be told in terms of its singularity and specificity but only indirectly through other stories: 'I would suggest that the interest of *Hiroshima mon amour* lies in how it explores the possibility of a faithful history in the very indirectness of this telling.'[8] This, of course, raises profound ethical and epistemological questions about truth and authenticity. Theories of trauma have often stressed that sufferers feel that the experience does not belong to them but to someone else. A 'truer' reading of history may therefore be dependent on showing 'through other stories' rather than the idea of the 'purity' and 'authenticity' of first-hand experience (an argument that I will pursue in the next chapter). Once again, the substitution of one thing for another that this process entails can only be viewed as a 'screen memory' if that expression is understood in terms of a complex dynamic of condensation and displacement of meaning which often accompanies the experience of trauma rather than as an instrumentalist tool to efface another memory.

Seeing the intersections of different traumatic moments in cultural memory (one of the lessons we learn from Caruth's approach) displaces the singularity of Holocaust memory across different sites, not in order to conflate them in a universal theory of trauma (which is the possible danger of Caruth's approach) or to efface the specificity or betray the 'authenticity' of the event, but to define a tension between one and another, and between singularity and generality inevitably contained in representations of trauma. In the terms I am using here, then, one might say that Holocaust memory and concentrationary memory are interconnected in the same way, so that the specificity of the genocide and the more general idea of the concentrationary universe which places humanity as a whole at risk are neither opposites nor the same but occupy a space between the two.[9] This chapter considers this tension between Holocaust memory and concentrationary memory by focusing on the overlaps and intersections between representations of the Holocaust, colonialism and other forms of extreme violence. Reversing the gaze of the previous chapter, I will view three works that have become central to the canon of 'Holocaust literature' in French – Charlotte Delbo's trilogy *Auschwitz et après*, Georges Perec's *W ou le souvenir d'enfance* and Patrick Modiano's *Dora Bruder* – to show that Holocaust literature is always in dialogue with other stories of horror and violence.

Charlotte Delbo: *Auschwitz et après / Auschwitz and after*

Charlotte Delbo only decided to publish her writings on her experience in Auschwitz-Birkenau twenty years after the end of the war, first in the form of a text entitled *La Convoi du 24 janvier* (1965) and then a trilogy under the general title *Auschwitz et après* (1970–1971). However, she had earlier published *Les Belles lettres* (1961), an essay consisting of letters and comments on the Algerian War of Independence. In his fascinating analysis of this often overlooked work, Michael Rothberg suggests that the essay illustrates the '"multidirectionality" of memory' in a post-war France 'buffeted simultaneously by the non-identical, yet overlapping and equally conflictual legacies of the Nazi occupation and the unraveling project of colonialism'.[10] Rothberg seeks to demonstrate how Delbo's essay intervenes in the construction of collective memory in the public sphere. He suggests that, by bringing together and 'recirculating' literature on French torture in Algeria and genocide in Europe twenty years before, Delbo's text actively refashions a public conception of memory of both, without conflating the two events or losing sight of the specificity of each. Rothberg notes that the 'multidirectional' aspect of Delbo's work that he identifies in *Les Belles lettres* can also be seen in the *Auschwitz et après* trilogy, specifically with regard to questions of 'voice, testimony, and public intimacy'.[11] Colin Davis reinforces this important point. In relation to the epigraph to the first volume of the trilogy, *Aucun de nous ne reviendra*, where Delbo writes, 'Today, I am not sure that what I wrote is true. I am certain it is truthful',[12] Davis observes 'the author or narrator cannot simply *tell the truth* because she does not fully possess the meaning of her own testimony'.[13] In Delbo's terms, and those of Caruth mentioned above, a more 'truthful' testimony cannot avoid the stories of others because they are an integral part of her own voice. Using these insights as a guide, I would like to demonstrate how the testimonial memoirs of *Auschwitz et après* are premised on a poetics and politics of interconnected memories.

The title of Delbo's trilogy, *Auschwitz et après*, is a key to a vision which operates not only in relation to one time but across time. Two incidents in the second book in the trilogy, *Une Connaissance inutile*

(*Useless Knowledge*) explicitly connect two distinct moments of brutality and resistance through a perceived similarity: the first is a description of the resistance and execution of four prisoners of the Nazis during the Second World War, which is related to a similar act of resistance and execution of an Algerian in 1960 (recounted in the magazine *L'Express*); the second is a description of one of the most brutal SS officers helping one of the prisoners rethread her shoelaces, which is related to a similar incident in the Vietnam War when Lieutenant William L. Calley, who was to be tried for the assassination of 109 South Vietnamese civilians, is described by his sister as having saved and cared for a lost Vietnamese girl and having suffered distress when she eventually fled from him (recounted in the *New York Post*, 28 November 1969).[14] These analogies might seem strange interruptions in Delbo's narrative of Auschwitz. However, a poetic structure of blurrings and overlappings of time and place has already prepared us for slippages of this sort. In the first text in the trilogy, *Aucun de nous ne reviendra*, in a section entitled 'The Dummies' ('Mannequins'), the sight of naked bodies laid out on the snow triggers a Proustian recall of a hot summer's day in Paris before the war when the narrator saw the delivery of a number of unclothed and hairless tailor's dummies outside a shop.[15] This uncanny moment leaves the narrator (and the reader) in a strange in-between state as she tries to comprehend the dividing line between living and dead bodies, the one haunting the other. Shortly after this flashback, a description in the camp of watching a skeletal, child-like woman in the snow, whose naked body is covered only in a blanket, is suddenly interrupted by a jump forward in time to the moment of writing after the war: 'Presently I am writing this story in a cafe – it is turning into a story'.[16] Here, Delbo blurs the moment of the *énoncé* in the past with the moment of the *énonciation* in the present to create an *entrecroisement* of times. Moreover, the slight modification of the language describing the present moment of writing when it is later repeated ('And now I am sitting in a café, writing this text')[17] enhances the (uncanny) sensation of sameness and difference which the conflation of times creates and which is reproduced elsewhere in this text through the incessant repetition and modification of statements: for example, the repetition of 'there is/there are' ('il y a') at the beginning of the text which confuses the time of departure and the time of arrival at 'the largest station in the world' ('la plus grand gare du monde'); or the section headings 'One Day' ('Un jour'), 'The Next Day' ('Le lendemain'), 'The Same Day' ('Le même jour'), 'Daytime' ('Le jour'), 'Night' ('La nuit'), 'Morning' ('Le matin'), 'Evening' ('Le soir') and 'Sunday' ('Dimanche'), which highlight the fragmentation of clock time into a returning and overlapping cycle of time; or the modification of tenses at the end – 'None of us will return. None of us was meant to return' ('Aucun de nous ne reviendra. Aucun de nous n'aurait dû revenir') – which again constructs an uncanny temporality between past, present and future according to a blurring of sameness and difference. Delbo's poetic temporal structure interrupts our idea of the time of the camps by overlaying it with multiple times from elsewhere.

The same is, of course, true of place. The opening of *Aucun de nous ne reviendra* not only blurs the distinction between departure and arrival but also draws together space outside the camp ('Some came from Warsaw ..., some from Zagreb ..., some from the Danube') with camp space ('This is the station they reach, from wherever they came').[18] These connections are central to the tensions established between 'normal' life and camp life, horror and the everyday. The effect is to shock each space out of its separateness and specificity, not in order to conflate them but to create an uncanny overlap of distance and proximity. The specificity of the experience in Auschwitz cannot be told without reference to numerous 'elsewheres' invading the narrative. Delbo's narrative technique is more akin to the overlapping of times and places, and the blurrings of horror and the everyday and life and death, that one finds in *Nuit et brouillard*. It would therefore be more accurate to describe the trilogy as 'concentrationary' texts rather than Holocaust texts as such, as the singularity of the event is constantly disturbed (or haunted) by the shadow of other times and places.[19]

Delbo's 'testimony' is never singular, or rather it is a pluralized singularity (in the way that Jacques Derrida describes the 'singularity' of monolingualism in *Le Monolinguisme de l'autre, ou le prothèse de l'origine*, as I shall argue in chapter 6). Other voices speak through the narrating voice (other women, men, Jews, Roma and Sinti, other nationalities and so on) so that the relationship between the narrator and these others is again held in an in-between state in which the self is (in the terms of Cayrol and then Julia Kristeva) a stranger to itself.[20] In other words, Delbo's testimony (if one can call it that) is a polyphonic play in which the individual subject, other subjects and the collective (or collectives) are neither distinct nor the same but are profoundly interconnected in a new formation. If testimony is an acting out of trauma (as Shoshana Felman and Dori Laub famously argue),[21] then Delbo makes us ask: 'Whose trauma is being acted out?'. This is a presentation of testimony in which it is not simply the unspeakable nature of the event that returns (and, with it, the recognition of the limitations of human comprehension to capture the event) but also, in the words of Cathy Caruth used to introduce this chapter, 'the way we are implicated in each other's traumas'. Caruth's observation about *Hiroshima mon amour* is also applicable to Delbo's dramatization of trauma: 'The problem of knowing Hiroshima is not simply the problem of an outsider's knowing the inside of another's experience; more profoundly, the film dramatizes something that happens when two different experiences, absolutely alien to one another, are brought together'.[22]

The last section of *Aucun de nous ne reviendra*, entitled 'Springtime' ('Printemps'), dramatizes this process but draws it back specifically to the nature of memory. Spring is first presented in the text as rebirth through the death of others: 'In the spring men and women sprinkle ashes on drained marshland plowed for the first time. They fertilize the soil with human phosphates'.[23] When Spring returns at the end it is once again presented as the time at which bodies and the earth, life and death are barely distinguishable. This vision of Spring in the camps is then overlaid with a different memory of Spring ('Spring sang in the memory, in my memory') which associates it with Paris ('In the spring, we walk along the Seine's embankment, looking at the Louvre's plane trees …. In the spring, we walk across the Luxembourg gardens before going to the office').[24] However, there is a recognition that these are banal images of an idealized past ('And my memory finds only clichés'). This is immediately followed by a famous line from Apollinaire, '"O my memory, my beautiful ship"' ('Mon beau navire, ô ma mémoire'), and then the questions 'Where are you, my real memory? Where are you, my earthly memory?', which add to the repetitive questioning of memory in the lines 'Why am I the only one left with the ability to remember?', 'Why did I keep my memory?'.[25] At the end of the text memory is shown to be soiled and deathly ('My memory is drained of its sap. My memory has bled to death'). However, the final image is ambiguous – 'Far beyond the barbed-wire enclosure, spring is singing. Her eyes grew empty. And we lost our memory'.[26] This ambiguity about memory is then followed by the ambiguity of the tenses and positioning of the speaking voice in the last two lines of the text.

In this final section, memory cannot be located specifically in terms of place or time: the memory of the camps is overlaid with images of Paris, and it is never clear whether we are dealing with the memory of the narrator in the camp or the memory of the narrator at the moment of writing. Furthermore, it is not clear whether it is the memory of the narrator at all (at whatever time and place of recall), or whether it is someone else's memory. For example, the singular memory of '*ma mémoire*' is doubled by the collective memory of '*nous avons perdu la mémoire*'. Yet even the apparent singularity of '*ma mémoire*' is doubled by the line from Apollinaire, '*Mon beau navire, ô ma mémoire*'. The repetition of the line '*le printemps chantait dans ma mémoire*' recalls the missing title of the Apollinaire poem 'La Chanson du mal-aimé' from which the line is taken (and the poem's themes of blighted love, and experience and return) as well as the idea of lyrical poetry itself ('*la chanson*') which (in Adorno's famous dictum) is impossible after Auschwitz. The questions posed in the text – '*Où es-tu, ma vraie mémoire ? Où es-tu, ma mémoire terrestre ?*' – are never resolved because there is no simple resolution after Auschwitz. ('Memory returned to me / and with it suffering / which made me wander back / to the homeland of the unknown.')[27]

Language, memory and identity are now fragmented because they are perpetually haunted by the silent knowledge of loss and death ('I was there... How? I don't know. But was I really there? Was it me? Was I...').[28] In a portrayal of the 'choral' nature of Delbo's narrative voice, Luba Jurgenson sensitively highlights the ambiguity of *'le chant de la mémoire'* as it slips between seeking solidarities with others and tragic dissolution into the void:

> On several occasions in the trilogy, the song is evoked as a way of being together, which mitigates the impossibility of collective action or a shared voice. The song is what brings together isolated voices, merges them into a plurality in which the disappearance of the individual is absorbed into the continuity of the group. However, reinforcing the paradoxical dimension of the non-return, the 're-found time' of the third volume creates, alongside this polyphony of resistance, the thread of a tragic chorus which connects with that of the theatre of antiquity. In effect, the fifteen voices form a choir which slows down and amplifies the speech of the actor, her 'singular voice', validating it by their presence but at the cost of its dissolution into their phantom community.[29]

Memory in Delbo's trilogy is like the concentrationary memory of *Nuit et brouillard*: a present out of joint because of a constant deathly haunting (what Delbo will later name, in the posthumous *La Mémoire et les jours*, 'deep memory'/'la mémoire profonde' which haunts the everyday). Delbo's poetic dispersal of time across times, place across places and voice across voices creates an interpersonal space and time which has no single home or source. At the end of the final volume of the trilogy *Mesure de nos jours*, the voice of memory belongs not to any specific individual but between individuals and emerges only through the connection between traumas:

> As for me, I remember nothing. (Who was the one who said this?) Actually I remember nothing. When people ask me something about over there, I feel a kind of void opening before me and instead of being seized by vertigo and stepping back, I run and fall in head-long, plunging into the emptiness under my feet in order to escape. Only when I'm with all of you do I remember, or perhaps I ought to say recognize your own remembrances.[30]

Georges Perec: *W ou le souvenir d'enfance* / *W, or The Memory of Childhood*

At the beginning of *W ou le souvenir d'enfance*, Gaspard Winckler, the narrator of the story of W (one of the two narratives that make up the text), confronts his own troubled childhood. His recollections are a vague set of images of horror rather than any clear and precise memory:

Those ghost towns, those bloody contests (I believed I could still hear the shouting), those unfurled, wind-whipped banners came back to live in my dreams. Incomprehension, horror and fascination commingled in the bottomless pit of those memories. For years I sought out traces of my history, looking up maps and directories and piles of archives. I found nothing, and it sometimes seemed as though I had dreamt, that there had been only an unforgettable nightmare.[31]

The nightmare images of a traumatized imagination, composed of strange and frightening sights and sounds, will provide a core of lexical items or traces (the sea, military ensigns, bloody races) to be explored in the following pages. This feeling of horror is abstract. Though, like all types of trauma, it will need to ground itself (or, to use Perec's term, 'anchor' itself) by attaching itself obsessively to diverse objects, it will nevertheless resist containment and remain a generalized and permanent nightmare shadowing all conscious formulations. Hence, although the deaths of the parents of the narrator of the 'autobiographical' narrative during the Second World War and the Holocaust provide a clear source for the narrator's trauma, and account for the endless spiralling of writing around their absence, the Holocaust itself is not the only origin of the more general and unnameable horror to which the above passage alludes. This 'unforgettable nightmare' is composed of images which emanate from other sources too. The poetics of the text make us read this horror through the kaleidoscopic prism of different moments and sites of racialized violence.

If we consider the narrative of the island of W we see how these confused images of horror are informed not only by a Holocaust imagination but also by a colonial imagination, and that the two interconnect, overlap and slide into each other in a number of ways. The boat journey undertaken by the deaf and dumb boy Gaspard Winckler (whose name the narrator of W has adopted) and his mother Caecilia to seek a miracle cure for Gaspard is described in terms of a colonial expedition to foreign lands in search of utopia.[32] The name of Angus Pilgrim – one of the four other members of the crew whose bodies will eventually be found in the shipwreck – clearly signals the journey to the New World and the mixture of religion and the sword by which it will be colonized. The island of W is subsequently presented as a colonial settlement by Westerners – 'white, Western, and moreover, almost exclusively Aryan: Dutchmen, Germans, Scandinavians, scions of that proud class called WASPs in the United States' – whose utopian society will be founded on the Olympic ideal and dedicated to 'the greater glory of the Body'.[33] Perec describes the founders of W as 'the group of colonizers', talks of 'the origins of its colonizers'[34] and uses the language and tone of a military cartographer to describe the size, climate and vegetation of the island.

By the end of the text, the colonial settlement will have been transformed into a concentration camp and the Olympic ideal perverted into a form of grotesque dehumanization. This is effected through a play on words and signs (a poetics that I discuss further below) which allows meaning to splinter out across different sites and fields. Thus, the very terms used to define the colonial settlement of W resonate profoundly with the vocabulary and imagery of a fascist aesthetic. The glorification of the body on W takes on the aesthetic form of Aryanism – 'that bold discipline, those daily achievements, those neck-and-neck struggles, the intoxication of victory' – and clearly derives from the fascist visual style central to Leni Riefenstahl's famous filming of the 1936 Berlin Olympics for her film *Olympia* (1938), for W is 'a land where Sport is king, a nation of athletes where Sport and life unite in a single magnificent effort' and where 'the athletic vocation shapes the life of the State'.[35] Perec's island of athletes shows how the idealization of the male body in sport, and the rationalized institutional system constructed to make this cult of the body the central focus of society, are crucial to the racial thinking of both colonial and fascist aesthetic practice.

In his fascinating analysis of some of the shared institutional practices and aesthetic ideals of imperialism and fascism, Paul Gilroy locates sport as a central feature of a common aesthetic of the body. He cites a passage from *Mein Kampf* in which Hitler's racial thinking is clearly informed by a composite imperialist/fascist aesthetic around the body:

> it is not a function of the folkish state to breed a colony of peaceful aesthetes and physical degenerates. Not in the respectable shop keeper or virtuous old maid does it see its ideal of humanity, but in the defiant embodiment of manly strength and in women who are able to bring men into the world. And so sport does not exist only to make the individual strong, agile and bold; it should also toughen him and teach him to bear hardships.

Gilroy comments that '[t]hese words could almost have come from the pages of *Scouting for Boys* or *Rovering to Success*. They provide a strange, distorted echo of an older imperial ideal'.[36] Franck Evrard traces the roots of Perec's society of athletes back to the early nineteenth century and the military-inspired cult of uplifting physical exercise 'as the remedy for and solution to concerns about "the decadence of the race", and as a means of regeneration of the individual and the nation and the saving of civilization'.[37] Mastery of the body ('la maîtrise du corps') is at the heart of the disciplinary and surveillance society described by Michel Foucault in *Surveiller et punir* which will be exploited both by the colonial and the totalitarian state.[38]

These links between sport, race and power suggest that Perec's text is not only dealing with the horror of Auschwitz. The strange history of the major sporting arena in Paris, the Vélodrome d'hiver (Vel' d'hiv), to which W also clearly alludes, seems to confirm this. In the famous round-up (*rafle*) of 16–17 July 1942, Jews were brought to the stadium before being sent on to Drancy in the north of Paris and the camps in the east. Yet the Vel' d'hiv, demolished in 1959 to make way for a new stadium, the Palais des sports, was also the site of the round-up of about ten thousand Algerians following the demonstration of 17 October 1961. Rothberg notes the heading used by the weekly magazine *France Observateur* on 26 October 1961 under a photograph showing Algerians interned in the Palais des sports after the demonstration of 17 October: 'Does this remind you of anything?' ('Cela ne vous rappelle rien?'). Rothberg also recalls the same comparison made by Marguerite Duras in an article entitled 'The Two Ghettos' ('Les Deux ghettos') which also appeared in *France Observateur* (9 November 1961).[39] Writing two years later in her autobiography *La Force des choses*, Simone de Beauvoir observes 'ten thousand Algerians had been herded into the Vel' d'hiv, like the Jews at Drancy once before'.[40] In his (not uncontroversial) post-Foucauldian argument on the normalization of 'the camp' ('the camp' as the new *nomos*) in the biopolitical power relations of modern society, Giorgio Agamben cites the sporting arena (including the Vel' d'hiv) as one of the many spaces in which camp structures may appear:

> The stadium in Bari into which the Italian police in 1991 provisionally herded all illegal Albanian immigrants before sending them back to their country, the winter cycle-racing track in which the Vichy authorities gathered the Jews before consigning them to the Germans, the *Konzentrationslager fur Auslander* in Cottbus-Sielow in which the Weimar government gathered Jewish refugees from the East, or the *zones d'attentes* in French international airports in which foreigners asking for refugee status are detained will then all equally be camps. In all these cases, an apparently innocuous space (for example, the Hôtel Arcades in Roissy) actually delimits a space in which the normal order is de facto suspended.[41]

The confused images and vague sense of an 'unforgettable nightmare' that beset both narrators in *W ou le souvenir d'enfance* thus spring from a complex history of the racialization of bodies in Western society. In Perec's case, it has produced a consciousness in which the idealization of the male body in racial thought is always shadowed by the denigration and dismemberment of other bodies which fail to match the racialized ideal. The childhood fantasy of W to which the 'autobiographical' narrator has returned is thus inevitably accompanied by the negative image shadowing 'the greater glory of the Body' previously recounted:

> From this point on, there are memories – fleeting, persistent, trivial, burdensome – but there is nothing that binds them together. They are like that unjoined-up writing, made of separate letters unable to forge themselves into a word, which was my writing up to the age of seventeen or eighteen, or like the dissociated, dislocated drawings whose scattered elements almost

never managed to connect up and with which, at the time of 'W', roughly, that is, between my eleventh and fifteenth year, I filled whole exercise books: human figures unrelated to the ground which was supposed to support them, ships with sails that did not touch the masts and masts which did not fit into the hulls, machines of war, engines of death, flying machines and implausible mechanical vehicles with disconnected nozzles, discontinuous cordage, disengaged wheels rotating in the void; the wings of the planes were detached from their fuselages, the legs of the athletes were separated from their trunks, their arms were out of their torsos, their hands gave them no grasp.[42]

The second part of this remarkable passage can, on one level, be read as the symptoms of a young mind traumatized by machines of destruction in which the fantasy of the perfect body of W is overshadowed by fears of the fragmented body and loss of 'anchoring' ('ancrage'). When read in the context of the first part of the passage, this traumatized imagination is clearly inscribed within the space of a fragmented language and memory. Seen in the wider context of the text, we are presented with visions of idealized and dismembered bodies, utopian visions and the 'engines of death'. Seen in the wider context of Perec's poetic practice, we are presented with a set of signs which, like the fragmented body or machine parts, will be assembled, disassembled and reassembled *ad infinitum* (thus mimicking, according to Freud, the foundational structuring fantasies of the ego on wholeness and fragmentation). The effect of this constant articulation and disarticulation of lexical items is to constitute a set of signs whose meaning will always be doubled by resonances from elsewhere to constitute a series of overlapping semantic fields which share a common vocabulary. Like Freud's dream condensation or the example of the palimpsest, the text explores different but overlapping visions of utopias and nightmares, of fantasies of perfect forms and the anxieties born of fragmentation, destruction, violence and loss. The writing is a journey through a personal and historical lexicon drawn from both a colonial and a Holocaust imaginary (especially concerning the body). This broken and reassembled language constitutes the post-apocalyptic landscape of the text in which meaning can only ever be deferred from one site to another and, at best, a temporary suspension following catastrophic violence and loss.[43]

Perec gives us a number of clues as to his method of memory, imagination and writing which make it clear that the overlapping of a Holocaust and a colonial imaginary according to a shared vocabulary is not simply an arbitrary reading of the text but a fundamental part of its poetics. In the brief abstract which appears on the back cover of the book, Perec describes the connection between the two narratives as follows:

In this book there are two texts which simply alternate; you might almost believe they had nothing in common, but they are in fact inextricably bound up with each other, as though neither could exist on its own, as though it was only their coming together, the distant light they cast on each other, that could make apparent what is never quite said in one, never quite said in the other, but said only in their fragile overlapping.[44]

This practice of only being able to see one thing through another, and conceiving art as the 'fragile overlapping' between apparently distinct elements, is closely related to what the 'autobiographical' narrator calls his 'frustrated left-handedness' ('gaucherie contrariée'), by which he is unable to distinguish between opposites. He cannot tell left from right in a bobsleigh race, during his driving test and when he rows, nor can he distinguish between grave and acute accents or between concave and convex. Of particular interest (in terms of my wider discussion) is his failure to see metaphor and metonymy and a paradigm and a sytagm as opposites. He is obsessed with mnemonics ('les procédés mnémotechniques') by which words are derived, in condensed form, from other words.[45] Hence, the search for a miracle cure which ends in catastrophe, the transformation of a sporting utopia into a concentration camp, the overlapping of a colonial adventure and the Holocaust, and so on are examples of this imagination which blurs the contours between supposedly 'distinct' semantic fields. Signs are inherently unstable and multivalent. They are sites of condensation and displacement of meaning, sites of substitution of one thing for another and connection between different elements, sites of metaphor and metonymy. Memory and imagination are indistinguishable from the play of writing which operates on a paradigmatic and syntagmatic axis at the same time. As Michael Sheringham observes, it is the process of writing itself which draws together all the signs in play: 'Writing is the point at which memory, biography, identity, and loss coincide.'[46]

This oxymoronic imagination presumably explains the 'autobiographical' narrator's fascination with fairly obscure military figures like le Général de Larminat, Thierry Argenlieu and Charles de Foucauld, all of whom were either war heroes who were also involved in colonial activities or military men who were also members of the religious order (or both, as in the case of Charles de Foucauld, an army officer in Algeria and Tunisia in the late nineteenth century who later became ordained as a priest and lived a hermit-like existence in Algeria before being brutally killed).[47] The Christ-like depiction of the death of Charles de Foucauld – 'I remember the death of Charles de Foucauld: he is tied to a post, the fatal bullet has gone straight through his eye, and blood runs down his cheek' – when seen in conjunction with his colonial military early life, captures that strange blend of conquest and piety, brutality and utopianism epitomized by W.[48] And is the image that hovers as a ghost-like presence behind these hybrid figures (though never mentioned explicitly) that of Saint Sebastian, the famous 'soldier-saint' in early Christian mythology? After all, Sebastian is the patron saint of athletes and soldiers.

Yet the fascination with obscure military figures is far more complex than a simple blurring of opposites, as the military (like all other signs) is a link in numerous chains of meaning. The narrator of W once joined but is now running away from the army. For the 'autobiographical' narrator, military life is associated with his father:

> My father was a soldier for a very short time. Nonetheless, when I think of him, I always think of a soldier …. At a particular time in my life … the love I felt for my father became bound up with a passionate craze for tin soldiers …; one day I saw in [a shop] window a crouching soldier carrying a field telephone. I remembered my father had been in the communication corps, and this toy soldier, which I bought the very next day, became the regular centrepiece of all the tactical and strategic manœuvres which I performed with my little army.[49]

Soldiers have therefore become both substitutes for the father and objects of fear. They contain, in condensed form, a complex network of meaning in which love and killing, noble bodies and broken bodies are profoundly imbricated.

Doubles abound in the text: two narratives, two Gaspard Wincklers, two mothers with the same name, and so on.[50] Yet the 'fragile overlapping' between 'opposites' means that the doubling of one identity by another, or the substitution of one thing for another, does not efface the substituted object but acts as a mark or trace which contains the other within it to create a composite term. A consideration of the imbrications of Jewish and Christian symbols is indicative of this process. The 'autobiographical' narrator believes he remembers, just prior to his departure from his mother at the Gare de Lyon in 1942, 'that she injured herself one day and her hand was pierced through. She wore the star'.[51] This 'memory' appears shortly after note 24 describing marks on his own hands and will be part of a chain of meaning comprising the mother, marks, stigmata, holes and so on. In one sense, the pierced hand, given its obvious Christian connotations, seems an unlikely symbol to associate with the absence and subsequent death of the Jewish mother in the Holocaust,. However, if we see it as part of a sequence of *entrecroisements* in the text between Jew and Christian it acquires a logic particular to the work of the writing. The very first memory of the 'autobiographical' narrator at the age of three is that of being seated in the centre of the room at the back of his grandmother's shop, surrounded by his family, with Yiddish newspapers scattered around. Much to the delight of his family, the three-year-old child identifies a Hebrew letter which is described in writing ('the sign was supposedly shaped like a square with a gap in its lower left-hand corner'), then represented graphically in the text, and finally given the name either as 'gammeth, or gammel'.[52] The narrator then records, 'the subject, the softness, the lighting of the whole scene are, for me, reminiscent of a painting, maybe a Rembrandt or maybe an invented one, which might have been called "Jesus amid the Doctors'".[53] Two notes written by the narrator rectify the original narrative. The first explains that there is a letter 'gimmel' in the Hebrew alphabet (not 'gammeth' or 'gammel') but that the one traced by his younger self was more likely a 'mem' or 'M' and that his fascination for deciphering Hebrew letters took place at another time and place. The second note concerns the imaginary representation of this scene: 'In this memory, or pseudo-memory, Jesus is a newborn infant surrounded by kindly old men. All the paintings entitled "Jesus amid the Doctors" depict him as an adult. The picture I am referring to here, if it exists, is much more likely to be a "Presentation in the Temple"'.[54]

The 'autobiographical' narrator's first memory/image therefore contains at its centre a Hebrew letter which metamorphoses into the image of 'Jesus amid the Doctors'. The 'gammeth', 'gammel' or 'gimmel' is 'open-ended'; literally, because it is not a closed square but has 'a gap in its lower left-hand corner', and metaphorically, because the signifier will 'open out' onto a bewildering number of meanings traced in the text, including the name of the 'autobiographical' narrator/author ('There is in fact a letter called "Gimmel" which I like to think could be the initial of my first name')[55] and the swastika (*croix gammée*) of Nazism, the ultimate 'closed' sign for the repression of all plural meaning and the implementation of the single truth.[56] Like the mother, whose absence will provoke the endless string of signs or marks as displacements of that void, so the Hebrew letter (ambiguous in its form and meaning) will be transformed into other signs or marks which spring from and refer back to that point, both disguising that open-endedness in images, meanings and representations, and giving rise to different forms and meaning.

In the mind of the narrator, the image of the infant Jesus overlays, and is profoundly articulated with, the deciphering of the Hebrew letter. Jewish origins are thus not presented as roots which, in essentialist fashion, will shed a clear and unambiguous light on the narrator's identity. They can never be perceived as a simple presence. Rather, they are already caught up in a complex signifying system whose signs are constantly in the process of transformation and metamorphosis. Viewed in this way, the mother's stigmata or the Jewish child represented as the infant Jesus are neither opposites nor a paradox; they designate the imbrications and *entrecroisements* of a Jewish past in a Christian world, where the former has become progressively hidden by, but is nevertheless embedded in, the latter, and whose (re)tracing constitutes the trajectory of memory, identity and writing. In similar fashion, the Christianized name of 'Perec' becomes the sign (mark) which both hides and reveals the absent Jewish origins of the Peretz/Perez family who, as Maranos in Spain (*conversos*), would have disguised their Jewish origins and mimicked their Christian neighbours in order to survive under the Inquisition;[57] the Christianized names of the parents, André and Cécile, contain the traces of their Jewish origins as Icek Judko and Cyrla respectively; and the young narrator's Jewish background will be progressively overlaid with his convent education and his baptism in the summer of 1943 (on the recommendation of Father David who, according to the narrator's aunt, was himself 'a converted Jew').[58] The whole process of 'assimilation' is both a masking and a revelation of identity, camouflaging the traces of the past by overlaying them with a new set of signs, but, like a palimpsest, allowing those very traces to be retrieved beneath the surface.[59]

The visible object is therefore profoundly attached to the hidden object in a ceaseless game of hide and seek, masking and revelation, resembling Freud's description of the child's game of fort/da.[60] So, when the 'autobiographical' narrator traces the dizzying transformations of his name – '"Bretzel" is in fact merely a diminutive form (Beretzele) of Beretz, and Beretz, like Baruch or Barek, is formed from the same root as Peretz – in Arabic, if not in Hebrew, B and P are one and the same letter'[61] – or when the narrator of *W* tells us that he will write in the style of Ishmael (referring, presumably, both to the narrator of Melville's *Moby Dick* and Abraham's outcast son),[62] we must extend the composite term Christian-Jew to the more hybrid term of Christian-Jew-Arab.[63] The description of three of the five heraldic symbols on the letter sent to the narrator of *W* by Otto Apfelstahl is another key to the condensation and displacement of meaning at work in the text:

> Yet it was not a matter of abstract symbols; they were not chevrons, for example, or stripes or lozenges, but figures that were somehow double, with precise but ambiguous designs which seemed to be open to several different interpretations, without it being possible to decide on a satisfactory choice: one of them could just about have been a sinuous serpent with bay leaves for scales, another might have been a hand that was simultaneously a root; the third was equally a nest and a brazier, or a crown of thorns, or a burning bush, or even an impaled heart.[64]

If critics have commented at length on the *aller-retour* in the text between the two narratives, past and present, fact and fiction, truth and falsehood, memory and imagination, presence and absence, showing and hiding, wholeness and fragmentation and so on, very few have made similar comments about the same process operating with regard to the Holocaust and other moments of horror. Claude Burgelin alludes to a reading of this sort when he comments:

> the text should not be seen in terms of a single meaning. Perec has constructed this counter-utopia so that it relates to a range of different social systems, which are nevertheless linked in terms of their common perversion of the notions of law and freedom. Savagery is, first and foremost, a society whose only form of regulation is that of competition.[65]

More generally, Leslie Hill talks of the connections between times and spaces in Perec's writing in terms of a palimpsest: 'The real, which, according to Perec, is the object of all his efforts as a writer, is a palimpsest composed of different places and sites, different texts and spaces'.[66] However, there has been little critical development of either of these insightful observations, even though Perec's poetics of the 'fragile overlapping' invites a reading in which the Holocaust is, also, not a discreet event but only derives its meaning (never fixed, always deferred, always in suspension) from its relation to other signs from elsewhere. Thus, the multiple transformations of the letter W (itself a composite of two Vs which, placed one on top of the other, make X) give material form to the connections between empire and the Holocaust as W transmutes from being the first letter in the name of Wilson, who is the colonial founder of the island 'W' and the origin of its name, to its graphical presence in the Nazi swastika.[67]

Due to this obsessive reworking of lexical items, the quote at the end of the text from Rousset's *L'Univers concentrationnaire* can be read as a condensation of different contexts rather than the designation of the Holocaust as the only marker of dehumanization and loss. On an explicit level, the cruel disciplining of the body that takes place on W is equated with the structures of the concentration camp as described by Rousset, in which sport has been transformed into a mode of dehumanization. However, the connections that have previously been established in the text between colonial aspirations, sporting prowess and the disciplining of the body allow us to read this passage implicitly as the formation of an imperial and not simply fascist aesthetic. Perec's text shows how Rousset's concentrationary universe refers not only to the structures of the Nazi machine but also to broader Western structures of competition, utopianism, mastery and violence; that is, 'two worlds, the world of the Masters and the world of slaves'.[68] In fact, as Warren Motte observes, the intersection between the two narratives allows the concentrationary universe to permeate the world of the 'autobiographical' narrator's childhood: 'at every point, as Perec details instances of childish brutality, arbitrary injustice, and oppression, his narrative calls out to the concentrationary universe. As if he had in fact followed his mother into the camps'.[69] In effect, Perec offers us a way of reading Rousset not simply in terms of the concentration camps but in terms of a far wider 'camp' mentality (in Gilroy's terms and those of Rousset himself) which is deeply inscribed in the Western cultural and political imaginary and predicated on a horrific history of racialized violence. We will read the last lines of the text with this broader (Agambenian?) concept of the 'camp' in mind which, regrettably, has a life beyond its colonial and Holocaust variations: 'I have forgotten what reasons I had at the age of twelve for choosing Tierra del Fuego as the site of W. Pinochet's fascists have provided my fantasy with a final echo: several of the islands in that area are today deportation camps'.[70] The textual world of disarticulation and rearticulation of lexical items parallels the historical recycling of a racialized 'camp' mentality.

Patrick Modiano: *Dora Bruder*

A similar imbrication of colonial and Holocaust detail can be located in Patrick Modiano's *Dora Bruder*, in which the narrator traces the disappearance of a young Jewish girl in Paris during the Second World War. The immediate memories evoked by the Bruders' address on the Boulevard Ornano in Paris relate, first, to the narrator's childhood when he passed the Clignancourt barracks ('la caserne Clignancourt') with his mother, then to a Sunday in 1958 when he witnessed 'at every crossroads, groups of anti-riot police because of the events in Algeria', and finally to a visit to the area in the winter of 1965 to see a friend, leading the narrator to wonder, 'What had been the purpose of this barracks? I had been told that it housed colonial troops'.[71] The gateway to a story that will turn out to be about Occupation and the Holocaust is, thus, the image of a colonial barracks and events in Algeria, not incidents or places related directly to the Holocaust.

The narrator will discover that Dora's father Ernest – whose family will, as Jews, eventually be victims of French collaboration with the Nazis – was, by a strange twist of fate, in the French Foreign Legion at the beginning of the 1920s and therefore himself involved in colonial military operations 'sent to pacify those territories in Morocco not yet under French control'. 'The barracks in Belfort and Nancy' and then 'the barracks in Mèknes, Fez or Marrakesh', imagined by the narrator as locations where the young legionnaire might have been stationed, are reminders of 'la caserne Clignancourt' earlier and link the heart of metropolitan France more explicitly with the colonial adventure.[72] More significantly, 'the prison, the "camp" or rather the internment centre of Les Tourelles', in which Dora will be imprisoned before being transferred to the transit camp of Drancy, 'was [itself] on the site of a former colonial infantry barracks, the Tourelles barracks, at 141 boulevard Mortier'.[73] When the narrator visits this site in the present (now a *zone militaire*), none of this history (first as a colonial barracks, then as an internment camp during the war) is apparent: 'I thought that nobody remembers anything. Behind the wall stretched a no-man's land, an empty zone of amnesia'.[74] Yet the traces of the past are covered over, not obliterated, and the task of writing will be to penetrate this 'empty zone':

> However, beneath this thick layer of amnesia one could occasionally sense something, a distant, muted echo but which one would not have been able to define precisely. It was like being on the edge of a magnetic field without a mechanism for picking up the waves.[75]

Modiano opens up Parisian city space to the sound waves of a complex and troubled past of loss and violence. City sites are points of intersection between personal and collective trajectories and between memory, history and imagination. The initial associations established between Clignancourt and Les Tourelles, and between the *'années noires'* and the Algerian War, will echo across subsequent mentions of these sites to establish knotted clusters of meaning. Hence, all the circulars and administrative directives related to Jews which lead to Dora's arrest and detention in the *'commissariat du quartier Clignancourt'*,[76] which will subsequently result in her transfer to the former barracks of Tourelles,[77] carry with them the affective and historical charge of other round-ups at other times. When Clignancourt reappears following a later section on Tourelles, it is connected to a different memory in the narrator's past when, at the age of twenty, he met an old second-hand dealer ('brocanteur') from a Polish Jewish family who used to live in the area at the same time as Dora. Dervila Cooke reminds us of some of the connections established here:

> The *'brocanteur'* of the second last section (*Dora* 134–139) is a particularly symbolic point of connection between Dora, Albert Modiano and Modiano himself, in his Jewishness and his links with Clignancourt and especially the la Plaine area. The reader is invited to make further links between the *'juif polonais'* who sold suitcases in the Clignancourt *'puces'* and this junk salesman, who is also of Polish Jewish stock and once had a stand in that market (*Dora* 135–137). This *brocanteur*, who is such a strong linking force, and who puts the new and the forgotten to new use, dealing in bits and pieces, is a symbol of Modiano's own approach in the recording of fragments of lives.[78]

True enough, yet the cluster of connections that has formed around Clignancourt must also include the first memory associated with the site relating to the Algerian War. If the metaphorical use of the *'brocanteur'* is, as Cooke rightly suggests, illustrative of Modiano's method in the text (and, indeed, in his oeuvre as a whole), then the recycling of elements across city sites and individuals ultimately establishes multiple associations between different histories and memories of violence in republican France.[79]

When the narrator asks the doctor, Jean Puyaubert, in 1965 to certify that he has a lung problem so that he can escape his military service (even though, at that time, there was no war), and when (by coincidence?) the poet Roger Gilbert-Lecomte sees the same doctor for the same reason, it is because the forms of bureaucratic and institutionalized dehumanization that curtailed Dora's life and others like her in the Holocaust, and would then do the same to others during the Algerian War, have not disappeared. As the narrator says, 'the thought of living in a barracks, as I had already done when I was a boarder at school between the ages of eleven and seventeen, seemed to me to be insurmountable'.[80] Like the post-war presence of the concentrationary universe in *Nuit et brouillard*, the life of the camp continues to haunt everyday life, just as the presence of Dora haunts the streets of Paris:

> I walk down empty roads. For me, they are empty even in the evening, when there are traffic jams, when people are hurrying to the metro. I can't help myself thinking of her and sensing an echo of her presence in certain neighbourhoods. The other evening, it was by the Gare du Nord.[81]

Thus, the ubiquitous coincidences in the text (of which the meeting with the *'brocanteur'* and the link between the narrator and Gilbert-Lecomte are just two examples), and the connections established between the narrator's life and that of Dora and his own father, between different pasts and the present, the real and the imagined, 'fact' and fiction, and memory and history, are only coincidences in the surrealist sense of 'objective chance encounters' (*le hasard objectif*). Repetitions and similarities are, paradoxically, both fortuitous and necessary encounters in city space with a personal and collective unconscious traumatized by violence, dehumanization and loss, which, like the area around la rue des Jardins-Saint-Paul, has been covered over 'to construct a sort of Swiss village'.[82] Modiano reinvents the bland and normalized surface of postmodern everyday life not through the injection of sexual desire and myth (as in surrealism) but rather through the summoning up of unspeakable violence and the installation of a camp culture. If *Dora Bruder* treads the path of the *flâneur* in the city streets of Paris and is, in a certain sense, like a contemporary remake of André Breton's *Nadja*, then one of the crucial differences is that the encounter with a repressed unconscious reveals not the re-enchanted world of everyday life but the horrors of wasted lives. As with Perec's *W ou le souvenir d'enfance*, dehumanizing administration, prisons and camps beset both the narrator's haunted imagination and the history of France that he uncovers.[83] It taps into a historical/cultural imaginary of prisons, camps and dehumanizing administration which acts as a sort of unconscious backdrop to modernization and consumer culture. The return of the repressed in this text is an echo of an oppressive past which reverberates in the present, one in which, in the final lines, 'the executioners, the regulations, the authorities of so-called occupation, the prisons, the barracks, the camps, History, time' have defiled humanity.[84]

Notes

1. Cathy Caruth, *Unclaimed Experience*, p. 24.
2. 'aura de terreur sacrée', Jacques Rancière, 'S'il y a de l'irreprésentable?' in *Le Destin des images* (La Fabrique, 2003), p. 125 / 'Are Some Things Unrepresentable?' in *The Future of the Image*, trans. Gregory Elliott (London and New York: Verso, 2007), p. 109 (first published in *Genre Humain* 36 (2001), 81–102), and Gillian Rose, *Mourning Becomes the*

Law: Philosophy and Representation (Cambridge and New York: Cambridge University Press, 1996), p. 43.

3. Rancière, 'S'il y a de l'irreprésentable?', p. 134 / 'Are Some Things Unrepresentable?', p. 118.

4. In this sense, it could be argued that even Lanzmann's *Shoah* is not simply a Holocaust film. It relies on an iconography (that of trains and rails, for example) which has its own unconscious history which does not lead back exclusively to the Nazis' extermination programme, and then generates a model of staging trauma which will, in turn, influence other attempts to document or film different traumatic events. In other words, the film operates within a wider context of an unconscious imaginary (personal and collective) that links it inevitably to other scenes. In his critique of *Shoah*, Dominic LaCapra notes that 'the scenes of the present state of the camp and ghetto sites will themselves be haunted by afterimages of films and photographs that almost everyone of a certain age (including Lanzmann's witnesses) has seen' (*History and Memory after Auschwitz*, p. 108). Libby Saxton observes that Godard's recycling, in *Histoire(s) du cinéma*, of the gesture of death performed by the train driver Gawkowski in *Shoah*, draws attention to the circulation and reinvention of images in the wider archive that subverts Lanzmann's own prohibition on the use of the archive: 'by tracing the complex ways in which images circulate on screens and in our memories, Godard's work also invites us to consider just how much of *Shoah*'s anamnesiac power comes – in spite of Lanzmann's claims – from the archive, from the images of atrocity we remember from elsewhere (including Godard's video-essay) which play in our minds but are refused to our eyes as we watch the film' (*Haunted Images*, p. 66). I would therefore agree with Saxton's suggestion that the process of staging, re-enactment and incarnation in *Shoah* is itself haunted by traces from elsewhere (see pp. 37–38).

5. Marianne Hirsch, *Family Frames: Photography, Narrative and Postmemory* (Cambridge, Mass.: Harvard University Press, 1997).

6. Katherine Hodgkin and Susannah Radstone question the equation between experience and truth which underlies the notion of the authenticity of memory (in contra-distinction to the fictional nature of representation): 'To privilege memory as a tool of truth, through which the statements of authority may be subverted or contradicted, we must assume a direct correspondence between the experience and how it is remembered' ('Introduction: Contested Pasts' in Katherine Hodgkin and Susannah Radstone (eds), *Contested Pasts: The Politics of Memory* (London and New York: Routledge, 2003), p. 2).

7. 'Pour se souvenir, même de façon solitaire et privée, il faut recourir à un médium langagier …. Il n'y a pas de mémoire sans langage. Or la médiation du langage est d'emblée de rang social', Paul Ricœur, 'Histoire et mémoire' in Antoine de Baecque et Christian Delage (eds), *De l'histoire au cinéma* (Éditions Complexe, 1998), p. 20.

8. Caruth, *Unclaimed Experience*, p. 27. Nancy Huston's *L'Empreinte de l'ange* (Actes Sud, 1998) also shows how the stories of the lovers Andràs and Saffie, and the different moments of violence they relate (the Holocaust, Communism and the Algerian War) only become recognizable (in a Benjaminian sense) once they are brought into contact with each other.

9. As I mentioned in chapter 2, the historical investigation of *Nuit et brouillard* by Sylvie Lindeperg in *'Nuit et brouillard', un film dans l'histoire* and by Lindeperg and Annette Wieviorka in *Univers concentrationnaire et génocide* shows how the evolution of the concentrationary universe and the project for genocide are separate but overlapping. In our introduction to *Concentrationary Cinema*, Griselda Pollock and I have tried to distinguish between the evolution of the two projects to bring back into focus the wider question of total domination that has often been lost from sight in the age of Holocaust memory. Yet we also recognize that this formal separation should not

obscure the interconnections in practice. One of the fascinations of *Nuit et brouillard* from this perspective is precisely that the mix of images used by Resnais (for example, some taken from the extermination camps and some from the concentration camps) blurs historical distinctions which can only be restored through the sort of painstaking and detailed historical analysis that Lindeperg has undertaken.

10. Rothberg, *Multidirectional Memory*, p. 208. Like Delbo, the ethnologist Germaine Tillion also made connections between torture by the French in Algeria and the terror of the Nazi era based on her own experience as a victim of the Nazis (Tillion was in Ravensbruck), but she did not pursue these links through literary expression.

11. Rothberg, *Multidirectional Memory*, p. 218. See also Nicole Thatcher: 'Her ability to empathise allows her to introduce herself in new situations after Auschwitz and to evoke more recent victims and survivors, such as the mothers of "the disappeared" in Argentina or inmates in the Soviet gulags ([Charlotte Delbo,] *La Mémoire et les jours*, 95–102, 135–138). This decision to testify for other oppressed people, transcending boundaries of time and place, displays a moralistic trend which is already detectable in the Trilogy' (*A Literary Analysis of Charlotte Delbo's Concentration Camp Re-presentation* (Lampeter: Edwin Mellen, 2000), p. 35).

12. 'Aujourd'hui, je ne suis pas sûre que ce que j'ai écrit soit vrai. Je suis sûre que c'est véridique'.

13. Davis, *Haunted Subjects*, p. 96. Davis follows Derrida in suggesting that the narrator in testimonial literature is not fully in possession of his or her own voice because there will always be a supplement that cannot be known or spoken: 'Delbo's writing suggests that secrecy as much as revelation is a key characteristic of testimonial literature. Her text preserves its right to say whilst not saying; it does not disclose or even know everything that might be hidden within it. The secrets of spectral others impinge on the vulnerable self and ensure that its testimony is only ever part of the full story, and perhaps not even the most important part' (p. 109).

14. Charlotte Delbo, *Une Connaissance inutile (Auschwitz et après 2)* (Minuit, 1970), pp. 31–32 and pp. 97–111 respectively / *Useless Knowledge* in *Auschwitz and after*, trans. Rosette C. Lamont (New Haven and London: Yale University Press, 1995), pp. 115–231, pp. 132–133 and pp. 172–180 respectively.

15. Delbo, *Aucun de nous ne reviendra*, p. 29 / *None of Us Will Return*, p. 17. A further analogy with Proust is that a fellow inmate, Yvonne P., drops her spoon prior to the involuntary memory. Delbo is clearly referring here also to the Nazis' use of the word *Figuren* as a euphemistic term to define the objectified and doll-like nature of the corpse. Hannah Arendt writes, '[t]otal power can be achieved and safeguarded only in a world of conditioned reflexes, of *marionettes* without the slightest trace of spontaneity' (Arendt, 'The Concentration Camps', p. 761, my emphasis).

16. 'Et maintenant je suis dans un café à écrire cette histoire – car cela devient une histoire', Delbo, *Aucun de nous ne reviendra*, p. 45 / *None of Us Will Return*, p. 26.

17. 'Et maintenant je suis dans un café à écrire ceci', Delbo, *Aucun de nous ne reviendra*, p. 49 / *None of Us Will Return*, p. 29.

18. 'il y a ceux qui viennent de Varsovie …, il y a ceux qui viennent de Zagreb …, il y a ceux qui viennent du Danube'; 'C'est à cette gare qu'ils arrivent, qu'ils viennent de n'importe où', Delbo, *Aucun de nous ne reviendra*, pp. 13 and 10 respectively / *None of Us Will Return*, pp. 5 and 3.

19. Thatcher distinguishes between 'concentrationary literature and genocidal literature' (literature of the concentration camps and the extermination camps respectively) but her use of the term 'concentrationary' is not informed by a Cayrolian approach to post-war art (*A Literary Analysis of Charlotte Delbo's Concentration Camp Re-presentation*, p. 2.) Philippe Mesnard, however, does remark on the proximity of Delbo's narration to the Cayrolian idea of the Lazarean ('Pourquoi Charlotte Delbo?' in *Témoigner entre*

histoire et mémoire: Dossier Charlotte Delbo, vol. 105 (Kimé, 2009), p. 21). For an interesting discussion of the distinction between '*la littérature concentrationnaire*' and '*la littérature génocidiaire*', see Parrau, *Écrire les camps*, pp. 16–19.

20. See Julia Kristeva, *Étrangers à nous-mêmes* (Fayard, 1988). In the opening section of *Aucun de nous ne reviendra*, 'Rue de l'arrivée, rue du départ', the third-person narration of the arrival of Jews at Auschwitz is overlaid with a first-person affectivity, hence blurring the dividing line between the narrating self and the Jewish other. Catherine Coquio's felicitous description of the tension between the personal and the collective in Delbo's narrative as 'an anxious accordion' ('un accordéon nerveux') is in terms of female intimacy and solidarity, whereas I believe that the voice is more ambiguous than that, both in terms of gender and in other stratifications. Coquio does, however, modify this gender divide later: 'In *Auschwitz et après*, "men" and "women" form two worlds which are distinct but not completely separated' ('Dans *Auschwitz et après*, "les hommes" et "les femmes" forment deux mondes distincts, mais jamais complètement séparés'). Catherine Coquio, 'La Tendresse d'Antigone: Charlotte Delbo, un témoignage au féminin' in *Témoigner entre histoire et mémoire*, pp. 145 and 146.

21. Shoshana Felman and Dori Laub, *Testimony: Crises of Witnessing in Literature, Psychoanalysis and History* (New York and London: Routledge, 1992).

22. Caruth, *Unclaimed Experience*, p. 34.

23. 'au printemps des hommes et des femmes répandent les cendres sur les marais asséchés pour la première fois labourés et fertilisent le sol avec du phosphate humain', Delbo, *Aucun de nous ne reviendra*, p. 18 / *None of Us Will Return*, p. 9.

24. 'Le printemps chantait dans ma mémoire – dans ma mémoire'; 'Au printemps, se promener le long des quais et les platanes du Louvre …. Au printemps, traverser le Luxembourg avant le bureau', Delbo, *Aucun de nous ne reviendra*, pp. 177 and 179 respectively / *None of Us Will Return*, pp. 111–112.

25. 'Et ma mémoire ne trouve que des clichés'; 'Où es-tu, ma vraie mémoire ? Où es-tu, ma mémoire terrestre ?'; 'Pourquoi seul de ces êtres avais-je conservé la mémoire ?', 'Pourquoi ai-je gardé la mémoire ?', Delbo, *Aucun de nous ne reviendra*, p. 179 / *None of Us Will Return*, p. 112.

26. 'Ma mémoire a perdu sa sève. Ma mémoire a perdu tout son sang'; 'Loin au-delà des barbelés, le printemps chante. Ses yeux se sont vidés. Et nous avons perdu la mémoire', Delbo, *Aucun de nous ne reviendra*, p. 181 / *None of Us Will Return*, p. 113.

27. 'La mémoire m'est revenue / et avec elle une souffrance / qui m'a fait m'en retourner / à la patrie de l'inconnu', Delbo, *Une Connaissance inutile*, p. 184 / *Useless Knowledge*, p. 225. The reference to Apollinaire is one of many literary references in Delbo's work, including especially Molière, Giraudoux and Proust. The narrating voice is split across literary citations as well as 'real' people.

28. 'J'étais là… Comment ? Je ne sais. Mais étais-je là ? Étais-je moi ? Étais-je…', Charlotte Delbo, *Mesure de nos jours (Auschwitz et après 3)* (Minuit, 1971), p. 12 / *The Measure of our Days* in *Auschwitz and after*, trans. Rosette C. Lamont (New Haven and London: Yale University Press, 1995), p. 236.

29. 'à plusieurs reprises au gré de la trilogie, le chant est évoqué comme un mode d'être ensemble venant pallier l'impossibilité d'action commune ou de parole partagée. Le chant est ce qui fait tenir ensemble les voix isolées, fondues en une pluralité où la disparition de l'individu est résorbée dans la pérennité du groupe. Cependant, creusant toujours plus profond la dimension paradoxale du non-retour, le "temps retrouvé" du troisième volume crée en filigrane, au côté de cette polyphonie de la résistance, une choralité tragique qui s'apparente à celle du théâtre de l'antiquité. Les quinze voix forment en effet un chœur démultipliant et amplifiant la parole de l'acteur, sa "voix singulière", la validant par leur présence, mais au prix de sa dissolution dans leur communauté fantôme', Luba Jurgenson, 'L'Identité narrative chez Charlotte Delbo: Un

Modèle chorale' in *Témoigner entre histoire et mémoire*, p. 73. Jurgenson also draws the conclusion that Delbo's 'choral' testimony is not simply about the Nazi camps but, 'written after the revelations of the 20th Congress of the Soviet Communist Party and after the Algerian War' ('écrite après les révélations du XXe Congrès du PC soviétique, après la guerre d'Algérie'), is also about the fractured recollections of all those who resisted political terror (p. 74).

30. 'Moi, je ne me souviens de rien. (Qui était celle qui disait cela ?) Je ne me souviens vraiment de rien. Quand on me demande quelque chose de là-bas, je sens une espèce de vide béant devant moi et, au lieu d'avoir le vertige et de m'en écarter, je m'y précipite, je plonge dans ce vide béant qui est devant moi pour me sauver. Il n'y a qu'avec vous que je me souvienne, ou plutôt non, je reconnais vos souvenirs', Delbo, *Mesure de nos jours*, pp. 197–198 / *The Measure of our Days*, p. 344.

31. 'mes rêves se peuplaient de ces villes fantômes, de ces courses sanglantes dont je croyais encore entendre les mille clameurs, de ces oriflammes déployées que le vent de la mer lacérait. L'incompréhension, l'horreur et la fascination se confondaient dans ces souvenirs sans fond. Longtemps j'ai cherché les traces de mon histoire, consulté des cartes et des annuaires, des monceaux d'archives. Je n'ai rien trouvé et il me semblait parfois que j'avais rêvé, qu'il n'y avait eu qu'un inoubliable cauchemar', Georges Perec, *W ou le souvenir d'enfance* (Denoel, 1975), pp. 13–14 / *W, or the Memory of Childhood*, trans. David Bellos (Jaffrey, New Hampshire: David R. Godine, 1988), p. 3.

32. Perec, *W ou le souvenir d'enfance*, p. 42 / *W, or the Memory of Childhood*, p. 24.

33. 'des Blancs, des Occidentaux, et même presque exclusivement des Anglo-Saxons : des Hollandais, des Allemands, des Scandinaves, des représentants de cette classe orgueilleuse qu'aux États-Unis on nomme les Wasp'; 'la plus grande gloire du Corps', Perec, *W ou le souvenir d'enfance*, p. 95 / *W, or the Memory of Childhood*, p. 67.

34. 'le groupe de colons' (trans. modified); 'la provenance des colons', Perec, *W ou le souvenir d'enfance*, pp. 94 and 95 respectively / *W, or the Memory of Childhood*, pp. 66 and 67.

35. 'cette discipline audacieuse, ... ces prouesses quotidiennes, cette lutte au coude à coude, cette ivresse que donne la victoire'; 'un pays où le sport est roi, une nation d'athlètes où le Sport et la vie se confondent en un même magnifique effort'; 'cette vocation athlétique détermine la vie de la Cité', Perec, *W ou le souvenir d'enfance*, p. 96 / *W, or the Memory of Childhood*, p. 67.

36. Gilroy, *Between Camps*, p. 166.

37. 'comme le remède et la solution aux préoccupations sur la « décadence de la race », et comme un moyen de régénération de l'individu, de sursaut national et de sauvetage de la civilisation', Franck Evrard, 'Mythologies et écriture du sport' in Louis Arsac (et al), *Analyses et réflexions sur Georges Perec, W ou le souvenir d'enfance* (Ellipses, 1997), p. 122.

38. Evrard, 'Mythologies et écriture du sport', pp. 122–123.

39. Rothberg, *Multidirectional Memory*, pp. 236–245.

40. 'Dix mille Algériens étaient parqués au Vel' d'Hiv, comme autrefois les Juifs à Drancy', Simone de Beauvoir, *La Force des choses*, vol. 2 (Gallimard, 1963), p. 435 / *Force of Circumstance*, trans. Richard Howard (Harmondsworth: Penguin, 1968), p. 614. De Beauvoir continues, 'Pouillon told us about a session in the Chamber during which Claudius Petit said to Frey: "Now we know what it means to be a German when the Nazis were in power!"; his words were greeted by a dead silence. It was five years since Marrou had reminded them of Buchenwald and the Gestapo; for years now, the French people had been just as much accomplices to what was going on as the Germans under Nazi rule; the belated uneasiness some of them were feeling about this fact did nothing to reconcile me with them' ('A la Chambre, au cours d'une séance que Pouillon nous raconta, Claudius Petit dit à Frey : "Nous savons maintenant ce que ça signifiait d'être allemands pendant le nazisme !" ; ses paroles tombèrent dans un silence de mort. Il y

avait plus de cinq ans que Marrou avait évoqué Buchenwald et la Gestapo ; pendant des années, les Français avaient accepté les mêmes complicités que les Allemands sous le régime nazi ; le malaise tardif que certains en éprouvaient ne me réconciliait pas avec eux', de Beauvoir, *La Force des choses*, pp. 436–437 / *Force of Circumstance*, p. 615). For a full account of French police brutality towards Algerians in the Palais des sports and in other holding centres after the demonstration of 17 October 1961, see House and Macmaster, *Paris 1961*, pp. 129–136. For a discussion of *W ou le souvenir d'enfance*, sport and Vichy, see Hans Hartje, 'W et l'histoire d'une enfance en France' in *Georges Perec et l'histoire*, Actes du colloque international de l'Institut de littérature comparée Université de Copenhague du 30 avril au 1er mai 1998, recueillis et publiés par Steen Bille Jorgensen et Carsten Sestoft (Copenhagen: Museum Tusculanum Press, 2000), pp. 53–66, and Nigel Saint, 'Drame de juillet, tragédie de l'été: Perec et Roland-Garros', *French Cultural Studies* 10 (1999), 173–178. In a strange disjunction between the cultural life of the photograph and its historical accuracy, the shot employed by Resnais in *Nuit et brouillard*, which supposedly depicts the round-up of Jews in the Vel' d'hiv, was actually an image of 'suspected collaborators rounded up in the same place shortly after the Liberation' ('des suspects de collaboration regroupés dans ce même lieu peu après la Libération'), Lindeperg, '*Nuit et brouillard*', un film dans l'histoire, p. 59. (There are no known photographs of the round-up of Jews in the Vel' d'hiv.) This is an example of the ability of the image to interrupt linear time and the specificity of place once it is put into circulation within cultural memory (see chapter 5 for a development of this discussion).

41. Agamben, *Homo Sacer*, p. 174.

42. 'Désormais, les souvenirs existent, fugaces ou tenaces, futiles ou pesants, mais rien ne les rassemble. Ils sont comme cette écriture non liée, faite de lettres isolées incapables de se souder entre elles pour former un mot, qui fut la mienne jusqu'à l'âge de dix-sept ou dix-huit ans, ou comme ces dessins dissociés, disloqués, dont les éléments épars ne parvenaient presque jamais à se relier les uns aux autres, et dont, à l'époque de W, entre, disons, ma onzième et ma quinzième année, je couvris des cahiers entiers : personnages que rien ne rattachait au sol qui était censé les supporter, navires dont les voilures ne tenaient pas aux mâts, ni les mâts à la coque, machines de guerre, engins de mort, aéroplanes et véhicules aux mécanismes improbables, avec leurs tuyères déconnectées, leurs filins interrompus, leurs roues tournant dans le vide ; les ailes des avions se détachaient du fuselage, les jambes des athlètes étaient séparées des troncs, les bras séparés des torses, les mains n'assuraient aucune prise', Perec, *W ou le souvenir d'enfance*, p. 97 / *W, or the Memory of Childhood*, p. 68.

43. For a fascinating reworking of Perec's connections between race, power and sport in relation to the Holocaust, see Philippe Grimbert's *Le Secret* (Grasset, 2004).

44. 'Il y a dans ce livre deux textes simplement alternés ; il pourrait presque sembler qu'ils n'ont rien en commun, mais ils sont inextricablement enchevêtrés, comme si aucun des deux ne pouvait exister seul, comme si de leur rencontre seule, de cette lumière lointaine qu'ils jettent l'un sur l'autre, pouvait se révéler ce qui n'est jamais tout à fait dit dans l'un, jamais tout à fait dit dans l'autre, mais seulement dans leur fragile intersection.'

45. Perec, *W ou le souvenir d'enfance*, pp. 184–185 / *W, or the Memory of Childhood*, pp. 135–136.

46. Michael Sheringham, *French Autobiography: Devices and Desires* (Oxford: Oxford University Press, 1993), p. 323. Other examples of a superimposition of distinct or opposite terms would include listing the historical events which took place on the day on which the 'autobiographical' narrator was born (conjoining the historical and the personal), the description of the island of W whose hostile coastline is in direct contrast to the hospitable and fertile interior (Perec, *W ou le souvenir d'enfance*, pp. 93–94 / *W, or*

the Memory of Childhood, pp. 65-66), and the deaths of Dumas's musketeers – 'Athos in his bed at the very instant that his son Raoul falls in Algeria, d'Artagnan swept off by a canon-ball at the siege of Maestricht, just after being appointed *maréchal*' ('Athos dans son lit au moment même ou tombe en Algérie son fils Raoul, d'Artagnan emporté par un boulet au siège de Maestricht alors qu'il vient d'être nommé maréchal'), (Perec, *W ou le souvenir d'enfance*, p. 196 / *W, or the Memory of Childhood*, p. 144).

47. Perec, *W ou le souvenir d'enfance*, pp. 204–205 / *W, or the Memory of Childhood*, pp. 149–151.

48. 'je me souviens de la mort de Charles de Foucauld : il est attaché à un poteau, la balle qui l'achève lui est entrée en plein dans l'œil, et le sang coule sur sa joue', Perec, *W ou le souvenir d'enfance*, p. 206 / *W, or the Memory of Childhood*, p. 151.

49. 'Mon père fut militaire pendant très peu de temps. Pourtant quand je pense à lui c'est toujours à un soldat que je pense …. A une certaine époque de ma vie … l'amour que je portais à mon père s'intégra dans une passion féroce pour les soldats de plomb …; Un jour même, voyant en vitrine un soldat accroupi porteur d'un téléphone de campagne, je me souvins que mon père était dans les transmissions et ce soldat, acheté le lendemain, devint le centre habituel des opérations stratégiques ou tactiques que j'entreprenais avec ma petite armée', Perec, *W ou le souvenir d'enfance*, pp. 46–48 / *W, or the Memory of Childhood*, pp. 27–29.

50. 'This whole history of breakage can only be narrated through the technique of doubling (the two narratives, two Gaspard Wincklers…). But, at the same time that the narrative structure contains these divisions, the strands of the writing weave a multiplicity of links which reconstitute the texture and the unity of a story, while still respecting the gaps' ('Toute cette histoire de cassure ne peut se raconter que dans le dédoublement (dédoublement des deux histoires, des deux Gaspard Winckler…). Mais, en même temps que la structure narrative met en place ces clivages, les fils de l'écriture tissent une multiplicité de liens qui recomposent, tout en respectant les trous, la trame et l'unité d'une histoire'), Claude Burgelin, *Georges Perec* (Seuil, 1988), pp. 150–151.

51. 'qu'elle se blessa un jour et eut la main transpercée. Elle porta l'étoile', Perec, *W ou le souvenir d'enfance*, p. 52 / *W, or the Memory of Childhood*, p. 32.

52. 'le signe aurait eu la forme d'un carré ouvert a son angle inférieur gauche'; 'gammeth, ou gammel', Perec, *W ou le souvenir d'enfance*, pp. 26 and 27 respectively / *W, or the Memory of Childhood*, p. 13.

53. 'La scène tout entière, par son thème, sa douceur, sa lumière, ressemble pour moi a un tableau, peut-être de Rembrandt ou peut-être inventé, qui se nommerait "Jésus en face des Docteurs"', Perec, *W ou le souvenir d'enfance*, p. 27 / *W, or the Memory of Childhood*, p. 13.

54. 'Dans ce souvenir ou pseudo-souvenir, Jésus est un nouveau-né entouré de vieillards bienveillants. Tous les tableaux intitulés "Jésus au milieu des Docteurs" le représentent adulte. Le tableau auquel je me réfère, s'il existe, est beaucoup plus vraisemblablement une "Présentation au Temple"', Perec, *W ou le souvenir d'enfance*, p. 28 / *W, or the Memory of Childhood*, p. 14.

55. 'Il existe en effet une lettre nommée "Gimmel" dont je me plais à croire qu'elle pourrait être l'initiale de mon prénom', Perec, *W ou le souvenir d'enfance*, p. 27 / *W, or the Memory of Childhood*, p. 14.

56. See Perec, *W ou le souvenir d'enfance*, p. 110 / *W, or the Memory of Childhood*, p. 77. Perec counters the fixed meaning of the swastika and its power over the other by opening it out onto an infinite range of other meanings, and thereby restoring the very otherness which its will to power would eradicate.

57. Perec, *W ou le souvenir d'enfance*, p. 56 / *W, or the Memory of Childhood*, pp. 35–36.

58. 'un juif converti', Perec, *W ou le souvenir d'enfance*, p. 130 / *W, or the Memory of Childhood*, p. 94.

59. It could also be said that the 'intersections' between Jewish and Christian signs (especially that of the '*main transpercée*' of Christ relocated on the Jewish mother who died in Auschwitz) serve the function of making visible what has been forgotten in the Christian myth of resurrection and transcendence. Shoshana Felman's comment on Paul Celan's poem 'Todesfuge' (Death Fugue) can shed an interesting light on the representation of the wound in Perec. Felman notes, in relation to Celan's poem:

> The Christian figure of the wound, traditionally viewed as the mythical vehicle and as the metaphoric means for a historical transcendence – for the erasure of Christ's death in the advent of Resurrection – is reinvested by the poem with the literal concreteness of the death camp blood and ashes, and is made thus to include, within the wound, not resurrection and historical transcendence, but the specificity of history – of the concrete historical reality of massacre and race annihilation – as unerasable and untranscendable. What Celan does, in this way, is to force the language of the Christian metaphorics to witness in effect the Holocaust, and be in turn witnessed by it (*Testimony: Crises of Witnessing in Literature, Psychoanalysis and History*, p. 30).

If Perec can also be said to 'force the language of the Christian metaphorics to witness in effect the Holocaust, and be in turn witnessed by it', then he is reinserting 'the unerasable and untranscendable' into a mythical system which is, precisely, predicated on 'resurrection and historical transcendence'. Perec's art, mindful of Adorno's dictum that to write poetry after Auschwitz is barbaric, must make visible silence, absence and death within its own signifying system rather than function simply as a means of forgetting or transcending them. My modification of Felman's argument would suggest, however, that the chains of meaning established in the writing mean that the open wound does not only bear witness to the Holocaust as the forgotten object.

60. 'I was like a child playing hide-and-seek, who doesn't know what he fears or wants more: to stay hidden, or to be found' ('je fus comme un enfant qui joue à cache-cache et qui ne sait pas ce qu'il craint où désire le plus : rester caché, être découvert'), Perec, *W ou le souvenir d'enfance*, p. 18 / *W, or the Memory of Childhood*, p. 7. According to Freud, the child 'manages' his or her separation from the mother through staging the process of separation and return, presence and absence. For an interesting application of Freud's fort/da theory to questions of trauma and mourning, see Eric L. Santner, *Stranded Objects: Mourning, Memory and Film in Postwar Germany* (Ithaca and London: Cornell University Press, 1990).

61. '"Bretzel" n'est d'ailleurs rien d'autre qu'un diminutif (Beretzele) de Beretz, et Beretz, comme Baruk ou Barek, est forgé sur la même racine que Peretz – en arabe, sinon en hébreu, B et P sont une seule et même lettre', Perec, *W ou le souvenir d'enfance*, p. 56 / *W, or the Memory of Childhood*, p. 35.

62. Perec, *W ou le souvenir d'enfance*, p. 14 / *W, or the Memory of Childhood*, p. 4.

63. In an interesting article on Perec and the Arab world, Anne Roche notes the use in *W ou le souvenir d'enfance* of 'the signifier *crouille* (p. 159 et passim), a racist slang term for 'Arab' that the inhabitants of the island of W use to designate the last ones left amongst them, the pariahs. This ... term is perhaps derived from the signifier *musulman* which, in the vocabulary of the concentration camps, was used to describe those prisoners who had lost all physical and mental control and who simply crouched, waiting for death' ('le signifiant « crouille » (p. 159 et passim), mot d'argot raciste, désignant les arabes, et que les habitants de l'île W emploient pour désigner les derniers d'entre eux, les parias. Ce ... terme est peut-être dérivé du signifiant « musulman » qui désignait, dans le vocabulaire des camps de concentration, les déportés qui avaient perdu tout ressort physique et mental et qui se tenaient accroupis, attendant la mort'), Anne Roche, 'Perec et le monde arabe' in *Georges Perec et l'histoire*, p. 159.

64. 'Il ne s'agissait pas pourtant de symboles abstraits, ce n'étaient pas des chevrons, par exemple, ni des bandes, ni des losanges, mais des figures en quelque sorte doubles, d'un dessin à la fois précis et ambigu, qui semblait pouvoir s'interpréter de plusieurs façons sans que l'on puisse jamais s'arrêter sur un choix satisfaisant : l'une aurait pu, à la rigueur, passer pour un serpent sinuant dont les écailles auraient été des lauriers, l'autre pour une main qui aurait été en même temps racine ; la troisième était aussi bien un nid qu'un brasier, ou une couronne d'épines, ou un buisson ardent, ou même un cœur transpercé', Perec, *W ou le souvenir d'enfance*, pp. 19–20 / *W, or the Memory of Childhood*, p. 8.

65. 'Il ne faudrait pas s'en tenir à une lecture sens unique. Perec a construit cette contre-utopie de façon que puissent s'y déchiffrer des systèmes sociaux divers, mais unis dans leur perversion des notions de loi et de liberté. La barbarie, c'est d'abord une société qui ne connaît comme loi régulatrice que la compétition', Burgelin, *Georges Perec*, p. 159.

66. 'Le réel, objet selon Perec de tous ses efforts d'écrivain, est un palimpseste constitué de différents lieux et sites, différents textes et espaces', Leslie Hill, 'Perec à Warwick' in Mireille Ribière (ed.), *Parcours Perec* (Lyon: Presses Universitaires de Lyon, 1990), p. 29. See also an interesting analysis by Laurent Olivier of Perec's 'archaeology of memory' in *W ou le souvenir d'enfance* in terms of a hybrid construction of a superimposition and stratification of traces (Laurent Olivier, 'L'Impossible archéologie de la mémoire: À propos de *W ou le souvenir d'enfance* de Georges Perec', *European Journal of Archaeology* 3, 3 (2000), 387–406).

67. Perec, *W ou le souvenir d'enfance*, pp. 94 and 110 respectively / *W, or the Memory of Childhood*, pp. 66 and 77.

68. 'deux mondes, celui des Maîtres et celui des esclaves', Perec, *W ou le souvenir d'enfance*, p. 218 / *W, or the Memory of Childhood*, p. 160.

69. Warren Motte, 'Georges Perec and the Broken Book', in Lawrence D. Kritzman (ed.), *Auschwitz and after: Race, Culture and 'the Jewish Question' in France* (London: Routledge, 1995), p. 241. Perec's overlaying of horror and the everyday in this way echoes Rousset and Cayrol and even Robert Antelme.

70. 'J'ai oublié les raisons qui, à douze ans, m'ont fait choisir la Terre de Feu pour y installer W : les fascistes de Pinochet se sont chargés de donner à mon fantasme une ultime résonance : plusieurs îlots de la Terre de Feu sont aujourd'hui des camps de déportation', Perec, *W ou le souvenir d'enfance*, p. 222 / *W, or the Memory of Childhood*, p. 164.

71. 'à chaque carrefour, des groupes de gardes mobiles, à cause des événements d'Algérie'; '[à] quoi avait-elle servi, cette caserne? On m'avait dit qu'elle abritait des troupes coloniales', Patrick Modiano, *Dora Bruder* (Gallimard, 1997), p. 8.

72. 'afin de pacifier les territoires encore insoumis du Maroc'; 'Les casernes de Belfort et de Nancy ... les casernes de Mèknes, de Fez ou de Marrakech', Modiano, *Dora Bruder*, pp. 23 and 24.

73. 'La prison, le « camp » ou plutôt le centre d'internement des Tourelles'; 'occupait les locaux d'une ancienne caserne d'infanterie coloniale, la caserne des Tourelles, au 141 boulevard Mortier', Modiano, *Dora Bruder*, p. 60.

74. 'Je me suis dit que plus personne ne se souvenait de rien. Derrière le mur s'étendait un no man's land, une zone de vide et d'oubli', Modiano, *Dora Bruder*, p. 130.

75. 'Et pourtant, sous cette couche épaisse d'amnésie, on sentait bien quelque chose, de temps en temps, un écho lointain, étouffé, mais on aurait été incapable de dire quoi, précisément. C'était comme de se trouver au bord d'un champ magnétique, sans pendule pour en capter les ondes', Modiano, *Dora Bruder*, p. 131.

76. Modiano, *Dora Bruder*, pp. 101–108.

77. Modiano, *Dora Bruder*, p. 111.

78. Dervila Cooke, 'Hollow Imprints: History, Literature and the Biographical in Patrick Modiano's *Dora Bruder', Journal of Modern Jewish Studies* 3, 2 (2004), p. 135.

79. Andreas Huyssen's notion of an 'urban palimpsest' applied to Berlin is, once again, a particularly appropriate term to describe Modiano's approach to Parisian city space in *Dora Bruder*: 'Berlin as palimpsest implies voids, illegibilities, and erasures, but it also offers a richness of traces and memories, restorations and new constructions that will mark the city as lived space' (*Present Pasts*, p. 84).

80. 'la perspective de vivre une vie de caserne comme je l'avais déjà vécue dans des pensionnats de onze à dix-sept ans me paraissait insurmontable', Modiano, *Dora Bruder*, p. 96.

81. 'Je marche à travers les rues vides. Pour moi elles le restent, même le soir, à l'heure des embouteillages, quand les gens se pressent vers les bouches de métro. Je ne peux pas m'empêcher de penser à elle et de sentir un écho de sa présence dans certains quartiers. L'autre soir, c'était près de la gare du Nord', Modiano, *Dora Bruder*, p. 144.

82. 'pour construire une sorte de village suisse', Modiano, *Dora Bruder*, p. 136. Is it just coincidence, too, that the witness at Dora's birth in 1926, Gaspard Meyer (p. 19), has the same first name as the narrator of the story of W and the young boy who has disappeared in Perec's text (Gaspard Winckler), and also that Dora's mother, Cécile, has the same name as Perec's mother and the mother of Gaspard (Caecilia) (and also one of the narrator's fellow inmates in Delbo's *Aucun de nous ne reviendra*)? In the following memory, there is also an echo of Daeninckx's description at the end of *Meurtres pour mémoire* of layers of the past uncovered beneath peeling strips of paper: 'The strips of painted paper that I had seen thirty years before in the rue des Jardins-Saint-Paul were the traces of bedrooms people had formerly slept in – rooms in which those of Dora's age had lived and where the police had come to round them up one day in July 1942', ('Les lambeaux de papiers peints que j'avais vus encore il y a trente ans rue des Jardins-Saint-Paul, c'étaient les traces de chambres où l'on avait habité jadis – les chambres où vivaient ceux et celles de l'âge de Dora que les policiers étaient venus chercher un jour de juillet 1942'), Modiano, *Dora Bruder*, pp. 136–137.

83. See for example the numerous references to Paris as prison on pp. 56, 60, 96, 130, 138. Similar connections occur in many of Modiano's other works, for example *Des Inconnues* (Gallimard, 1999) and *Un Pedigree* (Gallimard, 2005).

84. 'les bourreaux, les ordonnances, les autorités dites d'occupation, le Dépôt, les casernes, les camps, l'Histoire, le temps', Modiano, *Dora Bruder*, p. 145. Richard Golsan notes the following in relation to Modiano's technique in *Dora Bruder*:

> Foremost among these [literary strategies] is the blurring of the boundaries between (historical) reality and fiction evident, most obviously, in the status of 'Dora Bruder.' Also prominent is what might be described as the conflation of historical epochs, so many superimposed geological or archaeological beds whose many traces can be detected in the present. ... The Occupation is not the only past that emerges or, in some ways, merges into the present in *Dora Bruder*. In pursuing the traces of the deported girl in the streets and neighborhoods of Paris, Modiano finds himself confronted with other pasts, other troubled times in history, which his memory calls up but fails to integrate into any coherent vision or understanding of what has gone before. For example, he recalls 'the Boulevard Barbès and the Boulevard Ornano, deserted, on a Sunday afternoon in May 1958. On each corner were groups of Mobile Guards, because of the events in Algeria.' Here, as in so many other manifestations of Vichy's afterlife in the 1980s and 1990s, from the Barbie trial to the trial of Maurice Papon, efforts to come to terms with the memory and legacy of the Dark Years – whether in fiction or in real historical terms – are linked to, and somehow must pass through, the equally troubling memory of the Algerian War (*Vichy's Afterlife*, p. 46).

Golsan diagnoses Modiano's strategy only to critique it, as he believes that the conflation of different historical events detracts from the specificity of the event itself. My argument here, and throughout this book, is rather different: the conflation of times and places that one finds in *Dora Bruder* is crucial to the working of memory, time and imagination and offers us a non-linear way of perceiving history. Although it is right to say that a major superimposition in the text is between the Algerian War and the Dark Years, it is nevertheless missing the wider point that these events are themselves associated with a culture of prisons and camps which the narrator perceives elsewhere too. The traces of dehumanizing authority are attached to specific moments of violence but are not simply confined to them. The particular and the universal are held in an ambivalent state: this is not simply repetition of the same but an uncanny return, both same and different, familiar and yet new.

Chapter 5

THE MEMORY OF THE IMAGE

The image in a film is a mask, an allegory which is more or less discernible and changes with each new imprint.[1]

In the famous passage from the *Arcades Project* cited in chapter 1 of this book, Walter Benjamin reconfigures history by removing it from a linear and scientific framing and inserting it into the non-linear, spatial and poetic concept of the 'constellation' or the 'dialectical image'. The chronological distinctions between past, present and future of the former paradigm are transformed into the overlapping nature of past, present and future of the latter. Following the influences of Bergson, Proust, Surrealism and montage theory, Benjamin de-temporalizes memory and spatializes it so that it becomes a composite image. In his excellent discussion of Chris Marker's *La Jetée* to which I referred in chapter 2, Patrick Ffrench uses the felicitous term 'the memory of the image' to describe the way in which Marker reinvests the image with a complex layering of personal and collective histories. In this chapter I will use Ffrench's term as a way of reframing Benjamin's notion of the dialectical image and apply it to two films – Jean-Luc Godard's *Histoire(s) du cinéma* and Michael Haneke's *Caché* – which reconfigure history in fascinating ways.

Jean-Luc Godard: *Histoire(s) du cinéma*

Thus, in Godard, the interaction of two images engenders or traces a frontier which belongs to neither one nor the other.[2]

Montage is central to Godard's vast project *Histoire(s) du cinéma*. Montage allows Godard to combine in endless series diverse images taken from the vast archive of cinematic images and reshape our vision of history. Montage denies the notion of meaning inherent in the image itself (hence Godard's critique of André Bazin's prohibition of montage) and proposes instead the notion that meaning is produced in the space opened up by the interaction between images, as Deleuze observed about Godard's work long before the making of *Histoire(s)* (see the quotation above).[3] Montage aligns Godard's non-linear approach to history with Benjamin's notion of the image as a constellation in which past and present collide in a flash. Montage is at the heart of Godard's idea of memory as a present praxis of recollection and illumination (in the Benjaminian sense of the word) after missed encounters with the 'real', which could never be shown by a purely linear history. In the following discussion I will consider two sequences from *Histoire(s)* which highlight the way in which Godard's montage dramatizes palimpsestic memory and proposes a politics of representation.

Voyage au Congo

In Chapter 1b Godard combines image, text and sound around issues of race, fascism and cinema in complex interconnections. Cutting from the images of Lana Turner and Marilyn Monroe to a photo of an African woman, bare from the waist up, via Godard's pronouncement 'Phantom Africa' ('L'Afrique fantôme'), we are taken through a sequence concerning the image and Black Africa which eventually cuts to Mussolini, Hitler and 'ordinary fascism' ('*le fascisme ordinaire*'). One of the major threads here is the journey undertaken by André Gide and his lover (sometimes thought to be his nephew) Marc Allégret in Africa in 1927, which resulted in a book entitled *Voyage au Congo* by Gide (containing photos by Allégret), and a film of the same name by Allégret.[4] Godard uses text by Gide, critical of European colonization of Africa, and parts of Allégret's film, whose voyeuristic camera and 'ethnological' narration recording Congolese customs displays a more pronounced ethnocentric gaze on Black Africa than Gide's text. The intersection of this series with fast cutting of a shot of Mussolini in front of a camera and Hitler filmed from below with Mussolini's voice-over connects the racialized image of black skin with 1930s fascism and the history of the cinema itself.[5]

However, it is in the interstices between these images that these connections emerge more fully. Flashing on the screen amongst the above are the words *ombres blanches* ('white shadows'). *Ombres blanches* is the name given to the technique of projecting ghost-like white shadows through a magic lantern known as a fantascope, an early precursor of the film camera. The appearance of the white image is dependent on the dark shadows around it which are blocked off to allow the white shadows to appear. The letters of *ombres blanches* are consequently white against a black background, and are followed by the blue letters of the word *image* on a white background. Like a camera obscura – and following Marx on ideology and Fanon on the white mask imposed on the black body – the technique of *ombres blanches* inverts the real to give an image that we take to be the real. The 'lens' of racializing ideology which creates the 'phantom Africa' in the European imaginary (and, in the same instance, reifies the White goddesses Lana Turner and Marilyn Monroe) is then turned on Europe by Mussolini and Hitler (Mussolini is shown filming with a huge camera); colonialism and fascism are dependent on the same 'trick' performed by the image which is to be found at the origins of the history of the cinema. Godard seems to confirm Césaire's view of the 'boomerang effect' by which the 'image' of civilization used by Europeans in the colonies to dehumanize the colonized is brought back to Europe in the form of fascism.[6] However, unlike Césaire – but more like Benjamin – he shows how cinema (as a creator of 'the individual' and 'the crowd' in its aestheticization of politics) is directly involved in the mythology of the leader and the construction of the masses inherent in both fascism and colonialism.[7]

Godard also inserts into this sequence brief excerpts from the Errol Flynn film *Captain Blood* (1935) and the name Antonio das Mortes (the fictional character in two films of the 1960s by the Brazilian film-maker Glauber Rocha), both of which play on the same manipulation of black and white in ideological image construction. In *Captain Blood*, Flynn is captured, enslaved and then leads his fellow slaves to revolt and freedom in swashbuckling style. Hollywood's manipulation of the *ombres blanches* trick therefore inverts real slavery and colonization and transforms it into a heroic White story of daring and freedom. Antonio das Mortes, on the other hand, who first appears in the aptly named *Black God, White Devil* (1964), overturns White order in revolutionary style, hence showing the radical potential of cinema (just as the white letters of 'me, a Black' ('moi, un noir') on a black background invert the power relations inherent in 'ombres blanches'). The reappearance here of Godard's old formula, 'It's not a just image, it's just an image', warns us of the ambiguity of the image, while the repeated expression, 'Who is responsible for the disappearance of oppression? Us!' over Allégret's voyeuristic film and the non-voyeuristic image of a Black woman also shows the potential for both racialized and liberating modes of representation through the cinema.[8] In other words, Godard's montage seems to stage the struggle between oppression and liberation by unsettling the ideological fixity of the image and reinserting it within a dialectical view of history.

Delving further into the interstices between images in this sequence, we should note that *Ombre blanche* (*The White Shadow*) was also a film made in 1923 by Graham Cutts, on which the young Alfred Hitchcock cut his teeth as editor and art director. This is of interest for at least two reasons. First, Godard's pursuit through montage of the traces of one image in another creates connections that ripple out across the whole history of the cinema. Hitchcock ('the greatest creator of forms of the twentieth cenutry' / 'le plus grand créateur de formes du vingtième siècle', *Histoire(s) du cinéma*, Chapter 4a) is central to *Histoire(s)*, not least perhaps because of his early involvement in a film which gestures (in its name) to the illusion and power of film itself. 'Hitchcock' functions as a figure around which a vast number of different images, moments and ideas connect and coalesce (one of which could indeed be his later work on editing footage of the concentration camps taken by the Allies immediately after the liberation of the camps). To a lesser degree, Allégret has a similar function in *Histoire(s)* in this sequence. The Debrie Sept camera that Allégret used on his journey with Gide to Africa (a 35 mm still and cine camera marketed from 1922 onwards) is connected both with the *ombres blanches* precursor to film and with the subsequent cameras that are shown in abundance throughout *Histoire(s)*, including the one being manipulated by Mussolini. He therefore has a place in the technical/ideological construction of images which is particularly relevant here. Furthermore, in his post-war films, Allégret is largely credited with giving young actors a start in cinema, some of whom (like Jean-Paul Belmondo) would, of course, go on to work with Godard himself. Godard rewrites the history of the cinema through tracing the connections that linear history erases.

Second, the film *Ombre blanche* (though only referred to by title rather than explicitly through images) has a metaphorical bearing on *Histoire(s)*. In one scene the soul of a dead woman passes into her (living) twin sister; in another, the twin sister knocks over, in a car accident, her mad father whose sanity is then miraculously restored as he recognizes his daughter once again. There is a resemblance here between the recognition after an amnesiac experience which takes place in this film and the regaining of Suzanne's memory in the excerpt from Léonce Perret's 1912 film *Le Mystère des roches de Kador* which appears in Chapter 2a. Trond Lundemo's comment on Godard's use of the return of memory in Perret's film (which is triggered by Professor Williams's film projection of the re-staged trauma that induced Suzanne's amnesia) is relevant for *Ombre blanche* too, and indeed for Godard's method in general:

> This leaves us with a complex view of cinema's relation to memory: it constitutes the event as a kind of 're-meditation' but simultaneously performs a process of erasure. Memory turns into recollection through elimination, and cinema is viewed as a machine for the selection of images and the distribution of memory. Professor Williams's method of projecting images mirrors that of Godard as historian. As with the amnesiac in *Le Mystère des roches de Kador*, the images from the past in *Histoire(s)* are never of an original event, but rather a rewriting and an erasure.[9]

This casts a particular light on the memory of the image in *Histoire(s)*. As with Proust, the past has to be lost before it can be regained; the cinema works like a Proustian 'machine' between 'lost time' ('le temps perdu') and 'regained time' ('le temps retrouvé') (*Histoire(s) du cinéma*, Chapter 2b). And, as with Proust, what comes back once it has been lost is a far more profound memory because it includes (indeed, it is founded on) connections, associations and intersections that conscious memory cannot reach. The memory of the image is therefore its buried unconscious; within the single image lies the plural history of the cinema (hence the constant tension between singular and plural in the title of *Histoire(s)* and in the alternating inscriptions 'every history' / 'toutes les histoires' and 'one single history' / 'une histoire seule').[10] The past is latent ('the past is never dead. It hasn't even passed'); Orpheus can bring Eurydice back from the underworld of oblivion ('The cinema authorizes Orpheus to turn back without killing Eurydice').[11] 'Death and resurrection' performed by cinema is modernity's secular form of Renaissance art: it condenses into an image the weight of history. The image in question in the repeated phrase 'the image will appear at the time of the resurrection' ('[l]'image viendra au temps de la résurrection') (*Histoire(s) du cinéma*, Chapter 1b) is thus the Benjaminian image or constellation. What then appears in this epiphanous flash of light from the darkness is not the redemptive incarnation of a holy spirit but the infinite interconnecting traces of the ghosts of the past that haunt the present. The missed encounter (like trauma itself) can be re-staged through the montage of cinematic images, not in order to re-enact the moment beyond representation (as in Lanzmann's *Shoah*) but to involve the spectator in a process of reading the event historically.[12] The *'voyage au Congo'* undertaken by Gide and Allégret is therefore recast by its insertion within other 'journeys' through the tangled terrain of race and the cinema, which allows us to 'read' that journey historically.[13]

Juif/Allemand/Musulman

'You saw nothing in Hiroshima', *Hiroshima mon amour.*

The major encounter that cinema failed to record, according to Godard, and that therefore must be staged, was with the concentration camps ('forgetting the extermination is part of extermination' / 'l'oubli de l'extermination fait partie de l'extermination', *Histoire(s) du cinéma*, Chapter 1a). Unlike Lanzamnn's eschewal of representation in his staging of trauma in *Shoah*, Godard's montage, in which images of horror are combined with texts, images and sounds from elsewhere, produces a belated cinematic encounter of truly startling, and often shocking, import, which propels us into a new relationship with the event.[14]

In the final chapter of the film entitled 'Les Signes parmi nous' (*Histoire(s) du cinéma*, Chapter 4b), there is a sequence of images of women of different ages with the name Clio across them, the muse of History and the title of Charles Péguy's famous Bergsonian work on history and memory which is a constant reference point throughout *Histoire(s)*. Other text written across these images reads 'whoever wants to remember must dedicate himself to the absolute' and 'this beautiful chance that memory

Figure 5.1 Montage of Rembrandt's drawing of Elsje Christiaens hanging on a gibbet (1664), young Jewish woman with yellow star and Palestinian freedom fighter, Jean-Luc Godard, *Histoire(s) du cinéma* (1998)

becomes'.[15] This is followed by a sequence involving other women: the image of a Jewish woman at the time of the Second World War wearing a yellow star on her coat is superimposed first on Rembrandt's drawing of Elsje Christiaens, who was strung up on a pole after being executed by strangling as a punishment for killing her landlady with an axe, and then a photo of a female (Palestinian?) freedom fighter holding aloft a rifle (see Figure 5.1).

Shortly after, images of an editor feeding a reel of film through his fingers, accompanied by the sound of the whirring of the machine (another constant motif in *Histoire(s)*), contain a superimposed text which reads 'connecting things which have never yet been connected, and don't appear to be connectable' (and the sound of Godard's voice intoning 'the association of ideas is distant, distant').[16]

This simple description cannot do justice to the combinations at work here. For example, the image of the female freedom fighter only emerges gradually and, at first sight, the montage seems to suggest that the figure holding the rifle above her head is the Jewish woman with the yellow star. However, we can read some of the ways in which Godard retells the Holocaust by placing it within other histories of violence and suffering. Different images of victimhood, suffering and resistance are brought together in a way which shocks each out of their containment within a chronological historicist narrative, thus showing how the cinematic splicing and rearranging of images can produce a vertical idea of memory (proposed by Bergson and endorsed enthusiastically by Péguy) which redraws time in a non-causal way.[17] One of the effects here is to recontextualize the image of the yellow star (now atrophied because of over-exposure?) by juxtaposing it with other images of suffering and resistance, not in order to collapse history into a simplistic repetition of the same and to equate unproblematically the Holocaust and other instances of suffering, but to open up the question of similarity and difference, and simultaneity and distance, in new ways. What is the relation between the Jewish woman, the freedom fighter and Rembrandt's drawing of the dead girl on a pole? By means of what Rancière terms 'the clash of heterogeneous elements that provides a common measure', Godard's montage disrupts habitual associations to establish new connections.[18]

Images become more ambiguous in the continuation of the above sequence. The splicing of the reel of film is accompanied by a repetition of the phrase 'connecting things' (*'rapprocher les choses'*) and is then followed by a detail from Cézanne's painting 'Le Christ aux limbes' (1869).[19] This gives way to a young man with a machine gun accompanied by the anguished voice of a child speaking Arabic, the image of a dead man on the pavement in a pool of blood, and subsequently an image of a Palestinian woman standing in front of a barbed-wire fence holding a rifle. The return of the manipulation of the reel of film which stops and starts, accompanied by the sound of the clicking and whirring of the reel in the machine, is overlaid first with the word *Israel* and then the word *Ismael*. Next, an image of a man's face, wide-eyed and open-mouthed in an expression of horror, is overlaid with the word *Allemand* then *Juif*. A painting of a bloodied man in a blindfold being led by ropes tied around his hands then gives way to slow-motion film of soldiers dragging the dead body of a Holocaust victim, while added to the repeated words *Allemand* and *Juif* is the word *Musulman* and, finally, the title of Robert Antelme's famous work *L'Espèce humaine*.

In this sequence, the combinations achieved by the splicing of film and the *rapprochement* of distant and unexpected elements in time and space explicitly relate the horror of the Holocaust to the Israel–Palestine conflict. The connection is established in part by plays on words. First, '*Israel*' is replaced by '*Ismael*', the substitution of the *r* of the former for the *m* of the latter suggesting both the similarity and difference of Jews and Arabs, thus reproducing the original ambiguity of the relationship between Isaac and Ishmael, different because they are at the origin of Jewish and Arabic traditions respectively but similar in that they are half-brothers (as they are both sons of Abraham). Second, the word *Musulman* is both the term given for the corpse-like figure of the Jew in the camps who is not yet dead but no longer human, and, of course, the term for 'Muslim'. Yet these plays on words are in no way frivolous for they are an integral part of the production of what Junji Hori terms Godard's 'historical montage'. Hori cites Godard's reflection on the use of the term *musulman*:

> when one sees the corpse of a Jew dragged by two Germans in a concentration camp, we can call the corpse 'Muslim' .... We have to think through both, the camps and Lebanon or Algeria. What happened in Algeria is the aftermath.[20]

These articulations are disturbing, as the genocide is brought into a dialogue with other forms of violence and victimhood (and 'the Jew' appears to slide uncomfortably from one side of the perpetrator–victim equation to the other). However, the questions they raise about atrocity and suffering, perpetration of violence and victimhood open up a space of reflection on the relationship between specific instances of atrocity and the general nature of *'l'espèce humaine'* without providing easy answers.

However, the reduction of this sequence to relations between the Holocaust and the Israel–Palestine conflict, and between Jew and Arab (even if these are shown to be ambiguous) is itself an over-simplification of Godard's method. The inclusion of a Christian iconography of suffering, the intersection of different languages over the images (German, French, Arabic, English), and the presence of the cinematographer carrying out his montage from the cinematic archive of horror and suffering contribute to the unceasing process of translation and mediation of images and the construction of intersecting layers of meaning. If our image of the Holocaust is inevitably infected (and inflected) by other images from elsewhere, then it is also true to say that these other images (and indeed, culture in general) are, in turn, infected by the Holocaust.[21] No one image can be apprehended in isolation from other images ('one image can hide another', to play on the warning at French stations 'un train peut en cacher un autre'). Images in *Histoire(s)* are literally palimpsests as they are superimposed on one another or dissolve at different speeds into each other, leaving behind their traces.[22] Images treated in this way constitute the very matter of memory, as Céline Scemama observes: 'Godard's undertaking is to remember by interrogating the images themselves, because images have a memory and bear the imprints of their time. They are the very substance of memory'.[23] This is a dynamic and dialectical process of connection and transformation in which the image fragments into unstable signs to be deconstructed and reconstructed *ad infinitum* (what Rancière terms 'a metamorphic operativeness');[24] history is an open-ended play to be composed and recomposed without ever congealing into a fixed and final resurrection of the pieces (a dialectics which never achieves its synthesis).[25] Like the unstable image, the terms *Allemand, Juif, Musulman, Israel, Ismael* and so on are also decentred according to the perpetual process of condensation and displacement of meaning. Even the reappearance of the same elements – for example, the statement *'Rapprocher les choses'*, the flashing signs of titles like *'Histoire(s)'* and so on – are not simple repetitions but modifications of similarity according to the other elements with which they are formally juxtaposed.[26] Godard's montage thus denies the specificity of place and time (of meaning in general) by transforming 'specificity' into a dynamic play of interconnecting traces. By placing the horror-stricken face of the Jewish victim of the Holocaust in a series of similar but different faces of horror, Godard shocks the Holocaust out of its framing within any preceding aesthetic (the negative sublime, Hollywood's sentimentalized piety, and so on) to propel it (vertically, paradigmatically and dialectically) into history, or at least the history/histories of the cinema.[27]

Michael Haneke: *Caché*

[T]here is nothing more horrific than the tearing of memory.[28]

Although Michael Haneke's 2005 film *Caché* is an entirely different project to that of Godard's *Histoire(s)*, it is nevertheless interesting to bring them together in terms of their attention to the image.[29] Both reinvest the image with a memory composed of intersecting histories of racialized violence and consequently provoke us into reading history in the moment of the image. In the following discussion I will broach the question of a palimpsestic memory in *Caché* through Haneke's play on the cut.

First, there are the violent physical cuts and the consequent spilling of blood that punctuate the film: the beheading of the cock by the young Algerian boy Majid, the childlike drawings of this scene which accompany the videos sent to the home of Georges and Anne Laurent, the shadowy images of the young Majid armed with an axe advancing on the young Georges, and, most shocking of all, the suicidal throat-slitting of the older Majid. Second, there are violent cuts in the ties binding one character to another: the separation of the young Majid from his parents when they disappear from his life after the events of 17 October 1961 in Paris, the forcible separation of Majid from the Laurent family home shortly after these events, the disappearance of Georges's and Anne's son Pierrot, and the second abduction of Majid as an adult when, with his own son, he is arrested by the police, suspected of kidnapping Pierrot and leading a campaign of terror against the Laurent family. Third, there are the cuts that mark out the dividing lines between the protected zone of Georges's bourgeois life and the outside world – between public and private space, between ethnic groups, between the present and the past, and between the moment and history. Finally, there is the filmic cut which splices up the real into disconnected images, each one a violent abstraction from its surrounding contexts. *Caché* shows us that, cocooned in a world of dislocated images, we are cut off from our contact with the real and from our past. Exposure to the violence of the cut re-establishes connections that have been severed, returns us to an ethical position with regard to the other, and reinscribes human action within history.

Cuts and Connections

The long-held opening image of the façade of Georges's and Anne's house in the tranquil thirteenth *arrondissement* in Paris provides the initial setting in which the play on the cut is worked through in the film. Our inability to see what is happening (in fact, nothing is happening 'in plain sight')[30] is mimicked by Georges's inability to locate precisely the viewing position of the camera filming his house from the outside. The spectator and Georges are led to believe that the image we are watching hides something else, that the fixed image (of the sort that, we subsequently realize, acts like the surface décor for Georges's bourgeois lifestyle) contains its 'blind spots' and that what is visible is haunted by what is off-screen and outside the frame.[31] Haneke highlights the nature of the cinematic cut which fixes the flux of reality in a self-contained image by violently abstracting it from its surrounding contexts and, hence, making it unreadable. Filmic cuts are hidden incisions which separate and compartmentalize. But by dramatizing this process, Haneke reinscribes an awareness of the otherness of the image – what is hidden and repressed in the violent carving out of the cinematic image – suggesting the contamination of off-screen and on-screen spaces, or the complicity between them rather than their violent separation.

Paradoxically, then, the uncut image (the long take) will highlight the fact that its apparent seamlessness is actually the result of hidden cuts.[32] Georges's way of seeing has cut out what is troubling, in the same way that his later editing of his television arts programme will remove what may be troubling for his bourgeois audience ('it's becoming a bit theoretical' / 'ça devient un peu théorique', he says, when replaying the tape of the studio discussion of Rimbaud).[33] The recipients of this process of hidden cutting (the viewers of Georges's programme) are as complicit in the denial it implies as the spectators of the film we are watching (us). But by playing with the detective story genre, Haneke leads Georges and the spectator to an encounter with the repressed violence of the cut.

In *Caché*, the physical cuts, the severing of personal ties and the policed demarcation lines marking out privileged metropolitan space are the sites of violence and separation that have been repressed in Georges's sanitized world, the *hors champ* which bursts unexpected into the frame. The suddenness of Majid's slitting of his own throat is in stark contrast to the long take of the outside of Georges's house, as if it is the raw event that that bland façade has hidden from view.[34] Similarly, the naïve and childlike drawings of violence sent to Georges are the flip-side to the smooth screens and sets (and stylized violence) that make up the staged surface of his life, while the eruption of the other into Georges's personal space (the Black cyclist crossing Georges's path outside the police station, Majid's son forcing his way into Georges's office) dramatizes the hidden splitting and compartmentalization on which egalitarian republican France is constructed.[35]

The major moment of violence that has been cut from the visible image and from Georges's consciousness, which will return progressively in the film, is, of course, the Algerian War of Independence. We will learn how Majid's parents, working for Georges's parents at the time of the Algerian War, disappeared on the night of the FLN demonstration in Paris on 17 October 1961 and how Majid was subsequently sent away by Georges's parents because of the lies told by Georges. Questions of Georges's complicity, and indeed that of France as a whole, in crimes of horror forty years before are raised, little by little, as the layers of amnesia that have hidden them from view are stripped away from Georges's consciousness.

However, the structures of complicity exposed by dramatizing the violence of the cut announce a more complex view of hidden connections and memory than one that simply relates them to France's colonial and post-colonial relations with Algeria. As Haneke has observed himself, 'I think that every country has skeletons in its closet, which one can certainly apply to Austrian history as well. There's scarcely a country in Europe, perhaps none at all, even in the world, that isn't affected by this phenomenon'.[36] Haneke's treatment of ways of seeing and remembering establishes multiple interconnections between the visible and the repressed, so that what is hidden beneath the normalized surface of metropolitan everyday life is a cultural imaginary of overlapping layers of violence and trauma. In this sense, Haneke opens up the sanitized image to violence in a way that resembles Godard's approach in *Histoire(s)*. The image is transformed from a façade screening out reality into an indeterminate and over-determined site in which seeing is haunted by being seen, questions of guilt and responsibility for past events are intricately connected with present lives, and structures of complicity between different spaces are rendered visible. The scene in which news items on the television on the Iraq War, the Abu Ghraib torture trials and Israeli violence on the West Bank form the backdrop to the domestic drama of Pierrot's disappearance graphically demonstrates this point, as the bourgeois domestic space is invaded by diverse scenes of violence. What has been written out of the screen but will return to haunt Georges is a complex layering of images and multiple ways of seeing.[37]

The store of interconnecting and superimposed images that returns to haunt Georges is thus composed of different sites of horror in which, perhaps inevitably, echoes of the Holocaust invade the memory of a Franco-Algerian past (whether consciously intended on Haneke's part or not). For example, the childlike drawings sent to Georges recall other instances of children's involvement in situations of war and violence, especially the famous children's drawings from Terezin concentration camp outside Prague. The disappearance of Pierrot and of Majid's parents and the abduction of the young Majid remind us of war-time round-ups of young and old prior to their transportation to the death-camps.[38] On a broader level, the themes of complicity, responsibility and guilt in relation to crimes against humanity in the past that have been repressed in the present bind the 'Algeria syndrome' to the earlier 'Vichy syndrome' in the French cultural imaginary. Georges's emphatic denial of guilt – 'I am not responsible' ('Je ne suis pas responsable') he declares when challenged by Majid's son following Majid's suicide – recalls the statements made by SS officers and kapos in Resnais's *Nuit et brouillard*. These echoes of another scene of violence, trauma and separation shock the image out of its imprisonment within the banal surface of the everyday.

Like Godard, Haneke's transformation of the two-dimensional image into an over-determined site of cultural meaning evokes ambiguous inter-connecting stories of Muslim and Jew. Does the cutting of the cock's throat not recall the dietary laws of Islam (Hallal) and Judaism (in French, *Kascher/caché*?) which stipulate that animals for slaughter must be killed by having their throats cut to allow for the draining of the blood? Does the recurring image of Majid spitting blood that haunts Georges (invoking the play on words *cracher/caché*) evoke the Jewish tradition of mourning a lost relation?[39] Does the casting out of Majid from the family home recall the story of Abraham's son Ishmael who was cast out from the family home to wander in the desert with his mother Hagar?[40] Why is the name of Majid's father Hashem, which not only has an Arabic lineage in the form of the Hashemites but is also one of the Hebrew words for God?[41]

These reverberations of different scenes of violence and separation make our viewing of the penultimate scene of the film multi-layered. This is the moment of the return of the repressed when Georges dreams of the abduction of Majid as a young boy in 1961 (see Figure 5.2). Due to

Figure 5.2 Abduction of the young Majid, Michael Haneke, *Caché* (2005)

the complex layering of meaning mentioned above, not only the Algerian connection now penetrates Georges's dulled consciousness but also, I suggest, the nightmare world of the *rafles* (round-ups) of Jews during the Second World War (as the struggling Majid is forced into a car by a faceless man and woman) and possibly, hidden in a deeper recess, the splitting of Isaac and Ishmael, with their separate lines of descent (despite there being no explicit reference in the film to Georges as a Jew). Moreover, by situating the camera from the point of view of the young Georges hidden in the darkened space of the barn in the same position as the earlier scene in which the young Georges watches Majid beheading the cock,[42] Haneke overlays this moment with yet greater traumatic affect. The severing of the head from the bird's neck in the earlier scene and the severing of Majid from his surrogate family in this scene – both the result of Georges's betrayal and both metaphorically gesturing to the violent severing of the ties binding France to Algeria – are superimposed to constitute a sort of primal moment of cutting, separation and trauma. This is accompanied by a similar multi-layering of witnessing and complicity. As Georges is projected back in his dream to the darkened space of the barn, his adult look is overlaid both by the look of his younger self (it is, after all, young people who interrupt the smooth surfaces of bourgeois representation in the film, as they do in the earlier *Funny Games*) and by our own gaze as observers/voyeurs in the darkened space of the cinema. Film and spectatorship are therefore also implicated in the guilty secret that is here exposed.

The superimposition of different dramas of cutting, separation and trauma (personal and political) and of violence, witnessing and complicity opens up bourgeois metropolitan consciousness to a cultural imaginary informed by history. If history, then, has a way of biting back (as the 'shaggy dog' story recounted by the friend at the dinner party warns), then the image as palimpsest suggests that this history is a complex affair.[43]

Reading the Image

A comparison between the first and final scenes of *Caché* demonstrates how the return of a complex history is related to a sort of progressive reading, or pedagogy, of the image. In the first image, as we have noted, Georges is obsessed with finding the position from which seeing/filming took place but he cannot locate it. As Ezra and Sillars observe, 'Georges's response to Anne's opening word – Alors? (So?) – Rien (Nothing) – is one that closes off enquiry and denies the possibility of meaning'.[44] Georges is unable to 'read' the image (and neither can we as spectators) because there is no context which would help to orient us. There is simply an anxiety that the image is not self-sufficient and that its truth can only be understood by what lies outside it. It is this anxiety which sets in motion the search for an explanation. However, by the end of the film, the bland surface image at the beginning that cannot be read can now be said to be transformed into a palimpsest because it has, progressively, been provided with a layering or memory, culminating in the return of the repressed in the abduction of the child Majid.[45] It is precisely the memory of the image that establishes a way of seeing, reading and knowing ('the image that is read ... the image in the now of its recognizability', as Benjamin puts it in *The Arcades Project*). The intelligibility of the image therefore requires a reading which goes beyond the limitations of rational explanation (Georges's 'plotting' of space and time) to reawaken a profound memory which encompasses dream and history.[46] But it also establishes an *ethics* of looking which was absent at the beginning because it brings back not only the repressed scene itself but also the presence of the witness to that scene (Georges and the spectator are implicated in the event rather than cut off from it). The look can now read the dialectical movement of the image – the image not cut away from its context but perceived in terms of a montage of images; a look that can be aware of itself caught between innocence and guilt; a look which has now moved beyond solipsism towards history.

Hence, by the film's final sequence – another long-held image of a façade (Pierrot's school) recalling the long-held first image of the façade of the Laurents' house – we have acquired a way of reading the apparent banality of the image as screen. Though still not *visible*, multiple frames of reference are nevertheless *present* within this image and imbue it with a layered temporality and spatiality. Rather than nothing happening in plain sight (as at the beginning), the image endowed with its memory ensures that a whole architecture of meaning is present in this single fragment of the everyday. To those who feel frustrated at the end because the culprit is never revealed, I would suggest that they are still stuck in Georges's blindness of the beginning. For those who have acquired a way of reading the image, they will realize that far from the ending withholding its hidden secret, it actually makes it readable, not in the sense of answering the whodunit (that is neither here nor there), but in terms of the transformation of the image from a screen to a Benjaminian constellation, composed of multiple interconnections between the visible and the *hors champ* and between present and past.

The treatment of memory in *Caché* is a way of countering what Abdelkebir Khatibi terms, in the quotation used in the preface to this section, *'la déchirure de la mémoire'* (the tearing of memory). However, as Benjamin's constellation clearly announces and Godard's montage reinforces, the severed past that comes back into focus is neither a linear narrative nor a full and coherent account. Similarly, the return of 'depth' beneath the surface is not a realist depth but one in which surface and depth are in dialectical tension, whereby the visible is a saturated and over-determined site for a specific historical conjuncture ('dialectics at a standstill', as Benjamin so memorably puts it).[47] The final image is open-ended because, like all images, it is haunted by a complex layering of invisible material which can never coalesce neatly into a coherent whole. Montage and the long take provide ways of reading the image, instead, in terms of shocks, relations, superimpositions and structures of complicity. The particular and the universal are recast by placing them in a dialectical relationship with each other: violence and complicity are particularized (the film is about the history of France and Algeria), analogized (it is also about the Holocaust and modern forms of violence), and universalized (it reaches beyond all specificity) at the same time. In *Caché*, Haneke's 'constellations' counter the cut as an abstraction from history and the image as screen by dramatizing the sedimented and overlapping nature of individual and collective meaning. In this sense, the film is a powerful reminder of Benjamin's description of the critical point at which history is visible in the present moment.

'Un montage qui ne sépare rien'

Georges Didi-Huberman describes Alfred Hitchcock's editorial work on the filming of the concentration camps at the time of the liberation as follows:

> Hitchcock understood immediately that this form needed a montage that doesn't separate anything. First, the victims must not be separated from the executioners, meaning that the corpses of the prisoners must be shown under the very eyes of the German officials, and the consequent decision to make minimal cuts in the long panoramic shots of the filming, so frightening in their slowness; then, the camp itself must not be separated from its social environment, even though – or because – that environment was normal, quaint, rural, and even bucolic.[48]

The Hollywood director Samuel Fuller, in an interview discussion in 1988 of his twenty-minute filming of Falcenau concentration camp outside Prague in 1945 when, as a young man, he was part of the U.S. forces liberating Nazi-controlled Europe, describes a very similar technique to that employed by Hitchcock:

> This shot shows you how close the camp was to the village. Here are the houses; the camp was just behind. It's a shot with no cut, no editing. I just panned from the houses to the camp. See how close they are! I didn't make a single cut. It was essential not to. Playing on this mound, the children must surely have been able to see inside the camp.[49]

Hitchcock and Fuller seem to know instinctively that any cut in the filming of these moments of horror would divorce the image from its true context. Didi-Huberman's comments on Hitchcock are made in the context of his discussion of Godard's use of montage in *Histoire(s)*, to suggest that 'Godard says nothing less'.[50] But Haneke also shows us that separation and cutting remove horrific crimes from their historical and ethical environment. He counters this either through the long take which eschews the cut (like Hitchcock and Fuller), or through the use of a montage to connect apparently disparate times and spaces (unlike Georges who dislocates the image from its contexts, specifically in the editing suite at work and, in a more general sense, inside the cocooned metropolitan space in which he lives).[51] Both Godard and Haneke employ montage as a way of *thinking dialectically* ('a thinking form' / 'une forme qui pense', as Godard says of cinema in Chapter 3a of *Histoire(s)*); that is, putting together 'unlikely' elements to produce not an amalgam but a third element. Didi-Huberman observes that, in Godard's juxtaposition in Chapter 1a of *Histoire(s)* of the Holocaust victim and Elizabeth Taylor in *A Place in the Sun* (1951) via Georges Stevens's filming, '[w]hat this montage allows us to think is that the differences brought into play *belong to the same history* of war and of cinema'.[52] Reading the image (both images) takes place in the space opened up between them; this is the space in which history resides. This is the lesson that Benjamin teaches us when he says, '[o]nly dialectical images are genuinely historical'.

In *Le Destin des images*, Rancière also cites Godard in elaborating his thesis of a *'montage dialectique'* (which produces the shock of the heterogeneous) and a *'montage symbolique'* (which places disparate elements in the same continuum):

> Interminably to connect, as [Godard] does, a shot from one film with the title or dialogue of another, a sentence from a novel, a detail from a painting, the chorus of a song, a news photograph, or an advertising message, is always to do two things at once: to organize a clash and construct a continuum. The space of these clashes and that of the continuum can even bear the same name: History. History can indeed be two contradictory things: the discontinuous line of revealing clashes or the continuum of co-presence. The linkage of heterogeneous elements constructs and, at the same time, reflects a meaning of history that is displaced between these two poles.[53]

Rancière suggests that these two *'poétiques de l'image'* converge in contemporary art in an attempt to re-situate fragmented human activity ('a "loss of community" or undoing of the "social bond"') within a new sensibility of a shared history and world.[54] Didi-Huberman also places the emphasis on the power of montage to draw together the disparate. Both reflect on the primary function of the image (of art in general?) to reach out to the world and resist the ever-increasing atomization of our senses and our knowledge.[55]

Of course, the techniques of disassembling and reassembling described by Didi-Huberman and Rancière have a long lineage in modernism across the arts, through cubism, Apollinaire, Cendrars, surrealism, Eisenstein and so on. Yet Godard and Haneke have developed their own politico-aesthetic idiom in contemporary cinema to reinvent the power of these techniques. By constructing (in Rancière's words) 'the space of … clashes and that of the continuum', they both open up the image to history. Images are made to connect and comment on each other, not by collapsing one into the other but by searching out their points of similarity and difference. Montage challenges the fixity of the image by what Didi-Huberman, echoing Rancière, calls *'le travail dialectique de l'image'* and what I am calling the memory of the image. Like Godard's montage in *Histoire(s)*, Haneke's attention to the connections between the image and violence will also suggest that the history of war and the history of the cinema are part of the same history, for what is hidden is both a history of violence and the violent history of *'découpage'* (cutting) that has severed it from our consciousness.

In their different ways, *Histoire(s)* and *Caché* employ a Benjaminian approach to history to open up the memory of the image.[56] What cannot be read or comprehended in the initial encounter must be re-staged through the juxtaposition of images to allow a reading (always open-ended) to take place. In this sense, history, as Rancière suggests, is not dependent on verisimilitude and scientific 'fact' but (quite the reverse) the use of poetic figures like metaphor, montage and allegory that can connect the disparate.[57] The memory of the image in *Histoire(s)* and *Caché* is Benjamin's 'image in the now of its recognizability'.

Notes

1. 'L'image dans un film est un masque, une allégorie plus ou moins perceptible, changeant avec chacun', Cayrol and Durand, *Le Droit de regard*, p. 97.
2. 'Ainsi, chez Godard, l'interaction de deux images engendre ou trace une frontière qui n'appartient ni à l'un ni à l'autre', Deleuze, *Cinéma 2: L'Image-temps*, p. 236 / *Cinema 2: The Time-image*, p. 181.
3. 'If an image looked at separately clearly expresses something, if it can be interpreted and will not be transformed on contact with other images, those other images have no power over it and it will have no power over them, neither in terms of action or reaction. It is complete in itself and, in the cinematographer's system, unusable.' ('Si une image regardée à part exprime nettement quelque chose, si elle comporte une interprétation et ne se transformera pas au contact d'autres images, les autres images n'auront aucun pouvoir sur elle et elle n'aura aucun pouvoir sur les autres images, ni action ni réaction. Il est définitif et inutilisable dans le système du cinématographe'), Godard, *Histoire(s) du cinéma*, Chapter 1b.
4. In the narration, Godard does not mention Allégret by name but refers to him as 'the nephew of André Gide' ('le neveu d'André Gide').
5. As Rancière says of the relationship between cinema and history, the most interesting questions come to light 'only when one breaks from the subject/object relationship and tries to understand the two terms together, to see how the notions of cinema and history interconnect and, together, constitute a history' ('seulement lorsqu'on sort de ce rapport sujet/objet et qu'on essaie de saisir ensemble les deux termes, de voir comment la notion du cinéma et celle de l'histoire s'entre-appartiennent et composent

ensemble une histoire'), 'L'Historicité du cinéma' in Antoine de Baecque and Christian Delage (eds), *De l'histoire au cinéma* (Éditions Complexe, 1998), p. 45.

6. See also the long critique of Europe at the beginning of Chapter 3a of *Histoire(s) du cinéma*, especially the way barbarous acts by governments are dissembled through official rationalizations.

7. The connection made by Godard between cinema's construction of the star (Turner and Monroe) and dictators (Mussolini and Hitler) is one that André Bazin had made earlier: 'If Stalin, although living, can be the main character in a film, that is because he no longer simply has the stature of an ordinary human being but benefits from the transcendent status enjoyed by the gods and dead heroes; in other words, his aesthetic physiology is, fundamentally, no different from that of the Western film star' ('Si Staline, bien que vivant, peut être le personnage principal d'un film, c'est qu'il n'est plus à la mesure humaine et qu'il bénéficie de la transcendence qui caractérise les dieux vivants et les héros morts ; en d'autres termes, sa physiologie esthétique n'est pas fondamentalement différente de celle de la vedette occidentale'), 'Le Mythe de Staline dans le cinéma soviétique' in *Qu'est-ce que le cinéma 1* (Éditions du Cerf, 1958), p. 82. (I am grateful to Matthew John for drawing my attention to this quotation.) See also Edgar Morin, *Les Stars* (Éditions du Seuil, 1972).

8. 'Ce n'est pas une image juste, c'est juste une image'; 'De qui dépend que l'oppression disparaisse ? de nous !'.

9. Trond Lundemo, 'The Index and Erasure: Godard's Approach to Film History' in Michael Temple, James S. Williams and Michael Witt (eds), *For Ever Godard* (London: Black Dog Publishing, 2004), p. 385.

10. 'the image is neither *nothing*, nor *one*, nor *all*, precisely because it offers multiple singularities which are always susceptible to differences, or [to borrow Jacques Derrida's coinage] to "*différances*"' ('l'image n'est ni *rien*, ni *une*, ni *toute*, précisément parce qu'elle offre des singularités multiples toujours susceptible de différences, ou de "différances"'), Didi-Huberman, *Images malgré tout*, p. 152 / *Images in Spite of All*, p. 121.

11. 'Le passé n'est jamais mort. Il n'est même pas passé'; 'Le cinéma autorise Orphée de se retourner sans faire mourir Eurydice', *Histoire(s) du cinéma*, Chapter 2a and Chapter 3a respectively. The latter statement was 'the caption chosen by Godard for one of the photos illustrating the interview between Godard and Serge Daney about *Histoire(s) du cinéma*', ('légende choisie par Godard pour l'une des photos illustrant l'entretien fait par Serge Daney à propos des *Histoire(s) du cinéma*'), 'Godard fait des histoires', *Libération*, 26 December 1988, cited in Bellour, *L'Entre-images 2*, p. 137.

12. In Hitchcock's *Vertigo*, Scottie re-stages Madeleine's life in order to establish the truth. However, this 'resurrection' can only take place at the expense of Madeleine herself (the object of desire), as she is killed in the process. Heavily influenced by Hitchcock's film, Chris Marker also stages the desire for repetition of a moment from the past in ambivalent terms in *La Jetée*. As Janet Harbord observes, '[t]he man wishes to return to a former moment, a "twice-lived" moment of time. His fate is sealed by a desire for repetition, for an identical match, to experience the moment as it was then. The moment of the woman's awakening demonstrates the force of the current, of how the past can hold us in its thrall to the point where it assumes the features of the present. In this particular film, Marker allows us to experience memory and remembering both ways. It is the seduction of the past that lives with us and to which we are ineluctably drawn. And it is the need to grasp the matter of what has been in order to re-make it differently' (Marker, *La Jetée*, p. 5). The tension between loss and resurrection that we see in *Vertigo* and *La Jetée* is played out repeatedly in *Histoire(s)*.

13. As I mentioned in chapter 1, in Rouch and Morin's *Chronique d'un été*, the conversation between Rouch, Morin, Marceline and some African and French students (including the young Régis Debray) on the terrace of the Musée de l'Homme connects discussion of atrocity in the Belgian Congo and the war in Algeria with Marceline's experience as

a Jew in the concentration camps. Godard's *'voyage au Congo'* traces a similar trajectory and includes a reference to one of Rouch's previous 'ethnographic' documentaries (filmed in the Ivory Coast), *Moi, un Noir* (1958). This film pioneered the jump-cut that Godard admired in Rouch's work and then made a central feature of his own films.

14. For comparisons of Lanzmann's *Shoah* and Godard's *Histoire(s)*, see Didi-Huberman, 'Image-montage ou image-mensonge' ('Montage-image or Lie-image') in *Images malgré tout*, pp. 151–187 / *Images in Spite of All*, pp. 120–150. Libby Saxton gives an excellent account of the polemic between Lanzmann and Godard around representing the Holocaust ('The Missing Reel and the Unimaged Real: Godard/Lanzmann', *Haunted Images*, pp. 46–67). Regarding the 'shocking' nature of some of the montage sequences involving the Holocaust, these often consist of a juxtaposition of Holocaust images and pornography. The shock is obviously connected with images of bodies in which the sexualized, the mutilated and the abject overlap uncomfortably in Bataillean fashion. Griselda Pollock analyses the images of naked women in *Nuit et brouillard* to show how their sexual content renders them ambiguous as images of dehumanization, ('Death in the Image: The Responsibility of Aesthetics in *Night and Fog* (1955) and *Kapo* (1959)' in Pollock and Silverman (eds), *Concentrationary Cinema*, pp. 258–301). The unconscious sexual troping in *Nuit et brouillard* is made a conscious staging of the shock of opposites in *Histoire(s)*. (The overlaps between horror and the erotic might be said to be far more consciously staged in the opening of Resnais's *Hiroshima mon amour* when intertwined bodies referring simultaneously to the mutilation of the Holocaust and Hiroshima in the past and to love-making in the present force us to reflect on the possible connections between these different bodies.)

15. 'qui veut se souvenir doit se confier à l'absolu'; 'ce beau hasard que devient le souvenir'.

16. 'Rapprocher les choses qui n'ont encore jamais été rapprochées, et ne semblaient pas disposées à l'être'; 'l'association des idées est lointaine, lointaine'.

17. 'Can one recount time / time in itself / as it is / time as a thing / no, in truth / it would be a mad undertaking / a narrative in which it would be said / time passed / time went by / time took its course' ('Peut-on raconter le temps / le temps en lui-même / comme tel / et en soi / non, en vérité / ce serait une folle entreprise / un récit où il serait dit / le temps passait / il s'écoulait / le temps suivait son cours'), Godard, *Histoire(s) du cinéma*, Chapter 2a.

18. 'le choc des hétérogènes qui donne la mesure commune', Rancière, *Le Destin des images*, p. 65 / *The Future of the Image*, p. 55.

19. I am grateful to Nigel Saint for this information.

20. Junji Hori, 'Godard's Two Historiographies' in Temple, Williams and Witt (eds), *For Ever Godard*, p. 339. According to Céline Scemama, this is the only part of *Histoire(s)* in which, instead of allowing cinema to relate history, Godard speaks in its place and, consequently, ideology replaces thought. She cites an article by Michèle Cohen-Halimi and Francis Cohen ('Juifs martyrs, kamikazes: La Monstrueuse capture – Question à Jean-Luc Godard', *Les Temps modernes* 629 (2004/2005), 301–310) in which the authors accuse Godard of an outrageous amalgamation of the present plight of Palestinians and the suffering of Jews in the concentration camps ('*Histoire(s) du cinéma' de Jean-Luc Godard: La Force faible d'un art* (L'Harmattan, 2006), p. 18). However, I believe that this is a rather reductive reading of this sequence. The shock of montage functions equally well here as elsewhere and it may well be the case that the substitution of thought for ideology is the fault of the critics themselves rather than Godard.

21. Georges Bataille predicted the effect of horrific images from the Holocaust on post-war culture in his famous statement 'the image of Man is now inseparable from the gas chamber' ('l'image de l'homme est inséparable, désormais, d'une chambre à gaz'), *Critique*, 12 May 1947.

22. See the section 'Palimpsestes (images, textes, sons)' in Alexandre Castant, 'Histoire(s) du (son du) cinéma' in 'Où en est le God-Art?', *CinémAction* 109 (2003), pp. 207–208.

23. 'L'entreprise de Godard est ... de se remémorer en interrogeant les images elles mêmes, parce que les images se souviennent et portent les empreintes de leur temps. Elles sont la matière même de la mémoire', Scemama, *'Histoire(s) du cinéma' de Jean-Luc Godard*, p. 15. In her discussion of the relationship between Christian icons and images of the camps in *Histoire(s)*, Scemama suggests that Godard exposes the ways in which the Holocaust has been assimilated into a Christian iconography (pp. 176–177). My own view is that Godard's montage (like Perec's word play in *W*) establishes a more relational, dialectical and open-ended structure rather than one that should be read simply in terms of an instrumentalist understanding of screen memory.

24. 'une opérativité métamorphique', Rancière, *Le Destin des images*, p. 52 / *The Future of the Image*, pp. 41–42. Michael Temple relates the transformative power of art back to the discussion of Malraux and Péguy: 'looking to Malraux, Clio recognizes and enjoys "the power of metamorphosis possessed by art", the inexhaustible potential of change and human invention. For history also simply means the changing of forms, the metaphor or carrying over of the familiar into the strange, the regular and repeated twisting of the known sound or image into some new monstrous shape, a soon-to-be beautiful trope', Michael Temple, 'Big Rhythm and the Power of Metamorphosis: Some Models and Precursors for *Histoire(s) du cinéma*' in Michael Temple and James S. Williams (eds), *The Cinema Alone: Essays on the Work of Jean-Luc Godard 1985–2000* (Amsterdam: Amsterdam University Press, 2000), p. 94.

25. 'The miracle of the resurrection by the image never constitutes an explanation, nor an expiation or a solution. The historical enterprise does not aim to save anything, as no salvation is possible. Godard is concerned with history, not theology' ('Le miracle de la résurrection par l'image ne constitue jamais une explication ni une expiation ni une solution. L'entreprise historique ne vise pas à sauver quoi que ce soit, aucune rédemption n'est possible. Godard fait bien de l'histoire et non de la théologie'), Scemama, *'Histoire(s) du cinéma' de Jean-Luc Godard*, p. 19. Here, Scemama follows Didi-Huberman's critique of those critics (including Rancière) who see in Godard's repeated use of 'the Christian, Pauline dictum' ('le *dictum* chrétien, paulinien') 'the image will appear at the time of the Resurrection' ('[l]'*image viendra au temps de la résurrection*') a reductive and redemptive staging of the image within the figure of the Angel of Resurrection. I would endorse Didi-Huberman's Benjaminian perspective here in which the Angel of Resurrection is always 'set, dialectically, between totally conflicting image states' ('tendu, dialectiquement, entre des états d'image que tout oppose'), *Images malgré tout*, pp. 184–185 / *Images in Spite of All*, p. 148.

26. The same could be said of the 'repetitions' of '*nouvelle vague/vague nouvelle*', '*Histoire(s) du cinéma/Une histoire seule*', and so on.

27. The photos of the girl in a scarf peering out from a cattle-truck being transported to the camps and the little boy with his hands up in the Warsaw ghetto, both of which are used in Resnais's *Nuit et brouillard* and have since become iconic, even clichéd, images of the Holocaust because of over-exposure, are similarly reinvented when they appear in complex montages earlier (the former in Chapters 1b and 4b, the latter in Chapter 4b).

28. 'il n'y a de plus atroce que la déchirure de la mémoire', Khatibi, *La Mémoire tatouée*, p. 44.

29. Catherine Wheatley makes a qualified analogy between Godard and Haneke's earlier *Funny Games* (1997 and 2007) in relation to the 'project of counter-cinema', (*Michael Haneke's Cinema: The Ethics of the Image* (New York and Oxford: Berghahn, 2009), p. 87).

30. Elizabeth Ezra and Jane Sillars, '*Hidden* in Plain Sight', *Screen* 48, 2 (2007), 215–221.

31. Martine Beugnet, 'Blind Spot', *Screen* 48, 2 (2007), 227–231.

32. Perhaps the most famous cut in French film is the eye-slicing scene which opens Luis Buñuel's surrealist masterpiece *Un Chien andalou* that Godard uses in *Histoire(s)*

(Chapter 1b). Although Haneke dramatizes the cut in a different way in *Caché*, it could be said that the effect is, in part, similar in that, in all three cases, the knife that cuts gestures metaphorically to both the violent assault mounted by the camera eye and the cinematographer on the flux of reality to carve out an image and the rupture of the apparently seamless space of the image to announce other ways of seeing.

33. For other instances of cutting, censorship and following a prescribed script, see Ezra and Sillars, '*Hidden* in Plain Sight'.

34. These two shots are connected in our minds because they are both seen from the fixed camera position of the unseen observer. Yet they are also radically different in that the first image seems to be a still, while in the second there seems to be an exaggeration of movement. Haneke (like Resnais, Marker, Godard and many others before them going back to Dziga-Vertov's early experiments) is clearly playing on the tension between movement and stasis, the photograph and the moving image, and on the nature of time itself in his questioning of the relationship between cinema and truth. For a fuller discussion of this question in relation to 'concentrationary cinema', see Matthew John, 'Concentrationary Cinema', unpublished Ph.D. thesis (University of Leeds, 2012).

35. For a fuller discussion, see Max Silverman, 'The Empire Looks Back', *Screen* 48, 2 (2007), 245–249.

36. 'Je crois que chaque pays a des cadavres dans son placard, une chose que l'on peut aussi bien appliquer à l'histoire de l'Autriche. Vous ne trouverez pratiquement pas de pays en Europe, voire aucun, de par le monde, qui ne soit touché par ce phénomène', 'Interview: Michael Haneke, réalisateur de "Caché"', *Arte* (2006), http://www.arte-tv. com/fr/Impression/4982,CmC=876864,CmStyle+98682.html (accessed 2 September 2008). Haneke has made similar references to the broader applicability of his film. For example: 'I don't want my film to be seen as specifically about a French problem. It seems to me that, in every country, there are dark corners – dark stains where questions of collective guilt become important. I'm sure in the United States there are other parallel examples of dark stains on the collective unconscious', 'Collective Guilt and Individual Responsibility: An Interview with Michael Haneke', *Cinéaste* (2005), http://www.thefreelibrary.com/Collective+guilt+and+individual+responsibility:+an +interview+with…-a0144567341 (accessed 2 September 2008).

37. In her excellent article on the relationship between on-screen and off-screen space in *Caché*, in which she invokes Pascal Bonitzer's concept of a '*champ aveugle*' and Gilles Deleuze's concept of a 'radical Elsewhere', Libby Saxton also suggests that our 'blind spots' in the film are not simply related to a single repressed moment but to numerous 'personal and collective traumas that have been silenced' ('Secrets and Revelations: Off-screen Space in Michael Haneke's *Caché* (2005)', *Studies in French Cinema* 7, 1 (2007), p. 15). Haneke's attention to the relationship between on-screen and off-screen space is evident in previous films. In *Funny Games* (1997), for example, the major acts of violence take place off-screen.

38. One thinks especially here of the round-up of the Jewish children of Izieu organized by the Nazi Klaus Barbie in 1944, for which he was eventually tried in 1987. For a discussion of children and ethics in *Caché*, see Rothberg's chapter on 'Hidden Children: The Ethics of Multigenerational Memory after 1961' in *Multidirectional Memory*, pp. 267–308.

39. In Howard Jacobson's novel *Kalooki Nights*, a Jewish boy who loses his parents is said to be 'spitting blood and howling like an animal', the explanation being that 'spitting blood … was what Jewish sons were said to do when their parents died. It was a manner of speaking, a metaphor for the enormity of their grief', *Kalooki Nights* (London: Jonathan Cape, 2006), p. 53. In terms of the play on words of *caché/cracher*, we should also remember that *cracher des injures* means 'to hurl abuse' (which describes Georges's reactions to the Black cyclist, to Majid when Georges confronts him in his

flat, and to Majid's son), while *cachets* could refer to the painkillers taken by Georges to blot out painful reality before he dreams of the abduction of Majid.

40. I am grateful to Bryan Cheyette for passing on this insight by the writer Clive Sinclair.

41. The name 'Hashem' can be read in relation to the play in the film on the letter/word/ sound *hache*. *Hache* is, of course, the French word for 'axe', which plays a central role in the film as it used by the young Majid to cut off the cock's head and is then wielded by him as he advances on Georges in the latter's nightmare (*hache* + M for Majid?). It is also the first letter in 'History' in the expression Perec uses in *W ou le souvenir d'enfance*, 'History with a capital H' / 'l'Histoire avec sa grande H' (Perec, *W ou le souvenir d'enfance*, p. 17 / *W, or the Memory of Childhood*, p. 6) (I am grateful to David Walker for this observation), and is the central sound in the word *caché* itself. It could be said, then, that hidden in the word *caché* (*haché* meaning 'chopped up') is the secret but violent way in which the linear narrative of History cuts up reality into pieces (severing it from its contexts), papers over the cracks through seamless representation and anaesthetizes us from the pain of jagged edges.

42. Catherine Wheatley, 'Secrets, Lies and Videotape', *Sight and Sound* 16, 2 (2006), 36.

43. See Saxton, 'Secrets and Revelations', p. 11. Lisa Coulthard is right to suggest of the multi-layered structure of the penultimate sequence which blurs the personal, the cinematic and history: 'It is simultaneously a dream image …, an objective insert directed at the audience …, and a traumatic intrusion of that which will not be put to rest: history' ('Negative Ethics: The Missed Event in the French Films of Michael Haneke', *Studies in French Cinema* 11, 1 (2011), 79).

44. Ezra and Sillars, '*Hidden* in Plain Sight', p. 218.

45. In the same way, the sound of bird-song, footsteps and car doors closing that can be heard in both scenes is complemented in the later scene by the memory of the traumatic moment of Majid's violent abduction that the first scene has repressed (Ezra and Sillars, '*Hidden* in Plain Sight', pp. 220–221). In Proustian fashion, involuntary memory (Delbo's '*mémoire profonde*') is attached to the senses, not the mind. The play on the words *caché/haché* discussed above assumes a greater relevance within this broader context of the importance of the non-conceptual and non-visual (especially sound) as the trigger for the return of the repressed past. The sliding of signification in the play of sound underpins the dissolution of the fixed image and the certainties of metropolitan identity.

46. For a Benjaminian reading of the way in which images acquire 'intelligibility', see Didi-Huberman's discussion of Sam Fuller's *Falcenau* in 'Opening the Camps, Closing the Eyes'.

47. Benjamin, *The Arcades Project*, p. 463.

48. 'Hitchcock comprit immédiatement que cette forme exigeait *un montage qui ne sépare rien* : d'abord, il fallait ne pas séparer les victimes des bourreaux, c'est-à-dire montrer ensemble les cadavres des prisonniers sous les yeux mêmes des responsables allemands, d'où la décision de couper aussi peu que possible les longs panoramiques du tournage, si effrayants dans leur lenteur ; ensuite, il ne fallait ne pas séparer le camp lui-même de son environnement social, fût-il – où précisément parce qu'il était – normal, coquet, rural voire bucolique', Didi-Huberman, *Images malgré tout*, pp. 171–172 / *Images in Spite of All*, p. 137.

49. 'Ce plan vous montre à quel point le camp était proche du bourg. Voici les maisons ; le camp était derrière. C'est un plan sans coupe, sans montage. J'ai juste fait un panoramique depuis les maisons jusqu'au camp. Voyez comme ils sont proches ! Je n'ai fait aucune coupe. Il ne fallait pas en faire. En jouant sur cette butte, les enfants devaient sûrement voir à l'intérieur du camp', cited in Christian Delage and Vincent Guigeuno, *L'Historien et le film* (Gallimard, 2004), pp. 211–212. Sylvie Lindeperg describes the opening shot of Resnais's filming of Auschwitz in *Nuit et brouillard* in

a similar way: 'Thus, the function of the camera movements is not so much to draw the spectator into the setting of the camp as to point up the contiguity of the banal and horror to be expressed in Cayrol's first words' ('Ainsi les mouvements d'appareil ont-ils moins pour vocation de faire pénétrer le spectateur dans le décor du camp que de signaler la contiguité du banal et de l'horreur qu'exprimeront les premiers mots de Cayrol'), *'Nuit et brouillard', un film dans l'histoire*, p. 88; see also my 'Horror and the Everyday in Post-Holocaust France'). Haneke's use of children to open up repressed horror (especially the child-like drawings accompanying the videos) strangely echoes Fuller's description here of the importance of including the children's viewing position in the depiction of the atrocity of the camp.

50. 'Godard ne dit pas autre chose', Didi-Huberman, *Images malgré tout*, p. 172 / *Images in Spite of All*, p. 138.

51. The scene in *Caché* in which Georges and Anne go to the swimming pool to watch Pierrot in a race seems incongruous in terms of the film's themes. However, when seen in the context of investing the image with a memory that reintegrates it into history, we are reminded perhaps of Bernard's showing of the film of French soldiers diving into a pool while off duty in Algeria in Resnais's *Muriel* while he recounts the torture of Muriel. One of the few scenes of family cohesion in *Caché* is therefore connected to violence, in the same way that Resnais links leisure and violence in *Muriel*. What we cannot see (in both films) is nevertheless 'recounted' in other ways.

52. 'ce que donne à penser ce montage est donc bien que les différences mises en jeu *appartiennent à la même histoire* de la guerre et du cinéma', Didi-Huberman, *Images malgré tout*, pp. 182–183 / *Images in Spite of All*, p. 146. For a discussion of the same sequence in *Histoire(s)*, see also Rancière, *Le Destin des images*, p. 73 / *The Future of the Image*, pp. 62–63 and Saxton, *Haunted Images*, pp. 50–51.

53. 'Connecter sans fin, comme il le fait, un plan d'un film avec le titre ou le dialogue d'un autre, une phrase de roman, un détail de tableau, le refrain d'une chanson, une photographie d'actualité ou un message publicitaire, c'est toujours faire deux choses en même temps : organiser un choc et construire un continuum. L'espace des chocs et celui du continuum peuvent même porter le même nom, celui d'Histoire. L'Histoire, ce peut être en effet deux choses contradictoires : la ligne discontinue des chocs révélateurs ou le continuum de la co-présence. La liaison des hétérogènes construit et réfléchit en même temps un sens d'histoire qui se déplace entre ces deux pôles', Rancière, *Le Destin des images*, p. 70 / *The Future of the Image*, p. 60.

54. 'la "perte de monde" ou la défection du "lien social"', Rancière, *Le Destin des images*, p. 77 / *The Future of the Image*, p. 67.

55. Rancière's description of Godard's aesthetic practice in *Histoire(s)* could also be applied to Perec: 'The poetics of *Histoire(s)* simply radicalizes the aesthetic power of the sentence-image as a combination of opposites' ('La poétique des *Histoire(s)* ne fait que radicaliser la puissance esthétique de la phrase-image comme combinaison des opposés'), *Le Destin des images*, pp. 77–78 / *The Future of the Image*, p. 67.

56. For interesting discussions of Godard's Benjaminian approach to history in *Histoire(s)*, see Scemama, *'Histoire(s) du cinéma' de Jean-Luc Godard*, and Monica Dall'Asta, 'The (Im)possible History' in Temple, Williams and Witt (eds), *For Ever Godard*, pp. 350–363. Hélène Raymond uses a Benjaminian perspective on history to relate *Nuit et brouillard* to *Histoire(s)* (*Poétique du témoignage*, p. 75).

57. Citing Geoffrey Nowell-Smith's observation that montage, image and metaphor are 'interchangeable' in Eisenstein, Michael Witt suggests that Godard creates 'a series of elliptical equations: cinema = image = montage = metaphor = art. To compose images (make metaphors) is to resurrect moments of history, or, as Godard wrote by way of a prescient subtitle to *Histoire(s) du Cinéma* in his 1958 review of Léonard Keigel's film, *Malraux*: 'Art, in its own way, makes History come back to life' ('Montage, My Beautiful

Care, or Histories of the Cinematograph', in Michael Temple and James S. Williams (eds), *The Cinema Alone: Essays on the Work of Jean-Luc Godard 1985–2000* (Amsterdam: Amsterdam University Press, 2000), p. 50).

Chapter 6

MEMORY TRACES

In 'Freud and the scene of writing' ('Freud et la scène de l'écriture') in *L'Écriture et la différence*, Jacques Derrida follows Freud's formulation on memory as a palimpsest but, ultimately, points up what he sees as the limits of Freud's thought. According to Derrida, Freud makes a distinction between a pure perception and the inscription of the trace of the perception in the unconscious (the underlying 'pad'). However, as Derrida explains,

> pure perception does not exist: we are written only as we write, by the agency within us which always already keeps watch over perception, be it internal or external. The 'subject' of writing does not exist if we mean by that some sovereign solitude of the author. The subject of writing is a system of relations between strata: the Mystic Pad, the psyche, society, the world.[1]

For Derrida, then, we are already 'written on', which means that perception is as 'contaminated' by previous traces as the psychic mechanism which records the inscription in the unconscious. In contrast to Freud's formulation, Derrida posits a version of the trace which, no longer simply to be found in the unconscious but constitutive of *'la scène de l'écriture'*, disrupts the notion of the 'sovereignty' of the subject on which Freud's understanding of pure perception is premised:

> Thus, the Freudian conception of trace must be radicalized and extracted from the metaphysics of presence which still retains it …. The trace is the erasure of selfhood, of one's own presence, and is constituted by the threat or anguish of its irremediable disappearance, of the disappearance of its disappearance. An unerasable trace is not a trace, it is a full presence, an immobile and incorruptible substance, a son of God, a sign of parousia and not a seed, that is, a mortal germ.[2]

Derrida's version of the trace as a way of undoing the self, subverting the metaphysics of presence, and incorporating the anxiety of its own disappearance is remarkably close to Cayrol's vision (and that of Marker) of the Lazarean hero estranged from his 'self' because permanently haunted by his own death (though, to the best of my knowledge, Derrida never engaged directly with the work of either Cayrol or Marker). Derrida's view of memory also rejoins that of Cayrol and Marker in terms of a superimposition and cross-contamination of layers of traces ('a system of relations between strata') which subvert the binary distinctions that Derrida locates in Freud's formulation between surface and depth, present and past, and presence and absence. Derrida converts Freud's palimpsest into an intertextual play of incomplete (rather than permanent) traces whose meaning is always deferred onto other traces in an unceasing scene of inscription (*'écriture'*). He thus provides a more hybrid and dynamic version of the palimpsest in which the membrane between experience in the world and psychic recording in the individual unconscious is far more porous and fluid than Freud's rather static model had led us to believe.

The first section of this chapter will consider a short 'autobiographical' story by Hélène Cixous entitled 'Bare Feet' ('Pieds nus)' and Derrida's *Monolingualism of the Other; or, The Prosthesis of Origin* (*Le Monolinguisme de l'autre, ou le prothèse de l'origine*) through the lens of the memory trace as a form of dynamic, palimpsestic memory. The second section extends this discussion to consider the photo-text *Guyane: Traces-mémoires du bagne* by the Martinican writer Patrick Chamoiseau and the German-Algerian photographer Rodolphe Hammadi.

Hélène Cixous's 'Pieds nus' and Jacques Derrida's *Le Monolinguisme de l'autre, ou le prothèse de l'origine*

In 'Pieds nus' Cixous returns to her childhood as a young Francophone Jewish girl growing up in Oran in Algeria. However, as one might expect from Cixous, this is no simple autobiography. Memories of the past are intercut with the self-conscious narrative constructions of the present of writing, the innocence of childhood is inseparable from the knowing backward look of the adult, and the purity of nature, the sense of the eternal and the organic wholeness of Oran are undercut by the work of historical division on that city. The oppositions between autobiography and fiction, past and present, personal affect and historical fact, are recast to challenge the sovereignty of essences and the myth of origins.

'*Noeuds de mémoire*' are particularly apparent in the story's central episode. In October 1940, when Cixous was three years old, the Vichy state abrogated the Crémieux decree of October 1870, which had granted full citizenship to the Jews of Algeria, through the introduction of the infamous measures known as the *Statut des juifs*. Cixous describes the effect of this event on her family:

> It was in 1941 that my father was no longer a doctor or a soldier or a Frenchman or anything at all. That we were pariahs consoled me in an

obscure way, like true beings, like barefoot beings on the path of the Planters among the tombs. In order to survive my father became a pedicurist. I don't know why Vichy, which had taken the care of bodies away from him, still left him the care of corns. ... Finally we had come out right: we were no longer part of the oppressors. It seemed to me that New Time was opening before me. I knew the peace of the poor and the execution of the outlaw. Without a homeland, without a ghastly heritage, with a chicken on the balcony, we were unbelievably happy, like savages absolved from sin.[3]

The sense of displacement effected by this event of being transformed into pariahs is experienced by the young girl, paradoxically, as a consolation due to the rediscovery of authenticity. Cixous explores the metaphor of 'feet' to create links between the 'true beings' that the family has become after the loss of citizenship and the colonial oppressed, those who had 'a chicken on the balcony', whose homeland had been appropriated years before and who had never been granted citizenship by the occupying power in the first place. As *'pieds nus'*, innocent like savages in the Planters' land and relieved of the 'ghastly heritage' of European colonization, the family has a new freedom (at least in the eyes of the young girl) as it now finds itself outside the oppressive structures of the state. The image of the dethroned father, ejected from the body politic and banished to its antipodes to tend to feet, is symbolic of a new existence outside the law. (The English translation fails to capture the play on words in French between *'corps'* (body) and *'les cors aux pieds'* (corns).)

However, this is no simplistic idyll of a search for freedom, a return to nature and an unambiguous alignment of Jew and Muslim (or Berber) as victims of oppression. Liberation from the structures of the law also carries with it the mark of exclusion from the law. The pariah (or *'étranjuif'* as Cixous names this figure elsewhere) has an ambivalent status, straddling the boundaries between inclusion and exclusion, and evoking a radical sense of self-alienation. The remainder of the story will extend the metaphor of feet to develop the theme of ambivalence. The young girl is given a pair of white sandals, an event equal in significance to the abrogation of the Crémieux decree, since the barefoot child is now adorned, once more, with the trappings of culture, the law and 'civilization'. Through acquisition of the sandals she is transformed into a queen or an emperor, the chicken becomes a rooster with two crests, and the noble savage absolved from sin is now the proud owner of property, rushing 'from sin to sin', desperate to gain the approbation of the father, 'for, as all narratives tell us, for triumph to be triumphant it must be reflected in the light green eyes of the father'.[4] However, this return to culture and the law of the father is itself rendered ambivalent in the story's dénouement. As if drawn ineluctably to her fate, 'because without wanting to I had read the whole Book written in advance on the walls',[5] the girl submits to the siren call of a six-year-old Algerian shoeshine boy who opens a box of red polish and smears her white sandal with 'a greasy layer of thick blood'.[6] Finally, in response to this assault, the girl adopts a ploy. The story ends as follows: 'I acted like a child, refined. I told him that I had to go home and get money to pay him. I extricated myself from the trap and moved away with dignity, my foot red as a scream, blood on my soul for eternity.'[7]

The different sequences of the story construct a perpetual tension between inclusion and exclusion on a number of levels. Reinstated in the realm of the metropolitan and colonial symbolic order through the acquisition of the new sandals, the girl is thrust back into a situation of power, mastery, sin and guilt. She is consequently deprived of her sense of authenticity, liberation and identification with the oppressed brought about by the abrogation of the Crémieux decree: 'I confessed. I was guilty before his tribunal, the acquittal I had enjoyed since Vichy was of no value whatsoever. I lived in the rue Philippe on the second floor, and I had been given sandals that were almost entirely new. I confessed.'[8] As Ronnie Scharfman observes '(t)he painful ambiguity of her ethnic position and statelessness is compounded by her very slight social and economic privilege'.[9] Although she feels guilt in the drama of colonialism, because she is from the European quarter, in the drama of patriarchy she is, on the contrary, the victim of 'the lust of hatred, the first shimmer of desire',[10] and, finally, extracts her dignified revenge. The 'blood on [her] soul for eternity' at the end is ambiguous as it gestures both to the sexual assault on her virginity that she must endure and to the colonial assault on the Algerian boy that she is, it seems, also fated to carry out. Along with the removal of citizenship for Algerian Jews in 1940, these are instances whereby the mark of the other leaves its indelible trace on (and compromises the mastery of) the self.

In 'Pieds nus', different demarcations are carved out by the conflicting identifications of Jewishness, woman and colonizer (or *'pied noir'*, the term that is never mentioned overtly in the text but which is evoked implicitly in the title as the permanent shadow of *'pieds nus'*). This conflict of subject positions does not simply point up the non-essentialist and hybrid nature of identity; it also suggests a historical collision by which histories of patriarchy, anti-semitism and colonialism are not different histories at all but are profoundly imbricated, inextricably linked, and leave their indelible marks on subjects. If Vichy's removal of French citizenship for Algerian Jews will exclude the young girl from the French state and promote an identification with the oppressed of colonialism (thus constructing a sense of solidarity between Jews and the Muslims and Berbers of Algeria), the action of the shoeshine boy will cast her back in the role of colonizer and break the fragile bond between the 'community' of the oppressed. However, the resistance of the shoeshine boy in the colonial encounter is itself shadowed by the resistance of the young girl in the encounter between the sexes.

Cixous transforms her *'enfance algérienne'* (the title of the collection of stories in which 'Pieds nus' appears), or what she terms elsewhere her *'Algériance'* (a hybrid term composed of *Algérie, alliance* and possibly other terms), into a complex personal and historical conjuncture in which colonialism, the exclusion of the Jew and patriarchy intersect in conflicting ways.[11] By the end of the story, bare feet and covered feet, innocence and guilt, nature and culture, and the personal and the collective, are not simple oppositions for each has left its mark on the other. The removal of citizenship by being branded and stigmatized as 'Jew', the 'wound' inflicted on the young girl's sandals by the Algerian boy, and the ruse by which she extracts herself from his trap are all traces of otherness which mark the self. Like Cixous's 'stigmata' captured in her invented term *'noblessures'* (translated as either 'noblewounds', 'ourwounds', 'ournoblewounds' or even, by Jacqueline Rose, as 'woundednus'),[12] they disturb the sovereignty of the self over the other, the sovereignty of the colonizing power over the colonized, and the sovereignty of the racist state over the Jew. These marks, as signs of identification, are ultimately ambivalent: they signal both a belonging to and exclusion from a home, a community and an identity, and evoke the inevitable failure of mastery and self-presence. From the point of view of 'knotted intersections', they constitute the traces of cultural/historical inter-dependence which render problematic all essentialist accounts of the self and the community.

Cixous's text owes much to Derrida's *Le Monolinguisme de l'autre, ou le prothèse de l'origine* (hereafter *Le Monolinguisme*) which had been published the previous year (1996). Like Cixous, Derrida was a Francophone Jew who grew up in Algeria. In *Le Monolinguisme* he also refers to the abrogation of the Crémieux decree in 1940 as the critical moment at which the ambivalence of belonging is crystallized.[13] Derrida makes the link between this event and language: the nature of citizenship for the Algerian Jew – *'precarious, recent, threatened'*, because it was granted then taken away brutally and unilaterally by the state[14] – inevitably leaves its 'mark upon this belonging or non-belonging *of* language, this affiliation *to* language, this assignation to what is peacefully called a language'.[15] Like Cixous, the mark of the other both defines an identification with and an exclusion from the self and community. If, in the Cixous story, the 'wound' inflicted on the new shoes disturbs the possession and mastery of the young girl over her identity, in Derrida's text language is one's own yet never fully owned as a possession, like a body with an artificial limb:

> But who exactly possesses it? And whom does it possess? Is language in possession, ever a possessing or possessed possession? Possessed or possessing in exclusive possession, like a piece of personal property? What of this being-at-home [*être chez soi*] in language toward which we never cease returning?[16]

Hence, the paradoxical statement 'I only have one language; it is not mine',[17] which opens the text and is then repeated numerous times afterwards, is a performative announcement of the impossibility of the unified, homogeneous and possessed language, just as it is of the disorder of identity ('trouble de l'identité') which is also repeated through the text (and recalls Rimbaud's famous statement 'I is an other' / 'Je est un autre').

The move that Derrida makes from the specific autobiographical moment of the loss of citizenship in Algeria in 1940 (which is also a specific historical moment) to the universal lesson about the alterity of language and identity and the impossibility of mastery and belonging (whether on the part of the colonizer or the host) is central to understanding the paradox above. The illusion of what Derrida terms 'the hegemony of the homogeneous' means that the singular is never complete in its singularity (as it is always alienated from within, haunted by its own otherness) and the autobiographical can never recount a unified self;[18] but neither can the universal ever constitute a fixed law for all under the banner of sameness, nor can the historical narrate unproblematically the past. The oppositions between the singular and the universal and between the personal and the historical are undone at the same time as the opposition between self and other as discreet categories.[19] The Jew in Algeria in 1940 ends up being both no different from anyone else (the precarious nature of his/her status as citizen is the universal lesson about the ambivalent nature of one's 'own' language and *'le trouble de l'identité'*) and unique (as Derrida says, 'I do not know whether there are other examples of this in the history of modern nation-states, examples of such a deprivation of citizenship decreed for tens and tens of thousands of people at a time').[20] Similarly, the relationship between Jews and language in the works of Franz Rosensweig, Hannah Arendt and Emmanuel Lévinas discussed by Derrida in the long note on each of these is both the universal lesson of being an exile from one's own home and the very specific historical situation of the Jew under conditions of modernity.[21] As Derrida says, '"my case" [is] at once typical and uncommon'.[22] He is only exemplary in the sense of being both the same and different at the same time (which is to redefine the 'exemplary' itself to incorporate difference). As Geoffrey Bennington succinctly observes, 'every singularity is in this way *exemplary*'.[23] Derrida's playful statement to Abdelkebir Khatibi – 'dear Abdelkebir, between the two of us, I consider myself to be the *most* Franco-Maghrebian, and perhaps even the *only* Franco-Maghrebian here' – is to be understood in the same way.[24] Unlike Khatibi, he does not fit any of the categories available for classifying Francophone-Maghrebian speakers: 'Francophone French speakers who are not Maghrebian ..., "Francophones" who are neither French nor Maghrebian ..., French-speaking Maghrebians who are not and have never been French' (he places Khatibi in the latter category).[25] The fact that Derrida escapes all taxonomy by being in-between ('I am perhaps the only one here who can call himself at once a Maghrebian (which is not a citizenship) and a French citizen. One and the other at the same time'),[26] allows him to proclaim his singularity and, simultaneously, to read his indecipherability as a universal principle. In opposition to a simple alignment of discreet languages, cultures and identities (monolingualism as opposed to plurilingualism, monoculturalism as opposed to multiculturalism or cultural diversity), Derrida posits an experience which is 'neither monolingual, nor bilingual, nor plurilingual …, neither one, nor two, nor two + *n*', but one whose 'monolanguage remains incalculable' because it is both singular and plural at the same time.[27]

The centrality of the abrogation of the Crémieux decree for both Derrida and Cixous becomes clearer in the light of the tension between the singular and the universal: it is a mark inscribed on the self (more appropriately, a violent assault or traumatic inscription, like the red polish smeared on Cixoux's white sandals) which delineates (and stigmatizes) Jewish difference and singularity by exclusion from the collectivity. But it is also, at the same time, a trace of the wider historical process which produces difference, singularity and community in the first place. Comparing his own work on the wound of circumcision to Cixous's notion of *'noblessures'*, Derrida captures the tension between singularity and universality signified by the mark in a discussion with Cixous and Jacqueline Rose in 2004:

> I would say the ambiguity in my text on circumcision, the equivocality in this text, has to do with the fact that, on the one hand, I insist on the singularity, the irrepressibility of the wound, circumcision, my own circumcision, which is irreplaceable, it's a wound which structures myself as an absolute singularity. But, on the other hand, I suggest that there are analogies between the Jewish circumcision and every kind of wound which constitutes a community. At the origin of any identity, or cultural identity or nationality, there is something like a circumcision, there is a mark on the body, an ineffaceable mark on the body and this wound is universal. So I postulate between the two and I want to say both things at the same time. On the one hand it is absolutely irreplaceable and on the other hand there are circumcisions everywhere, even outside the Jewish or Islamic communities. That's the ambiguity of the mark on the body.[28]

The mark both distinguishes one thing from another and relates one thing to another. Hence, the intersections in *Le Monolinguisme de l'autre* between the Jewish experience, Islamic communities and European colonization in Algeria, and between the personal account (autobiography) and history are every bit as 'knotted' as those in Cixous's 'Pieds nus'. Derrida refuses a Jewish identity defined according to 'the hegemony of the homogeneous' (either from within the Jewish 'community' or, like Sartre in *Réflexions sur la question juive*, from without) but depicts it, instead, as caught in a no-man's-land between belonging and exclusion, between the personal and the general, between historical specificity and universal validity, hence reducing binary opposites to redundant categories. Elsewhere, I have criticized the adoption of 'the Jew' in postmodern theory as a trope or allegory of the decentred self, of exile, nomadism and otherness (especially with regard to Jean-François Lyotard's *Heidegger et 'les juifs'*).[29] However, Cixous and Derrida force us to modify this position. Historical specificity has not been evacuated here for the sake of allegory, and neither has the singular experience of growing up as a Jew in Algeria become testimony to the new universalism of alterity. It is simply that historical specificity and singularity are always in a 'precarious' relationship with their exemplary status.[30]

My concern to tease out the tension between the universal and the particular in these works by Cixous and Derrida by showing the inevitable traces of otherness in any 'singularity' is not, primarily, to highlight the philosophical challenge they pose to dualist thinking. Instead, I wish to shed light on ways in which they reveal the 'knotted intersections' between 'different' histories (in keeping with Nicholas Harrison's definition of 'Pieds nus' as 'a knotted, elusive account of a process of self-identification')[31] and hence refute essentialist and reductive readings. As Jane Hiddleston remarks in relation to *Le Monolinguisme de l'autre*, '[t]he text is condemned to a constant and paradoxical movement against each stance it adopts'.[32] 'Pieds nus' and *Le Monolinguisme de l'autre* open up the possibility of viewing Jewish diasporic history, 'indigenous' Algerian history, and the history of colonialism (to which one may add the histories of language, culture and patriarchy) not as separate histories, not even as histories which intersect at certain moments, but as sites in which the singular and plural coincide, the trace of the one is in the other, and the Jew and the non-Jew (like self and other) must be apprehended between sameness and difference. If cultural memory connected with post-colonial and Jewish histories could accommodate this 'fusion of horizons', in Gilroy's terms, it would go some way to challenging essentialist versions of difference and rewriting our narratives of the past.

Patrick Chamoiseau and Rodolphe Hammadi: *Guyane: Traces-mémoires du bagne*

> Work camps or death camps: there were obviously differences; but a penal colony is a penal colony; all these prisoners resembled, in my eyes, those who had been deported: the same extended foreheads and wild eyes.[33]

The short collaborative work *Guyane: Traces-mémoires du bagne* (hereafter Guyane) by the Martinican writer Patrick Chamoiseau and the German-Algerian photographer Rodolphe Hammadi opens with a commentary on the way in which the History and Memory of colonialism (with capital letters) are written by the colonizers. Monuments and documents testify to the victors' point of view. But, asks Chamoiseau, how might one write things differently, so that the histories and memories (with small letters) that official narratives have erased can be heard?

Produced as part of a series of photo-texts for the *Caisse nationale des monuments historiques et des sites* documenting France's major heritage sites, this slight book on the French penal colony in French Guiana (founded in 1852 for the transportation and imprisonment of French convicts and political prisoners and eventually closed in 1946)[34] is not only a critical response to the official writing of history but also a riposte to the republican story of national memory recounted in Pierre Nora's *Les Lieux de mémoire*. Chamoiseau explicitly replaces '*lieux de mémoire*' with the notion of '*traces-mémoires*' or memory-traces.[35] Citing his Martinican compatriot Edouard Glissant on writing an alternative history 'from below', Chamoiseau defines the scope of his project with Hammadi as follows:

> In the Americas of the plantations (be it in Guiana, in the foothills of the continental plate, or the arc of the Antilles), to visualize the trajectories of the diverse peoples who found themselves there, we must reinvent the notion of the monument and deconstruct the notion of heritage. Beneath the written History of colonialism, we must find the trace of histories. Beneath the haughty Memory of forts and edifices, we must find the unfamiliar places where the lives of these collectivities took shape.[36]

Hence, from the opening of the text, Europe is related to the Americas, and the victim populations of Guiana are related to other victim populations of colonial rule ('Amerindians, African slaves, Hindus, immigrants from Syria, Lebanon, China').[37] Chamoiseau also draws on his own origins as a native of Martinique, and its colonial history. Yet the challenge to monolinear, 'monumental' national history opens up forgotten channels not only between metropolitan France and colonized peoples but also between different sites of transportation, imprisonment and dehumanization. Through text and image, Chamoiseau and Hammadi transform the narrowly circumscribed surface of the ruins of the penal colony into a complex network of echoes and reverberations across space and time.

The Shapes and Sounds of the Memory-trace

What poetics of text and image do Chamoiseau and Hammadi employ in *Guyane* to convert the linear and monovalent narrative of the monument into the hybrid and multivalent vision of the memory-trace? Ruins testify to the impermanence rather than fixity of place, the discontinuities rather than linearity of time. They are, by their very nature, a sign of transformation and transience. Similar to but different from the buildings they once were, ruins are always haunted by a past; they are present but also bear witness to an absence. In the here and now but in the process of sinking into oblivion, they inhabit an in-between state, between past and present, presence and absence, visibility and invisibility. In this sense, ruins are uncanny: still recognizable though freed from the constraints of familiarity and use-value because of the ravages of time, they are strange and unknowable.[38] The bars, bolts, nails, locks, doors and walls which were once functional now 'transform into new meanings'.[39] Hence, 'the memory-Trace is born from the erosion and chaotic destruction of buildings, materials and meanings' (see Figure 6.1).[40] In surrealist fashion, defamiliarized objects become a kaleidoscope of colour, shape, shade and sound whose fluidity shatters the spatio-temporal constraints of the present of the penal colony.

The ruins therefore already inhabit a spatio-temporal no-man's-land between here and there, now and then, the familiar and the unfamiliar.[41] Ruins allow the echoes of the memory-trace to reverberate out from the fixity of the monument: 'The memory-Traces of the penal colony are broken, diffuse, scattered. We cannot approach them in the way we would approach the façade of a Cistercian abbey or a Romanesque church'.[42] Geometrical design partakes of the rigidity of the monument (and the monolinearity of Western narrative),[43] while the strange shapes of the ruins occupy a hinterland between coherence and chaos:

Figure 6.1 Ruins of the former penal colony in French Guiana, Rodolphe Hammadi (photographer), Patrick Chamoiseau and Rodolphe Hammadi, *Guyane: Traces-mémoires du bagne* (1994)

everything comes back to elementary forms and the resonances of these elementary forms: squares, circles, triangles, straight and curved lines, trapeziums, and their infinite connections. The functional rubs shoulders with the abstract, the familiar with the unfamiliar, immediate sense with hidden meanings. This is a primeval broth, a chaotic harmony whose only constant remains the emotion of the memory of the penal colony. The wear and tear born from abandonment tie together [*nouent*] this assemblage according to the imperceptible – yet sovereign – aesthetic of an interior necessity.[44]

The aesthetic principle at work in the 'resonances of these elementary forms' is a dynamic tension between shape and meaning. The memory-trace is a *noeud de mémoire* because of its capacity to trigger diverse memories and connect disparate detail.[45]

Hammadi's photos are part of the same (fundamentally modernist) aesthetic construction of the memory-trace. Oblique angles, odd juxtapositions between foregrounds and backgrounds disturbing perspective, and views framed in such a way that the object of perception dissolves into a play of shape and shading blur the clarity of distinction between 'different' spaces, volumes and shapes and splinter the meaning of the image. Here, as in the passage above, the aesthetic of the memory-trace is fundamentally one of deconstruction and reconstruction founded on the loosening of old connections and the creation of new ones ('[t]he wear and tear born from abandonment tie together [*nouent*] this assemblage according to the imperceptible – yet sovereign – aesthetic of an interior necessity'). Knotting is indeed Chamoiseau's metaphor of choice to describe the aesthetic device of making connections between disparate objects – 'moss connects everything' ('la mousse noue le tout'), 'knotted ironwork' ('un noeud de feraille'), 'the walls have knotted ancient pacts with enormous roots' ('[l]es murs ont noué de vieux pactes avec d'énormes racines')[46] – while Hammadi's photos similarly transform the site into a series of abstract 'assemblages' of shape, line and colour.

By transforming the ruins into knots of meaning, text and image connect the material remains with the human forms that inhabited this site:

Flesh knows how to erode stone. At Saint-Laurent, or on the islands, you have to see the signs of erosion. These broken or curved steps, the darkness more pronounced around openings, this particular patina which bears witness to an everyday gesture. Flesh has become a sculptor and a painter. The rubbing (the encounter) between man and stone, man and iron, was subtle. We must look at the rounded corners, assess the ferocity of these gates still intact and onto which who knows how many bodies were shattered. On the paths, we have to imagine this rectilinear centre which seems to remember the disciplined trudge of silent and anxious prisoners.[47]

The memory-trace is thus formed from the connections made (or imagined) between the shapes and sounds of the ruins and the inmates, and also between the visitors to the site (the writer, the photographer and the readers and viewers of their work) and the lives of others before them. In the photos, we are invited to imagine the ruins haunted by humanity, the visible haunted by the invisible, to create a play of presence and absence. In the text, the associations between different linguistic fields (the human and the material) create the same in-between state: 'the skin of the walls', 'the iron cried its rust into the wood', 'Sometimes, prosthetic limbs of ironwork are embedded in the living skin of the walls'.[48]

Chamoiseau and Hammadi dissolve the fixed meanings of word and image in the same way that the ruins have transformed the shape, stature and design of the original buildings. The transformation of the fixed monument into the memory-trace is therefore the poetic transformation of word and image into the echoes, resonances and reverberations of memory:

> *Transportation camp.* It is written above. Camp. Transportation. In silhouette behind these terms are rules, statutes, an order of suffering, a track leading to death or breaking point. What does it matter what they mean. The two coupled words are like carved inscriptions. This is not a naming, rather a flicker of memories.[49]

> Doors which are no longer doors, hinges unsure of their identity, windows which breathe, walls which enclose nothing, ironwork suddenly rendered strange... We must forget these words and find others. All these apparent meanings are suddenly thrown into an anxious state, primary meanings disaggregated, a sort of unravelling of signification incited by the wandering nature of my advance and my spirit. I am open to sensation.[50]

Chamoiseau calls on artists of all sorts to bring the memory-traces to life and travel beyond the frontiers of entrenched meaning. This is, then, a poetic journey amongst the ruins of the penal colony. Echoes and evocations are provoked by the resonances established in the encounter with the deserted ruins of the camp, writer and photographer broaching their subject not through the tourist gaze but with the sensibility of the wandering poet: 'And here I am amongst the memory-Traces of the penal colony of Guiana, not as a visitor but as a wanderer, not as a *flâneur* but as one who digresses'.[51] The Baudelairean spirit guiding this 'wandering' ('errance') and 'digression' ('divagation') is key to conjuring up other worlds, so that the bland surface of the present opens out on a kaleidoscopic canvas of space-time superimposition that Chamoiseau calls 'sedimented memories' ('des mémoires sédimentées').[52] As he says in the last lines of the text, '[h]ere, the conservationist will be of the tribe of poets. And conservation will be a poetics'.[53]

Camps and Colonies

The poetic evocation of '*des mémoires sédimentées*' in *Guyane* suggests that the memory-trace is an over-determined site in which the singularity of the moment is invaded by the complex layering of history. Although Chamoiseau warns of the dangers of historical writing as such – 'It would be better not to write the history of the penal colony but to attempt, instead, to apprehend the murmurs of the memory-Traces' – history returns in the murmurs of the memory-Traces themselves.[54] But this history is not the singular, monolinear and reductive History (with a capital *H*), bolstered by its monuments (as the opening of the book has forewarned), but is a history pluralized and hybridized by the memory-traces. The resonances of the past in the present – 'the resonances come from everywhere, from the colour, the matter, the stone, the iron, the shade, the flashes of light' – are the raw material of the poet-historian; that is, he or she who knows how to evoke the sound, the colour and the shapes of the memory-trace within which real history lies, in the sense of a Benjaminian constellation.[55]

The aesthetic structure of the memory-trace, whose meanings are 'constantly evolving, with diverse ramifications',[56] is therefore a condensation, or palimpsestic sedimentation, of other historical moments of transportation, imprisonment and dehumanization:

> But today's memory-Traces not only bear witness to the history of the penal-colony …. They have accumulated, over time, indefinable memories. They have associated long, moss-grown sighs with the vitality of the forest which today seems to knot them into a jewel-case. The building becomes ruin and the ruin becomes open-memories according to a spontaneous movement produced by an invisible accumulation.[57]

This 'invisible accumulation' is the result of layers of superimposed resonances and evocations, rather like the language of a symbolist poem. It is true (as we have seen) that Chamoiseau links the inmates of the penal colony to other victims of oppression and will also compare the lives of the inmates with those of slaves in Louisiana.[58] But these direct references to other times and places are rare. Instead, echoes, evocations, doublings and hauntings of other spaces and times are triggered by the similarities between different moments arising from the (Proustian) encounter with the deserted ruins of the penal colony.

The treatment of Alfred Dreyfus on Devil's Island is indicative of this approach. The first two of Hammadi's photos are of the cell in which Dreyfus was imprisoned at the turn of the twentieth century for treason, and the final photo is of a tower known as the 'tour Dreyfus'. But there is no mention of Dreyfus in the text, the most famous prisoner ever to be held on Devil's Island. His presence, and with it the history of anti-semitism, is evoked rather than mentioned explicitly so that the ghost of one form of racialized violence overlaps with that of others in this space, a shadow of the past (*ombre*/'shadow' is a word that recurs throughout the text and is an integral part of the image-constellations) mingling with the other shadows formed by the crumbling buildings.

However, it is the echoes of other camps of horror that have also left their mark on the material remains of certain sites that are evoked most vividly by the memory-traces of the penal colony: 'these buildings were places of imprisonment, spaces of security, camps in the woods, artisans' workshops, sheds, ovens, animal parks, hospitals, administrative services'; 'Camp. Transportation. …[A]n order of suffering, a track leading to death'.[59] These references to transportation, tracks leading to death, camps and ovens (and the bizarre assortment of everyday objects and activities and those connected with horror referred to above) inevitably (and palimpsestically) overlay this space and time with the memory of the Nazi concentrationary universe half a century earlier. The 'wandering' journey undertaken by writer and photographer in the remains of the penal colony in French Guiana, and the exploration of traces of memory in this site, cannot but recall the two major explorations of sites of horrific racialized violence in post-war French culture, Resnais's *Nuit et brouillard* and Lanzmann's *Shoah*.

It is *Nuit et brouillard* that is so vividly recalled by Chamoiseau and Hammadi in *Guyane*. So, for example, the description of the 'the stale smell of sour soup' echoes the image of an inmate sipping a weak broth in *Nuit et brouillard* which is accompanied by the comment 'the soup was diuretic';[60] 'lime or coal-fired ovens'[61] recall the Nazi ovens for the incineration of bodies; the 'nails which clawed the walls' echo the description by Cayrol at Auschwitz of a 'ceiling furrowed by nails';[62] 'a mad grass stubbornly sprouting from the stone' echoes Cayrol's description of 'a strange grass [which] has grown up and covered the ground' or, at the end of *Nuit et brouillard*, the description of 'the faithful grass [which] has returned on the parade ground around the blocks'.[63] Chamoiseau's description of the prisoners of the penal colony ('*les bagnards*') focuses on 'the burning fever of their look. As if the last energy of the will to live had attached itself to the fragile freedom of their eyes'. And, to remove any doubt about the reference being made, he adds, 'We have already seen this in other camps of despair', conjuring up the image in *Nuit et brouillard* of an inmate at Auschwitz staring out from his bunk, another of inmates looking out wide-eyed across the barbed wire, and the narrator's comment that 'finally, all the prisoners resemble each other. They align themselves on the timeless model of dying with open eyes'.[64] Other descriptions will similarly evoke the Nazi concentrationary universe – 'a haggard-looking mass, numbered, pouring out in confused ranks in their striped uniform – the whole of humanity dehumanized'; 'The numbers are confused with drawings, with scratches, with the blackened moss: they cover the skin of the wall with a worrying tattoo. No man's name, no address: simply numbers'; 'Night in the barracks'; 'The fearful night' – so that memories of French penitentiary practice, French colonialism and the Nazi camps are overlaid to create an image-constellation of meaning.[65]

The repetition of the marching of boots recorded by Chamoiseau – 'I hear the regular step of boots'; 'this rectilinear centre which seems to remember the disciplined trudge of silent and anxious prisoners'[66] – not only recalls the same image in *Nuit et brouillard* but also evokes, in a similar way, the Benjaminian 'double ground' or superimposition of different times provoked by the tread (both sound and trace) of feet. Yet, as Chamoiseau notes, repetition and difference are always in an anxious relationship: 'When we retrace our steps, meanings are not the same, lights and shades are modified, other details appear, other points are highlighted, other smells and other sensations arise from the colours; everything is alive and stimulates the spirit.'[67] Chamoiseau's following image of footsteps in the present captures perfectly the complex, knotted and delicate relationship between the different elements involved in the memory-trace, and especially between recall, preservation and effacement: 'And the tread is so heavy that the steps, their middle caved in for a long time, seem to give way once more under the hesitating foot'.[68] Hence, although walking now on the same earth that was trodden by the prisoners in the past ('And the ground bears witness to them: the earth, the stone, the cement have been friends to hordes of wrecked humanity'),[69] in the same way that the film crew's footsteps retrace the steps of the inmates at Auschwitz-Birkenau in *Nuit et brouillard*, the relationship between past and present, and us and them, occupies a space between sameness and difference. Just as *Nuit et brouillard* refers allegorically to another site of racialized violence (the Algerian War of Independence), but without collapsing one scene of horror into the other, so the memory traces of the penal colony establish an uncanny space of repetition and difference, connecting but not collapsing the two concentrationary systems of French Guiana and Nazi Germany.

Hammadi's photos also recall distinctive features of Resnais's film in the portrayal of the camp. A majority of the images are shot through window-frames, ironwork, barred doors, open doors and other framings to create a tension between inside the buildings of the camp and the lush vegetation of the outside world.[70] One's eye is held between the here and now of the camp and the light and shade, colours and shapes of elsewhere. The classic opening of *Nuit et brouillard* plays precisely on shifting perspectives across the barbed wire at Auschwitz and a tension between the camp and the surrounding countryside, horror and the everyday. In other photos, it is not the tension in perspective between here and there, inside and outside, that disturbs our vision but, on the contrary, no perspective at all so that proximity to the object makes us lose any purchase on what it is. The interior of dilapidated cells is simply an intertwining of wood and wall, shape, shade and colour, more an abstract design or collage than anything familiar.[71] This, too, is a device employed by Resnais as, for example, when a darkened screen only becomes recognizable as a mound of hair as the camera slowly withdraws and keeps its distance, or, conversely, when the camera panning around the gas chamber focuses in on a corner of wall and ceiling to highlight the scratch marks left by frantic victims. Just as Cayrol warns us that we need to know how to read the abstract inscription left by scratch marks on the ceiling as a sign, so the unfamiliar shapes of Hammadi's photos incite us to read the remains as complex signs.

Sliding perspectives, uncertain positioning, the questioning eye, and the transformation of the familiar into the unfamiliar are all techniques employed by Resnais in the filming of the concentration camps and adopted in this text by Hammadi to record the penal colony. The quest for the human traces and inscriptions left on the material remains of the colony discussed by Chamoiseau in the text, which is itself a fundamental aspect of *Nuit et brouillard* (not least in the example of the scratch marks on the ceiling), are vividly displayed in the photos.[72] In part, they humanize these places of dehumanization. Elsewhere, the words written above doors and gates ('Cells', 'Blockhaus', 'Library', 'Court-room' 'Punishment area') are the dehumanizing inscriptions that Chamoiseau, following Cayrol, ironically critiques as concentrationary language.[73] The ambiguities of human inscription are captured movingly in Hammadi's photos; the memory-trace recalls both humanity and its denial. Nowhere is this more apparent than in the photo of the entrance to the camp which has the words *'Camp de la transportation'* written above the archway.[74] Chamoiseau discusses the yawning gap between the words and the reality they designate, but it is only Hammadi's photo that reminds us of the mocking words *'Arbeit macht frei'* over the entrance to Auschwitz.

Finally, Chamoiseau's description of the murals painted over a period of eight years by one of the prisoners in the Church of Saint-Joseph d'Iracoubo as 'a noble cry' recalls the endless cry of suffering which closes *Nuit et brouillard*, and Chamoiseau's image of a ruined wall transformed into 'a worrying stele' evokes the final image of Resnais's film.[75] Text and image overlay one camp with another, one site of terror with another, and highlight the interconnections inherent in cultural memory. In her profound book on space in the works of Patrick Chamoiseau, Lorna Milne discusses parallels between traumatic memory related to the Holocaust and that related to the history of Martinique.[76] However, the memory-traces explored in the penal colony in Guiana do not so much relate one trauma to another (which implies their separate and relative status) as connect and overlay them in a complex network of meaning. The memory-traces are, in Gilroy's words, 'between camps' rather than within them.

The Remains of the Day

In her fascinating discussion of fascism and representation (to which I referred in chapter 4), the philosopher Gillian Rose criticizes the different techniques we employ (consciously and unconsciously) to distance ourselves from responsibility for acts of horrific violence. Using the metaphor of stages of the day, she suggests that if the beginnings of the day announce brave new worlds of human perfection (fascism and communism), and the middle of the day sees us reflecting on the catastrophe of these unfulfilled promises ('the broken middle', as Rose calls it), then it is only at the remains of the day that we can look back at 'the ruins of the morning's hope, the actuality of the broken middles' to assess the day not as external observers of a damaged history but in terms of our fraught and complex relationship with that history, and with representation itself.[77] Rose argues that Kazuo Ishiguro's 1989 novel *The Remains of the Day* (and the 1993 Merchant Ivory film version) is just such a mature reflection as it does not represent fascism by leaving our own integrity intact (in the manner of a film like Steven Spielberg's *Schindler's List*, for example) or denounce representation entirely (in the manner of pronouncements by Claude Lanzmann on representations of the Holocaust), but engages with representation to expose us to our own complicity with and response to the 'fascist' hold that representation inevitably exerts over us. Rose suggests that being at the remains of the day – after the false dawns of utopian ideologies and the 'broken middles' of sanctimonious critique – entails an awareness of the ambiguities of our compromised position as a basis for moral action.

I propose that *Guyane* also shows us at the remains of the day. The wandering journey undertaken by Chamoiseau and Hammadi through the remains of the penal colony is undoubtedly a challenge to the haughty ideals of the colonial project and to the 'History' written and monuments erected to inscribe it in fact. But the awakening of memory-traces by writer and photographer in the ruins of this utopian project does not simply expose the folly of power from the position of the self-righteous victim who has been written out of history. In Rose's terms, this would leave us still at the middle of the day, our sentimentality left intact as we look back, voyeuristically, at the ruins of empire-building.[78] The 'sedimented memories' of the memory-traces leave us at the remains of the day because they deny us any such vantage point or privileged perspective outside the knots of memory within which we ourselves are located (what Rose calls 'the fascism of representation'). By transforming the site of the ruins into a haunted space, the memory-trace conjoins past and present, here and there, today's observers and former actors, in such a way as to preclude voyeuristic distance. In the 'ambiguous zone' of the ruins, binary distinctions dissolve into a more complex space. The monument and the memory-trace are not opposites; the memory-trace is, instead, the paradoxical in-between state in which the autonomy, power and self-presence of the monument are doubled by their own connectedness, vulnerability and absence. Hammadi's photos capture this paradox perfectly as they show both the solidity and the evanescence of buildings, the porous relationship between culture and nature as the luxurious vegetation reclaims the site of the colony, and the ambiguous positions of inside and outside as the angles and perspectives fracture clear delineations and distinctions. Chamoiseau describes the mix of humanity and inhumanity of the penal colony in oxymoronic terms (and using a vocabulary which once again recalls the concentration camps) as 'a hallucinating concentration of what makes up Man: a combustion of light and shade, of light in shade and shade which illuminates'.[79]

At the remains of the day, distinctions are blurred and opposites confused: 'The prisoner and the prison guard were linked together in the same gasp in which the overwhelming desire to survive and the all-embracing nature of the power to punish mired both in the same rot'.[80] The reality of this space is one of collusion ('In the transportation camp … we should stop in the shadows, and wait for this testimony of a morbid collusion between the prisoner and the shadow'), complicity ('I confess that the shadow was complicitous and the light was not always so') and contamination (the trace of one in the other).[81] The remains of the day offer a vision in which the singularity of the present metamorphoses into a paradoxical constellation which denies the dichotomy between singularity and plurality (in the manner proposed by Derrida in *Le Monolinguisme de l'autre*). Chamoiseau's hybrid (and impossible) term '*la Trace-mémoires*' captures this paradox perfectly by connecting the upper-case *T* and singular noun of *Trace* with the lower-case *m* and plural noun of *mémoires*. It suggests that History and histories, and the monument and memory-traces, are both singular and plural at the same time, one always in the other. Chamoiseau states this clearly: 'The memory-Trace is both collective and individual, vertical and horizontal, of one community and trans-communitarian, fixed and mobile, and fragile'.[82] Writing about Martinique in *Ecrire en pays dominé* (1997), he describes this hybrid network once again through the metaphor of the knot: 'I am announcing here a site [*un Lieu*] …, a sovereign Meta-nation, mixed and tangled with all the countries in the world, haughty and interdependent, knotted and unknotted in the Stone-World [*Pierre-Monde*].'[83]

Reading *Guyane* as a poetico-historical meditation on memory 'at the remains of the day' gives us a particular way of understanding palimpsestic memory ('*noeuds de mémoire*') in relation to racialized violence, horror and dehumanization. The knots of the memory-trace mean that we are never simply there where we find ourselves but split across different times and spaces. We are situated within a complex history with no possibility of escape to take a distanced view. To pretend otherwise is to indulge in the folly of hubris and mastery which leads to the erection of camps and colonies. Guyane: *Traces-mémoires du bagne* offers us hope that this folly can one day be avoided, by offering us not total liberation from a camp mentality but an awareness of our complicity in the very site on which that mentality is founded.

Notes

1. 'la perception pure n'existe pas : nous ne sommes écrits qu'en écrivant, par l'instance en nous qui toujours déjà surveille la perception, qu'elle soit interne ou externe. Le 'sujet' de l'écriture n'existe pas si l'on entend par là quelque solitude souveraine de l'écrivain. Le sujet de l'écriture est un système de rapports entre les couches : du bloc magique, du psychique, de la société, du monde', Jacques Derrida, *L'Écriture et la différence* (Seuil, 1967), p. 335 / *Writing and Difference*, trans. Alan Bass (London: Routledge, 2011), p. 285.
2. 'Il faut donc radicaliser le concept freudien de trace et l'extraire de la métaphysique de la présence qui le retient encore …. La trace est l'effacement de soi, de sa propre présence, elle est constituée par la menace ou l'angoisse de sa disparition irrémédiable, de la disparition de sa disparition. Une trace ineffaçable n'est pas une trace, c'est une présence pleine, une substance immobile et incorruptible, un fils de Dieu, un signe de la parousie et non une semence, c'est-à-dire un germe mortel', Derrida, *L'Écriture et la différence*, p. 339 / *Writing and Difference*, p. 289. For an extended discussion of Derrida's engagement with Freud's note on the magic writing pad in 'Freud et la scène de l'écriture', see Christopher Johnson, *System and Writing in the Philosophy of Jacques Derrida* (Cambridge: Cambridge University Press, 1993), pp. 65–108.
3. 'C'était en 1941 mon père n'était plus ni médecin ni militaire ni français ni rien. Que nous fussions parias cela obscurément me soulageait, comme d'être vrais, comme d'être pieds nus sur le chemin des Planteurs parmi les tombes. Pour survivre mon père se fit pédicure. Je ne sais pas pourquoi Vichy qui lui ôtait le soin des corps lui avait cependant abandonné les cors aux pieds. … Enfin nous étions tombés dans le juste : nous ne faisions plus partie des oppresseurs. Il me sembla que le Temps Neuf s'ouvrait devant moi. Je connus la paix des pauvres et l'exultation des hors-la-loi. Sans patrie, sans affreux héritage, avec une poule sur le balcon, nous étions incroyablement heureux comme des sauvages absous de pécher', Hélène Cixous, 'Pieds nus' in *Une Enfance algérienne, textes inédits recueillis par Leïla Sebbar* (Gallimard, 1997), p. 60 / 'Bare Feet' in *An Algerian Childhood: A Collection of Autobiographical Narratives*. trans. Marjolijn de Jager (Minnesota: Ruminator Books, 2001), p. 56.
4. 'de péché en péché'; '[c]ar, tous les récits le disent, pour qu'un triomphe soit triomphal, il faut qu'il se reflète dans les yeux vert clair du père', Cixous, 'Pieds nus', p. 61 / 'Bare Feet', p. 57.
5. 'sans l'avoir voulu j'avais lu tout le livre écrit d'avance sur les murs', Cixous, 'Pieds nus', p. 61 / 'Bare Feet', p. 57.
6. 'une grasse couche de sang épais', Cixous, 'Pieds nus', p. 63 / 'Bare Feet', p. 59.
7. 'Je me fis infantile, distinguée. Je lui dis que je devais rentrer chez moi chercher l'argent pour le payer. Je me dégageai du piège, et je m'éloignai d'un pas digne, le pied rouge comme un cri, du sang sur l'âme pour l'éternité', Cixous, 'Pieds nus', p. 63 / 'Bare Feet', p. 59.
8. 'J'avouai. J'étais coupable. Devant son tribunal, à lui, l'acquittement dont je jouissais à mes yeux depuis Vichy n'avait aucune valeur. J'habitais rue Philippe au deuxième étage et j'avais des sandales données à l'état neuf. J'avouai.' Cixous, 'Pieds nus', p. 62 / 'Bare Feet', p. 58.
9. Ronnie Scharfman, 'Cixous, Derrida, and the Vichy Years in Algeria' in H. Adlai Murdoch and Anne Donadey (eds), *Postcolonial Theory and Francophone Literary Studies*

(Gainesville: University Press of Florida, 2005), p. 91. In her essay, Scharfman mentions 'Pieds nus' but mainly considers other Cixous texts concerning her childhood in Algeria, including 'Lettre à Zohra Drif' and 'Mon Algériance'. She also discusses Derrida's *Le Monolinguisme de l'autre* in a wider consideration of Derrida's early years in Algeria. Scharfman brings these texts together to 'interrogate the genealogy of wordplay in relation to an ethics of solidarity' (p. 87).

10. 'la convoitise de la haine, la première lueur du désir', 'Pieds nus', p. 62 / 'Bare Feet', p. 58.

11. Hélène Cixous, 'Mon Algériance' in *Les Inrockuptibles* 115 (20 August–2 September 1997), 71–74. This essay contains the same drama of the encounter with the Algerian shoeshine boy as that recounted in 'Pieds nus'.

12. Hélène Cixous and Jacques Derrida (chaired by Jacqueline Rose), 'The Language of Others', Jewish Book Week (March 2004), http://jewishbookweek.com/archive/010304e/transcripts2.php.

13. See Nancy Wood, 'Remembering the Jews of Algeria' in *Vectors of Memory: Legacies of Trauma in Postwar Europe* (Oxford: Berg, 1999).

14. 'précaire, récente, menacée', Jacques Derrida, *Le Monolinguisme de l'autre, ou le prothèse de l'origine* (Galilée, 1996), p. 33 / *Monolingualism of the Other; or, The Prosthesis of Origin*, trans. Patrick Mensah (Stanford, California: Stanford University Press, 1998), p. 15.

15. 'marque sur cette appartenance ou non-appartenance *de* la langue, sur cette affiliation de la langue, sur cette affiliation *à* la langue, sur cette assignation à ce qu'on appelle tranquillement une langue', Derrida, *Le Monolinguisme de l'autre*, p. 35 / *Monolingualism of the Other*, pp. 16–17.

16. 'Mais qui la possède au juste ? Et qui possède-t-elle ? Est-elle jamais en possession, la langue, une possession possédante ou possédée ? Possédée ou possédant en propre, comme un bien propre ? Quoi de cet être-chez-soi dans la langue vers lequel nous ne cesserons de faire retour ?', Derrida, *Le Monolinguisme de l'autre*, pp. 35–36 / *Monolingualism of the Other*, p. 17.

17. 'Je n'ai qu'une langue, ce n'est pas la mienne', Derrida, *Le Monolinguisme de l'autre*, p. 13 / *Monolingualism of the Other*, p. 1.

18. 'l'hégémonie de l'homogène', Derrida, *Le Monolinguisme de l'autre*, p. 69 / *Monolingualism of the Other*, p. 40.

19. See Jane Hiddleston, 'Derrida, Autobiography and Postcoloniality', *French Cultural Studies* 16 (2005), 291–304 and Michael Syrotinski, *Deconstruction and the Postcolonial: At the Limits of Theory* (Liverpool: Liverpool University Press, 2007), pp. 15–24.

20. 'je ne sais pas s'il y en a d'autres exemples, dans l'histoire des États-nations modernes, des exemples d'une telle privation de citoyenneté décrétée pour des dizaines et des dizaines de milliers de personnes à la fois', Derrida, *Le Monolinguisme de l'autre*, p. 36 / *Monolingualism of the Other*, p. 17.

21. See Derrida, *Le Monolinguisme de l'autre*, pp. 91–114 / *Monolingualism of the Other*, pp. 78–93.

22. "'mon cas", c'est la situation, à la fois typique et singulière', Derrida, *Le Monolinguisme de l'autre*, p. 33 / *Monolingualism of the Other*, p. 15.

23. Geoffrey Bennington, 'Double Tonguing: Derrida's Monolingualism', *Tympanum* 4 (2000), http://www.usc.edu/dept/comp-lit/tympanum/4/bennington.html.

24. 'Cher Abdelkebir, vois-tu, je me considère ici comme le *plus* franco-maghrébin de nous deux, et peut-être même le *seul* franco-maghrébin', Derrida, *Le Monolinguisme de l'autre*, p. 29 / *Monolingualism of the Other*, p. 29. The text originated as a keynote address delivered by Derrida at a conference in 1992 at Louisiana State University at which Abdelkebir Khatibi was present.

25. 'Français francophones qui ne sont pas des maghrébins …', "francophones" qui ne sont ni français ni maghrébins …, des maghrébins francophones qui ne sont pas et n'ont

jamais été Français', Derrida, *Le Monolinguisme de l'autre*, pp. 29–30 / *Monolingualism of the Other*, p. 12.

26. 'je suis ici, peut-être, seul, le *seul* à pouvoir me dire à la fois maghrébin (ce qui n'est pas une citoyenneté) et citoyen français. À la fois l'un et l'autre', Derrida, *Le Monolinguisme de l'autre*, p. 30 / *Monolingualism of the Other*, p. 13.

27. 'ni monolingue, ni bilingue, ni plurilingue …[,] ni une, ni deux, ni deux + *n*'; 'monolangue demeure incalculable', Derrida, *Le Monolinguisme de l'autre*, p. 55 / *Monolingualism of the Other*, pp. 29 and 30 respectively.

28. Hélène Cixous and Jacques Derrida, 'The Language of Others'. See also Derrida's 'Circumfession' in Geoffrey Bennington and Jacques Derrida, *Jacques Derrida* (Chicago: Chicago University Press, 1993). Khatibi, with whom Derrida is in dialogue in *Le Monolinguisme de l'autre*, also relates the mark of circumcision to the traces of *écriture* in his work. His metaphorical use of the tattoo as an overlaying of imprints in the process of memory in *La Mémoire tatouée* could also reference those other marks imprinted on the bodies of camp prisoners. The way in which wounds in Perec's *W* are displaced from one body to another exemplifies Derrida's statements about the ambivalence of marks on the body; they are both profound inscriptions on an individual body and the mark of a wider history.

29. Max Silverman, 'Re-figuring "the Jew" in France' in Bryan Cheyette and Laura Marcus (eds), *Modernity, Culture and 'the Jew'* (Cambridge: Polity, 1998), pp. 197–208.

30. For readings of Cixous and Derrida reading each other (especially with regard to their Jewishness), see Jacques Derrida and Hélène Cixous, 'From the Word to Life: A Dialogue Between Jacques Derrida and Hélène Cixous', *New Literary History* 37, 1 (2006), 1–13.

31. Nicholas Harrison, 'Learning from Experience: Hélène Cixous's "Pieds nus"', *Paragraph* 27 (2004), 21–32.

32. Jane Hiddleston, 'Jacques Derrida: Colonialism, Philosophy and Autobiography' in Charles Forsdick and David Murphy (eds), *Postcolonial Thought in the French-speaking World* (Liverpool: Liverpool University Press, 2009), p. 60.

33. 'Camps de travail ou camps de mort : il y avait évidemment quelques différences ; mais un bagne est un bagne ; tous ces internés, je leur voyais les mêmes fronts démesurés, les mêmes yeux fous qu'aux déportés', Simone de Beauvoir, *Les Mandarins* (Gallimard, 1954), p. 362.

34. The penal colony consisted of the three islands known as the Île du Salut off the coast of French Guiana (Île Royale, Île Saint-Joseph and the most famous Île du Diable, or Devil's Island) and the mainland town of Korou. It was known as one of the most notorious penal colonies in the world because of its harsh and disease-infested conditions. For a fuller discussion of the colony in one of the few articles devoted solely to *Guyane*, see Andrew Stafford, 'Patrick Chamoiseau and Rodolphe Hammadi in the Penal Colony: Photo-text and Memory-traces', *Postcolonial Studies* 11, 1 (2008), 27–38.

35. Patrick Chamoiseau and Rodolphe Hammadi, *Guyane: Traces-mémoires du bagne* (Caisse nationale des monuments historiques et des sites, 1994), p. 16.

36. 'Dans l'Amérique des plantations (que ce soit en Guyane, sur les contreforts continentaux, ou dans l'arc antillais), pour distinguer les trajectoires des divers peuples qui se sont retrouvés là, il faut réinventer la notion de monument, déconstruire la notion de patrimoine. Dessous l'Histoire coloniale écrite, il faut trouver la trace des histoires. Dessous la mémoire hautaine des forts et des édifices, trouver les lieux insolites où se sont cristallisées les étapes déterminantes pour ces collectivités', Chamoiseau and Hammadi, *Guyane*, p. 15.

37. 'Amérindiens, esclaves africains, immigrants hindous, syro-libanais, chinois', Chamoiseau and Hammadi, *Guyane*, p. 13.

38. In her excellent book on memory in Chamoiseau's work, Maeve McCusker suggests that hidden places of memory have this ghostly quality throughout his writings: 'These places have a peculiarly spectral and uncanny quality in Chamoiseau's work, at once familiar and unfamiliar, representing what Freud would describe as that which "ought to remain hidden but which has come to light"', *Patrick Chamoiseau: Recovering Memory* (Liverpool: Liverpool University Press, 2007), p. 103. See also pp. 142–149 for a more detailed discussion of the uncanny in Chamoiseau's work.

39. 'dérivent vers de nouveaux sens', Chamoiseau and Hammadi, *Guyane*, p. 37.

40. 'La Trace-mémoires se lève des usures et des destructions chaotiques de bâtis, de matières et de sens', Chamoiseau and Hammadi, *Guyane*, p. 42. Chamoiseau switches between different terms for the memory-traces, sometimes putting *trace* and *memory* in the singular, sometimes in the plural. However, his preferred usage is to mix singular and plural, upper and lower case. In this instance, for example, *trace* is singular and with upper-case *T* while *memory* is plural with lower-case *m*. I will discuss the significance of this in the final section of the chapter.

41. Dylan Trigg affirms the spatio-temporal ambiguities of the ruins in his phenomenological study of memory and the sites of trauma: 'At the outset, we discover that the ruin is both polymorphous and temporally dynamic. That is, unlike the "felicitous" space that characterizes Bachelard's domestic enclosure, allowing time and space to coincide as unitary phenomenon, the formal features of the ruin are situated in an ambiguous zone, whereby what remains is defined by what is absent. With this ambiguity, the identity of place loses its certainty .... Instead of monumentalizing what remains, the ruin brings about a non-memory, a puncturing in spatio-temporal presence.' 'The Place of Trauma: Memory, Hauntings, and the Temporality of Ruins', *Memory Studies* 2, 1 (2009), p. 95.

42. 'Les Traces-mémoires du bagne sont brisées, diffuses, éparpillées. On ne peut pas les aborder comme on accosterait au fronton d'une abbaye cistercienne ou d'une église romane', Chamoiseau and Hammadi, *Guyane*, pp. 21–22.

43. Chamoiseau and Hammadi, *Guyane*, p. 22.

44. 'tout renvoie aux formes élémentaires et aux résonances de ces formes élémentaires : carrés, triangles, lignes droites et courbes, trapèzes, et leurs infinies conjonctions. Le fonctionnel côtoie l'abstrait, ce que l'on reconnaît pas ; ce qui apporte sens immédiat borde ce qui se dérobe, un bouillon primordial, une harmonie chaotique dont l'invariant premier demeure l'émotion du souvenir du bagne. Les usures provenant de l'abandon nouent cet assemblage selon l'esthétique imperceptible – mais souveraine – d'une nécessité intérieure', Chamoiseau and Hammadi, *Guyane*, pp. 41–42.

45. Chamoiseau has often defined the notion of memory-traces elsewhere (see for example, *Écrire en pays dominé* (Gallimard, 1997)). McCusker discusses his use of *trace* and *tracée* in relation to memory in *Patrick Chamoiseau: Recovering Memory* (Chapter 4, 'Memory Materialized: Traces of the Past', pp. 101–127). She cites Chamoiseau's definition of *trace-mémoires* in *Écrire en pays dominé* (p. 120): 'The Trace is a concrete mark: a drum, a tree, a boat, a basket, an area, a song, a path which leads out... *Memories* radiate out in the Trace, they inhabit it as an immaterial, emotionally charged presence. Their associations, *Memory-traces*, do not constitute monuments, nor do they crystallize to form a single memory: they are a play of interconnecting memories .... Their meanings are always in flux, not fixed into a single meaning like those of the monument' ('La Trace est marque concrète : tambour, arbre, bateau, panier, un quartier, une chanson, un sentier qui s'en va... Les *mémoires* irradient dans la Trace, elles l'habitent d'une présence-sans-matière offerte à l'émotion. Leurs associations, *Traces-mémoires*, ne font pas monuments, ni ne cristallisent une mémoire unique : elles sont le jeu des mémoires qui se sont emmêlées. ... Leurs significations demeurent évolutives, non-figées-univoques comme celles du monument'), p. 102.

46. Chamoiseau and Hammadi, *Guyane*, pp. 25, 27 and 39 respectively. See also pp. 24, 31, 37.

47. 'La chair sait user la pierre. À Saint-Laurent, ou dans les îles, il faut voir les usures. Ces marches brisées, ou incurvées, ce noir plus soutenu au bord des ouvertures, cette patine particulière qui témoigne d'un geste quotidien. La chair s'est faite sculpteur et peintre. Le frottement (l'affrontement) entre l'homme et la pierre, entre l'homme et la ferrure, était subtil. Il faut regarder les angles arrondis, supputer la férocité de ces grilles demeurées intactes sur lesquelles combien de chairs ont dû se fracasser. Il faut imaginer, dans les allées, ce centre rectiligne qui semble se souvenir des marches disciplinaires sous des charges de silence et d'angoisse', Chamoiseau and Hammadi, *Guyane*, p. 32.

48. 'la peau des murs'; 'le fer a pleuré sa rouille dans le bois'; '[d]ans la peau vivante des murs, parfois s'encastrent des prothèses de ferraille', Chamoiseau and Hammadi, *Guyane*, pp. 37, 38 and 41 respectively.

49. '*Camp de la transportation*. C'est écrit dessus. Camp. Transportation. Derrière ces termes se profilent des règles, des statuts, un classement de la souffrance, une voie tracée vers la mort ou la brisure. Qu'importe leur signification. Les deux mots accolés agissent comme des glyphes. Ce n'est plus une dénomination, c'est un clignotement de mémoires', Chamoiseau and Hammadi, *Guyane*, p. 25.

50. 'Les portes qui ne sont plus des portes, les gonds qui se questionnent, les fenêtres qui aspirent, les murs qui n'enferment rien, les ferrures tout soudain insolites... Il faudrait oublier ces mots-là et en trouver d'autres. Toutes ces significations initiales sont brusquement en équilibre tremblant dans le délitement de leurs sens premiers, une sorte d'effilochement que suscite la divagation de mon avancée et celle de mon esprit. Je suis disponible pour les sensations', Chamoiseau and Hammadi, *Guyane*, p. 44.

51. 'Et me voilà dans ces Traces-mémoires du bagne de Guyane, non pas en visite mais en errance, non pas en flânerie mais en divagation', Chamoiseau and Hammadi, *Guyane*, p. 43.

52. Chamoiseau and Hammadi, *Guyane*, p. 25.

53. 'Ici, le conservateur sera de l'engeance des poètes. Et la conservation sera une poétique', Chamoiseau and Hammadi, *Guyane*, p. 45. The influence of Baudelaire is particularly evident in Chamoiseau's depiction of the ambiguous position of the poet, caught between preservation and the ravages of time, sifting the confused bric-a-brac for traces of those exiled and crushed by history (see *Le Cygne*).

54. 'Il vaut mieux résister à l'écriture historique sur le bagne et tenter d'en percevoir ce que les Traces-mémoires nous murmurent', Chamoiseau and Hammadi, *Guyane*, pp. 23–24.

55. 'les résonances viennent de partout, de la couleur, de la matière, de la pierre, du fer, de l'ombre, des éclats de lumière', Chamoiseau and Hammadi, *Guyane*, p. 42. Godard's description of his own method in *Histoire(s) du cinéma* is strikingly similar to that employed by Chamoiseau and Hammadi here: 'with words, sounds, stones, colours, so that the space constructed might last beyond time' ('avec des mots, des sons, des pierres, des couleurs, à fin que l'espace mis en forme dure au-delà des âges'), Chapter 2b.

56. 'en constante évolution, en ramifications diffuses', Chamoiseau and Hammadi, *Guyane*, p. 17.

57. 'Mais les Traces-mémoires d'aujourd'hui ne témoignent pas que de l'histoire du bagne. ... Elles se sont, au fil du temps, chargées d'indéfinissables mémoires. Elles ont associé de longs soupirs moussus à la vitalité forestière qui semble aujourd'hui leur nouer un écrin. L'édifice devient ruine, et la ruine devient mémoires-ouvertes par une autonastie résultant d'une accumulation invisible', Chamoiseau and Hammadi, *Guyane*, pp. 23–24.

58. Chamoiseau and Hammadi, *Guyane*, p. 39.
59. 'Ces édifices étaient des lieux d'enfermement, des espaces de sécurité, des camps forestiers, des ateliers d'activité artisanales, hangars, fours, parcs animaliers, hôpitaux et services administratifs'; 'Camp. Transportation. … [U]n classement de la souffrance, une voie tracée vers la mort ou la brisure', Chamoiseau and Hammadi, *Guyane*, pp. 18 and 25 respectively.
60. 'relents de soupes aigres'; 'la soupe était diurétique', Chamoiseau and Hammadi, *Guyane*, p. 27; Cayrol, 'Nuit et brouillard (commentaire)', p. 27.
61. 'des fours à chaux ou des fours à charbon', Chamoiseau and Hammadi, *Guyane*, p. 28.
62. 'ongles qui griffaient les murs', Chamoiseau and Hammadi, *Guyane*, p. 28; 'ce plafond labouré par les ongles', Cayrol, 'Nuit et brouillard (commentaire)', p. 38.
63. 'une herbe folle qui s'obstine dans la pierre', Chamoiseau and Hammadi, *Guyane*, p. 32; 'une drôle d'herbe [qui] a poussé et recouvert la terre'; 'l'herbe fidèle [qui] est venue à nouveau sur les appel-platz autour des blocks', Cayrol, 'Nuit et brouillard (commentaire)', pp. 18 and 42.
64. 'la fièvre avide de leur regard. Comme si l'ultime énergie du vouloir-vivre installait ses assises dans la liberté fragile des yeux'; 'On a déjà vu cela dans d'autres camps de désespoirs', Chamoiseau and Hammadi, *Guyane*, p. 30; 'À la fin, tous les déportés se ressemblent. Ils s'alignent sur un modèle sans âge qui meurt les yeux ouverts', Cayrol, 'Nuit et brouillard (commentaire)', p. 33.
65. 'une masse hagarde, numérotée, s'écoulant confondue dans l'uniforme rayée – toute humanité déshumanisée'; 'Les chiffres se mêlent aux dessins, aux éraflures, aux mousses noirâtres, ils parachèvent la peau du mur d'un tatouage inquiétant. Pas de nom d'hommes, pas d'adresse : des chiffres'; 'Nuit dans la case commune'; 'La nuit est effrayante', Chamoiseau and Hammadi, *Guyane*, pp. 31, 35, 37 and 40 respectively.
66. 'J'entends le pas de la botte régulière'; 'ce centre rectiligne qui semble se souvenir des marches disciplinaire sous des charges de silence et d'angoisse', Chamoiseau and Hammadi, *Guyane*, pp. 29 and 32.
67. 'Quand on revient sur ses pas, les significations ne sont pas les mêmes, lumières et ombres ont évolué, d'autres détails apparaissent, d'autres importances se gonflent, d'autres odeurs et d'autres températures s'élèvent des couleurs, tout reste vivant et sollicite l'esprit', Chamoiseau and Hammadi, *Guyane*, p. 42.
68. 'Et le pas se fait si lourd que les marches, brisées en leur centre depuis longtemps, semblent s'effondrer encore sous le pied qui hésite', Chamoiseau and Hammadi, *Guyane*, p. 41.
69. 'Et le sol en témoigne : de terre, de pierre, de ciment, il a été l'ami de bien des épaves humaines', Chamoiseau and Hammadi, *Guyane*, p. 36.
70. See the photographs on pp. 47, 52, 55, 58–59, 63, 65, 73, 84, 87–89 and 108–109.
71. See the photographs on pp. 62 and 68–69.
72. See the photographs on pp. 54, 62, 112 and 113.
73. 'Cellules'; 'Blockhaus'; 'Bibliothèque'; 'Prétoire'; 'Quartier disciplinaire', Chamoiseau and Hammadi, *Guyane*, pp. 52, 82–83, 86, 88 and 89 respectively.
74. Chamoiseau and Hammadi, *Guyane*, pp. 98–99.
75. 'un cri généreux'; 'une stèle troublante', Chamoiseau and Hammadi, *Guyane*, pp. 40 and 43.
76. Lorna Milne, *Patrick Chamoiseau: Espaces d'une écriture antillaise* (Amsterdam and New York: Rodopi, 2006), pp. 44–49.
77. Rose, *Mourning Becomes the Law*. See chapter 2, 'Beginnings of the Day: Fascism and Representation' (pp. 41–62), p. 42.
78. Defining our paradoxical situation as caught between the poles of '[t]he representation of Fascism and the fascism of representation', Rose critiques simplistic portrayals of the opposition between oppressors and oppressed: '[t]he representation of Fascism

and the fascism of representation does not work with the opposition between the agent of imperial domination and the oppressed other. It points out that "the other" is also an agent, enraged and invested; while the idea of the monolithic, imperialist agent amounts to the consolidation and reification of power, the dilemma of which is thereby disowned. The representation of Fascism and the fascism of representation does not oppose the idea of totalizing power to the degrading of its others, nor does it propose cultural pluralism as its expiation. It understands all agents *in power and out of it* to face the dilemma of asserting their moral will solely to guard their particular interests.' Rose, *Mourning Becomes the Law*, p. 62.

79. 'un concentré hallucinant de ce qui fait l'homme : déflagrations d'ombres et de lumières, de lumières dans l'ombre et d'ombres qui éclairent', Chamoiseau and Hammadi, *Guyane*, p. 19.

80. 'Le forçat et le gardien se retrouvaient liés dans le même hoquet où la démesure du désir de survivre et la toute-puissance du pouvoir de punir entraînaient, pour l'un et pour l'autre, un pourrissement égal', *Guyane*, pp. 29–30.

81. 'Dans le camp de la transportation ... il faut s'arrêter dans ces ombres, et attendre ce témoignage d'une collusion morbide entre le forçat et l'ombre'; 'J'avoue que l'ombre était complice et que la lumière ne l'était pas toujours', Chamoiseau and Hammadi, *Guyane*, pp. 33 and 34 respectively.

82. 'La Trace-mémoires est à la fois collective et individuelle, verticale et horizontale, de communauté et trans-communautaire, immuable et mobile, et fragile', Chamoiseau and Hammadi, *Guyane*, p. 17.

83. Cited in Milne, *Patrick Chamoiseau: Espaces d'une écriture antillaise*, p. 182. Stones appear in the quote by Victor Segalen that Chamoiseau uses as a preface to *Guyane*: 'Alone, immobile against the tide, here are the memorial Stones that no order of erosion can touch or loosen. They remain.' As McCusker says of stones in Chamoiseau's work, emphasizing the ambiguous temporality in his writing, '[t]hese ancient formations are at once outside time and deeply imbricated in it; they suggest a connection to a time beyond memory, while they simultaneously – by virtue of their very age and physical scale – encourage reflection on the past. It is through their timelessness, indeed, that they can be made to speak to every time' (*Patrick Chamoiseau: Recovering Memory*, p. 117).

Chapter 7

COSMOPOLITICAL MEMORY

In recent years there has been a growing body of work on the nature of memory in a transnational, transcultural and global age. Marianne Hirsch's felicitous term 'postmemory' provides us with a way of viewing memory uncoupled from its attachment to direct personal experience:

> Postmemory is a powerful and very particular form of memory precisely because its connection to its object or source is mediated not through recollection but through an imaginative investment and creation .... Postmemory characterizes the experience of those who grow up dominated by narratives that preceded their birth, whose own belated stories are evacuated by the stories of the previous generation shaped by traumatic events.[1]

Although specifically designating the memories of trauma received by children of survivors of the Holocaust, 'postmemory' nevertheless offers a more general way of understanding the deterritorialized nature of memory in a postmodern age. Andreas Huyssen notes how, in this global space of accelerated information flows, the Holocaust 'loses its quality as index of the specific historical event and begins to function as metaphor for other traumatic histories and memories'.[2] Alison Landsberg uses the term 'prosthetic memory' to describe a process in which 'the person does not simply apprehend a historical narrative but takes on a more personal, deeply felt memory of a past event through which he or she did not live'.[3] Aleida Assmann and Sebastian Conrad ask some of the important questions that arise from this new state of affairs:

> How are memories transformed, mutually eclipsed and politically contested as they reach a wider audience and move into a supranational arena of attention? How do memories spread and travel around the world? How are memories changed when they transcend their former habitat and move into the framework of global spectatorship, traffic and commerce? What role do the new media play in the construction and transmission of memories in a world of growing interconnectedness and intervisuality?[4]

New conditions clearly pose threats but also create new chances. The work of Daniel Levy and Natan Sznaider on the globalization of Holocaust memory shows that, although the disembedding of the Holocaust from its specific context risks losing its grounding in local personal and social histories, its transformation into what they call a 'cosmopolitan memory' can, nevertheless, also serve as a humanitarian and moral compass for victims of trauma in other sites of racialized violence.[5] However, for some, the use of Holocaust memory as a lesson for us all constitutes a new form of hegemony in the competitive memory stakes, and even a new manifestation of an old form of Western imperialism over the rest of the world.[6] The vicarious nature of memory once it loses its indexical link and becomes part of a global past is also double-edged. Although the imaginative and emotional investment in others' traumas may allow for new solidarities across the lines of race, nation and culture (as Landsberg suggests), the danger consists in banalization and revisionism, the umbilical cord attaching recollection to the original experience having been cut and the line between authenticity and construction (or reality and fiction) having become increasingly blurred. Moreover, we risk clothing ourselves in others' victimhood, which we have neither experienced nor properly understood, for the purpose of identity and, consequently, participating in a banal culture of empathy which is often more self- than other-oriented. Commenting on Cathy Caruth's statement that 'in a catastrophic age … trauma itself may provide the very link between cultures', Nancy Wood highlights the 'limits of the analogical enterprise' as follows: 'If we are all nominated as History's "survivors", merely by virtue of living vicariously through and after traumatic events, we risk diminishing the "incomprehensible pain" that real survivors of this century's catastrophes have suffered'.[7]

The seepage of traumatic memories into mass popular culture thus risks normalizing horror and reducing it to the saccharine content of a sugar-coated pill (hence Claude Lanzmann's opposition to a film like Steven Spielberg's *Schindler's List*). In her discussion of the ways in which images of horror have now become assimilated into the cultural mainstream, Libby Saxton cites Antoine de Baecque's observations on the legacy of a concentrationary iconography derived from the first images of the camps: 'Modern cinema was born out of those images, which have been ceaselessly at work in it, resurfacing in other forms, the to-camera look, the freeze-frame, documentary in fiction, the flashback, montage, contemplation, malaise, those specifically cinematographic figures that testify to the obsessive presence of the concentrationary palimpsest'.[8] Saxton also cites Gérard Wajcman who claims that it is not only representations of the body but the image in general that has been violated by those images from the camps: 'Today it is impossible to eliminate from the image of a body the resonance of the attack on the human image perpetrated in the gas chambers …. Images are no longer as they were before.'[9] This would be the realization of Resnais and Cayrol's worst fear: instead of being able to recognize and challenge the continued presence of the concentrationary universe in our midst, our culture has become saturated with its devices, strategies and iconography to such an extent that we are largely unaware and ignorant of its presence. Clearly this draws on the wider discussion of the camp as the new *nomos* of modern society associated with the ideas of Giorgio Agamben. In terms of cultural memory, these ideas suggest that a major danger today is a new amnesia in which shock, recognition and 'readability', essential for a politics of representation, have given way to the normalization of horror in contemporary society.[10]

These are very real problems arising from the new transmission, transformation and circulation of memories in an age of information technology. The synchronization of memories through new technologies risks dissolving uniqueness, singularity and plurality, which (coupled with spontaneity) were, for Hannah Arendt, the foundation stones of the human. In *La Transparence du mal*, Jean Baudrillard talks of the loss of a sense of history and reality in a media age, overtaken by the endless circulation of simulacra that bombard the senses and deny access to the real.[11] If this is indeed an accurate reflection of our condition today, then the memory-traces that Freud locates as deposited in the unconscious might simply be the recording of perceptions of simulations rather than the traces of real experience. As Geoffrey Hartman observes, '[t]his reality-loss Baudrillard links to our very capacity, now hugely expanded, for retrieving and disseminating knowledge: we gain a global information technology but it transmits images that could be simulacra'.[12] Hartman also reminds us that Walter Benjamin warned us of this loss of 'aura' long ago in his famous 1936 essay 'The Work of Art in the Age of Mechanical Reproduction'. The urbanist and cultural critic Paul Virilio has long argued that the homogenization of time through instantaneous information flows is the new form of totalitarian power in that it removes the space for reflection required for a genuine political and democratic culture to survive. The synchronization of modern time consciousness is the hypermodern logic of the camp mentality and forms the new tyranny of the subject. The philosopher Bernard Stiegler takes up many of Virilio's ideas in his critique of the industrialized synthesis of memory in societies in which the logic of production, consumption and exchange are the single overriding exigency in a globalized market. This is a dystopic (even 'catastrophist') vision in which memory has become detached from any sense of human subjectivity and forms part of a new totalizing power.[13]

By arguing in this book that palimpsestic memory synchronizes (or spatializes) memory traces from different sites of extreme violence (and by means of the very avant-garde techniques that Virilio sees as destructive of the human in modern art), I am proposing a model which risks endorsing the negative consequences outlined above. However, we need to clarify the terms of the debate about memory in a transnational, transcultural and information age. When the debate is framed in terms of what happens to local memories (or 'unique' memories) in a global age (How are they transformed? What is the role of new media? and so on), the risk is to assume the singularity, autonomy, specificity and authenticity of the memory in the first place (and its attachment to a specific individual or ethnocultural/national community) before mediatization and globalization refashioned it. Does 'Holocaust memory', for example, only become problematic when it moves from the particular to the universal via new channels of communication or was it always a problematic (or hybrid) category in the first place? If one views singularity and generality, and local and global not as binary opposites but as part of an ambivalent space of 'relationality' between sameness and difference, then the terms of the debate are not so clear-cut. The discussion of overlapping and interconnected traces in the work of all the writers and film-makers considered in this book clearly unsettles the autonomy, sovereignty and authenticity of memory and its connection to identity and community. It is not simply a question of how memory becomes pluralized, transformed or homogenized in a supranational space of accelerated information flows; it is also a question of rethinking the notion of the uniqueness, autonomy and homogeneity of individual and collective memory at a local level; in other words, challenging the formulations of Maurice Halbwachs, and then Pierre Nora, on the social construction of collective memory.[14] As I mentioned in chapter 4, the 'authenticity' and 'uniqueness' of traumatic recollection are themselves problematic, in part due to the very nature of testimony itself (which can never grasp the completeness of the original experience), in part due to the fact that memory is inevitably channelled through symbolic structures (that is, through structures that contain the traces of numerous elsewheres). The distinction between testimony and cultural memory (or, in Benjamin's terms, authenticity and reproduction) then becomes blurred, as Hirsch's idea of postmemory implies. Cultural memory is, by its very nature, a mediated and imagined form, whether it springs from direct or indirect experience.

This blurring of the distinction between lived and vicarious memory is perhaps one of the most vexed issues in an age of information overload, as Baudrillard, Virilio and many others have warned. Is it possible to maintain the specificity of the testimony of those who, as Rousset and Antelme say, feel the traumatic experience 'in their bones' while recognizing, at the same time, that the inscription of their experience draws it into the wider sphere of the circulation, transmission and reception of memory which affects us all? We need to be able to perceive these distinctions in terms other than those of absolute opposites. Let us remember that Derrida's critique of Freud's understanding of the memory-trace was precisely from the point of view of unsettling the notion of an autonomous subject prior to the traces of *'écriture'*. A broader way of framing the above question would perhaps be to ask, How can we maintain the distinction between memory and history (or the particular and the universal) while acknowledging their overlaps? This clearly requires a non-binary way of understanding memory, one which, as Huyssen observes, is in keeping with 'a new paradigm of thinking about time and space, history and geography'.[15] Perceiving memory as a palimpsest in the Derridean sense of a non-foundational interconnection of memory traces is a response to this question.

This would then be to suggest that the unique and the general, and the individual and the collective, are neither different nor the same but occupy a third space which, as Landsberg suggests in her definition of 'prosthetic memory', 'blur[s] the boundary between individual and collective memory [and] complicate[s] the distinction between memory and history'.[16] This does not deny the ways in which memory is transformed in an age of globalized information technologies; but it does suggest that the notion on which this argument often rests – namely, the loss of the singularity and uniqueness of memory – needs to be rethought. Memory has always been synchronous in a sense (as I have argued here) but synchronicity does not inevitably mean homogeneity and the path towards a totalizing mentality. Godard's montage in *Histoire(s) du cinéma* juxtaposes and superimposes a bewildering number of different images from different times and places, not to homogenize them but to place them in a dynamic, creative and open-ended relationship. As Didi-Huberman notes, following Benjamin, '[t]o make a montage does not mean to assimilate'.[17] Jacques Aumont says, in relation to Godard's *Histoire(s)*, that it is 'through montage that the cinema has access to reality, and also to memory'.[18] The connections that constitute this version of memory counter totalizing forms and new processes of amnesia rather than nourish them because the resulting relations form a disturbing and ambivalent knowledge. Memory as ambivalence is precisely what Godard's 1965 film *Alphaville* posits as the enemy of Virilio's bleak, dystopic vision of totalizing and homogenizing thought (or non-thought).[19] Can memory still be on the side of human freedom and thought or is it inevitably recuperated within the new processes of control, amnesia and denial of the human?

In an address to UNESCO in May 1991, Derrida reconsidered Kant's ideas on cosmopolitanism from a post-Kantian point of view. Derrida refashioned the teleological, state-bound, juridical and Eurocentric bias of Kant's cosmopolitanism, rejected the binary opposition between universalism and particularism upon which it is founded, and argued, ultimately, for a cosmopolitics based on an openness to the other and a new understanding of singularity. Fundamental to this vision is precisely the non-foundational interconnection of memory traces mentioned above. As Derrida noted in his address,

[p]hilosophy does not have one single memory. In its Greek name and its European memory, it has always been bastard, hybrid, grafted, multilinear

and polyglot; we must adjust our practice of the history of philosophy, of history and philosophy to this reality which was also an opportunity and which remains more than ever an opportunity.[20]

What Derrida says of the memory of philosophy could be said of memory in general. Whereas cosmopolitanism can only reproduce an Enlightenment view of the human and human society, Derrida's 'cosmopolitics' would relate to a post-Enlightenment 'democracy-to-come' (on a philosophical, ethical and political level). Viewed in this light, the globalization of Holocaust memory described by Levy and Sznaider would indeed be a 'cosmopolitan' memory in that it would assume a number of Enlightenment precepts, and would therefore not gesture to the sort of 'bastard, hybrid, grafted, multilinear and polyglot' memory described by Derrida.[21]

My consideration of works on extreme violence in this book through the lens of 'palimpsestic memory' has attempted to suggest that ambivalent connections between the particular and the universal may allow us to elaborate a post-Enlightenment version of memory and the human. In this sense, following Derrida, it could be called a 'cosmopolitical' memory. Benjamin's 'image' or 'constellation' had already gestured towards such a vision. All the works that I have discussed refashion the singularity of memory without collapsing it into an old universalism. They challenge our versions of discrete space and linear time, not to abandon us to thoughtless immersion in the new global flow of the instant but, on the contrary, to open up the instant to history. Landsberg is right to note that '[m]emory is not commonly imagined as a site of possibility for progressive politics'.[22] However, if the minimum requirement for a progressive politics is a space in which thought and dialogue can take place, then the poetics of palimpsestic memory can be an integral part of the 'democracy-to-come' (or what Agamben calls 'the new politics, which remains largely to be invented').[23] It would be neither individualist nor communitarian but would recognize the interconnections and the differences between individuals and groups. It would allow us to question the links between race, memory and identity in today's commemorative culture and hence challenge the basis of competition and conflict between 'communities'. And it would counter the normalization of horror by providing us with tools for exposing the strategies by which it has seeped unconsciously into popular culture. Like Arendt's fearful imagination and Cayrol's concentrationary art, it would make the present tremble by revealing the traces of elsewhere.[24]

The art of memory outlined in this study resembles our transformed perceptions of synchronous time and compressed space but gives us a critical lens through which to perceive identity and community, the moment and history in a 'liquid modern' world.[25] It provides no guarantee against reductive, commodified, instrumentalist or amnesia-inducing versions of our past. And it requires us to imagine a new, ethical site of memory once memory is no longer the property of an autonomous subject. At the very least, however, it offers an alternative vision of a critical space of relationality, without which the bleak prognostications on the future of 'the human' might well prove to be accurate. A paradigm of hybrid and overlapping rather than separate pasts, between the particular and the universal – a 'cosmopolitical' memory – could serve as a model for imagining new democratic solidarities in the future across the lines of race and nation commensurate with the interconnected world of the new millennium.

Notes

1. Hirsch, *Family Frames*, p. 22.
2. Huyssen, *Present Pasts*, p. 13.
3. Alison Landsberg, *Prosthetic Memory: The Transformation of American Remembrance in the Age of Mass Culture* (New York: Columbia University Press, 2004), p. 2.
4. Aleida Assmann and Sebastian Conrad, 'Introduction' in Aleida Assmann and Sebastian Conrad (eds), *Memory in a Global Age: Discourses, Practices and Trajectories* (London and New York: Palgrave Macmillan, 2010), p. 6.
5. See Daniel Levy and Natan Sznaider, 'Memory Unbound: The Holocaust and the Formation of Cosmopolitan Memory', *European Journal of Social Theory* 5, 1 (2002), 87–106, and *The Holocaust and Memory in the Global Age* (Philadelphia: Temple University Press, 2006).
6. See for example Brossat, *L'Épreuve du désastre*. Michael Bernstein characterizes the globalization of Holocaust memory as a new form of universalism (in fact, the last remaining universalism) in an age of catastrophe: 'In a sense, we are hypnotized by what one could call a monotheistic ideology of catastrophe. In such a view, there must be one exemplary cataclysm, one form of savagery unmatched by any others because only through a single, all-persuasive and all-sufficient instantiation of evil can the one truth about human nature emerge. To believe that different truths and conclusions arise in different contexts, and that each of these has an only local, and none a global, validity does not pitch the rhetorical or ideological stakes sufficiently high for a culture like ours, so deeply in love with the pathos of universalism' ('Homage to the Extreme: The Shoah and the Rhetoric of Catastrophe', *Times Literary Supplement* 4953 (6 March 1998), p. 7).
7. Wood, *Vectors of Memory*, p. 193. In *Le Juif imaginaire*, Alain Finkielkraut makes a similar criticism of the famous chant of solidarity with the oppressed, 'We are all German Jews' ('Nous sommes tous des juifs allemands'), by students in the 1968 demonstrations and sees this appropriation of the term 'Jew' as a sign of an instrumentalist use of the past for a superficial identity politics. However, Maurice Blanchot saw this chant as a sign of a new politics of refusal of humanist versions of identity. (See Blanchot's *Écrits politiques 1958–1993* (Gallimard, 2008). For an interesting discussion of the different responses by Finkielkraut and Blanchot to the 1968 slogan, see Sarah Hammerschlag, *The Figural Jew: Politics and Identity in Postwar French Thought* (Chicago: Chicago University Press, 2010), pp. 192–200.) Berthold Molden's discussion of the use of the Holocaust by left-wing intellectuals and activists at the time of the Vietnam War (Jean-Paul Sartre, Che Guevara, Stokeley Carmichael and others) highlights the interconnections at the time between critiques of colonialism, genocide and totalitarianism, and the composite

rather than compartmentalized approach to the notion of oppression and liberation embraced by the civil rights and counter-cultural generation around the world (see Berthold Molden, 'Vietnam, the New Left and the Holocaust: How the Cold War Changed Discourse on Genocide' in Assmann and Conrad (eds), *Memory in a Global Age*, pp. 79–96).

8. Antoine de Baecque, 'Premières images des camps: Quel cinéma après Auschwitz?', *Cahiers du cinéma* (November 2000), special issue, p. 66, cited in Saxton, *Haunted Images*, p. 4.

9. Gérard Wajcman, *L'Objet du siècle* (1998), p. 25, cited in Saxton, *Haunted Images*, p. 4.

10. Griselda Pollock and I have formulated the idea of a 'concentrationary imaginary' which has seeped into popular culture. Unlike Cayrol's concentrationary art, which was equipped to detect and expose the persistence of the concentrationary universe in contemporary society (see chapter 2), culture today has assimilated the concentrationary *'décor'* (to use Cayrol's word) but frequently fails to expose the horror which lurks behind it.

11. Jean Baudrillard, *La Transparence du mal* (Galilée, 1990).

12. Geoffrey H. Hartman, 'Introduction: Darkness Visible' in Hartman (ed.), *Holocaust Remembrance*, p. 11.

13. I am grateful to Ian James for these observations.

14. See for example Maurice Halbwachs, *Les Cadres sociaux de la mémoire* (Presses Universitaires de France, 1952), with *La Topographie légendaire des évangiles en terre sainte: Étude de mémoire collective* (Presses Universitaires de France, 1941), translated as *On Collective Memory* (Chicago: University of Chicago Press, 1992); Nora, *Les Lieux de mémoire*. Levy and Sznaider point out the irony in Nora's regret at the loss of memory today, when 'no longer is the nation-state the uncontested privileged site for the articulation of collective identity', as this was the very criticism aimed at the nation itself when, in the course of the nineteenth century, it displaced local communities as the container of collective memory. The nation, they argue, is no more 'authentic' as a community than the global in that both have to be 'imagined' to exist. However, having criticized the notion of a dichotomy between 'authentic' and 'imagined' communities underpinning the distinction between national and global memory, they then seem to re-institute (uncritically) the very same dichotomy to support Jan Assmann's distinction 'between communicative memory, based on group-specific carriers ... and cultural memories that can exist independent of its carriers'. As I argue here, this distinction (between 'experience' and 'representation') is as problematic as the one between 'authentic' and 'imagined' (Levy and Sznaider, 'Memory Unbound', pp. 90 and 91 respectively).

15. Huyssen, *Present Pasts*, p. 4.

16. Landsberg, *Prosthetic Memory*, p. 19.

17. 'monter n'est pas assimiler', Didi-Huberman, *Images malgré tout*, p. 190 / *Images in Spite of All*, p. 151.

18. 'en montant que le cinéma atteint la réalité, et aussi la mémoire', Jacques Aumont, *Amnésies: Fictions du cinéma d'après Jean-Luc Godard* (P.O.L., 1999), p. 165.

19. Virilio believes that cinema can *only* be on the side of 'non-thought' and is, ultimately, the ideological weapon of the military-industrial complex that dominates our lives: 'The cinema is not a new agora, a forum designed for civil and social life where migrants from around the world can enter into solidarity and communication, but rather a cenotaph' ('La salle de cinéma n'est pas une nouvelle agora, un forum destiné aux vivants de la Cité, où pourraient se rejoindre et communiquer des migrants venus du monde entier, mais bien un cénotaphe'), Paul Virilio, *Guerre et cinéma 1: Logistique de la perception* (Éditions de l'Étoile, 1984), p. 51.

20. 'La philosophie n'a pas une seule mémoire. Sous son nom grec et dans sa mémoire européenne, elle a toujours été bâtarde, hybride, greffée, multilinéaire, polyglotte et il nous faut ajuster notre pratique de l'histoire de la philosophie, de l'histoire et de la philosophie, à cette réalité qui fut aussi une chance et qui reste plus que jamais une chance', Jacques Derrida, *Le Droit à la philosophie du point de vue cosmopolitique* (Editions Verdier/UNESCO, 1997), p. 33. See also Jacques Derrida, *Cosmopolites de tous les pays, encore un effort!* (Galilée, 1997) / *On Cosmopolitanism*, trans. Mark Dooley, in Jacques Derrida, *On Cosmopolitanism and Forgiveness* (London: Routledge, 2001).

21. I would therefore endorse Rothberg's critique of the paradigm of 'cosmopolitan memory' proposed by Levy and Sznaider: 'Although highlighting universality, globalization, and cosmopolitanism, these critics narrate the history of Holocaust memory solely from the perspective of supposedly autonomous changes in the Holocaust's meanings. They subsequently occlude the active role that other histories and memories have played in stimulating many of those changes. Their "universalist" arguments are thus decidedly local and even occasionally parochial. By overlooking Holocaust memory's dialogic interactions with the legacies of colonialism, decolonization, racialization, and slavery, they not only simplify the history of Holocaust memory, they also end up producing a notion of morality that remains too singular and abstractly universal' (*Multidirectional Memory*, p. 265).

22. Landsberg, *Prosthetic Memory*, p. 141.

23. Agamben, *Homo Sacer*, p. 11.

24. As Édouard Glissant says, 'the world trembles, creolizes' ('le monde tremble, se créolise'), Édouard Glissant, *La Cohée du Lamentin: Poétique V* (Gallimard, 2005), p. 75.

25. Zygmunt Bauman, *Liquid Modernity* (Cambridge: Polity, 2000).

BIBLIOGRAPHY

(The place of publication of all French works cited is Paris unless otherwise stated.)

Agamben, Giorgio, *Homo Sacer: Sovereign Power and Bare Life* (Stanford: Stanford University Press, 1998 [1995]).

Alleg, Henri, *La Question* (Minuit, 1961).

Antelme, Robert, *L'Espèce humaine* (Gallimard, 1957 [1947]) / *The Human Race*, trans. Jeffrey Haight and Annie Mahler (Marlboro, Vermont: The Marlboro Press, 1992).

Arendt, Hannah, 'The Concentration Camps', *Partisan Review* 15 (1948), 743–763.

———, *The Origins of Totalitarianism* (London: Allen and Unwin, 1967).

———, 'Introduction. Walter Benjamin: 1892–1940' in Walter Benjamin, *Illuminations* (London: Collins-Fontana Books, 1973), pp. 7–58.

Assmann, Aleida and Sebastian Conrad, 'Introduction' in Aleida Assmann and Sebastian Conrad (eds), *Memory in a Global Age: Discourses, Practices and Trajectories* (London and New York: Palgrave Macmillan, 2010), pp. 1–16.

Aumont, Jacques, *Amnésies: Fictions du cinéma d'après Jean-Luc Godard* (P.O.L., 1999).

Bailbé, Claude, Michel Marie and Marie-Claire Ropars, *Muriel: Histoire d'une recherche* (Galilée, 1974).

Barthes, Roland, *La Chambre claire: Note sur la photographie* (Seuil, 1980).

———, 'Un Prolongement à la littérature de l'absurde', *Combat*, 21 September 1950, reprinted in *Jean Cayrol: Œuvre lazaréenne* (Seuil, 2007), pp. 761–762.

Bartov, Omer, *Mirrors of Destruction: War, Genocide, and Modern Identity* (Oxford and New York: Oxford University Press, 2000).

Bataille, Georges, *Critique*, 12 May 1947.

Baudrillard, Jean, *La Transparence du mal* (Galilée, 1990).

Bauman, Zygmunt, *Modernity and the Holocaust* (New York: Cornell University Press, 1989).

———, *Modernity and Ambivalence* (Cambridge: Polity, 1991).

———, *Liquid Modernity* (Cambridge: Polity, 2000).

Bazin, André, 'Le Mythe de Staline dans le cinéma soviétique' in *Qu'est-ce que le cinéma? 1* (Éditions du Cerf, 1958).

Beckett, Samuel and Georges Duthuit, *Proust, and, Three Dialogues* (London: Calder, 1965).

Bellour, Raymond, *L'Entre-images 2: Mots, images* (P.O.L., 1999).

Benjamin, Walter, 'Ninth Thesis on the Philosophy of History' in *Illuminations* (London: Collins-Fontana Books, 1973), p. 249.

———, 'On Some Motifs in Baudelaire' in *Illuminations* (London: Collins-Fontana Books, 1973), pp. 152–196.

———, 'The Image of Proust' in *Illuminations* (London: Collins-Fontana Books, 1973), pp. 197–210.

———, *The Arcades Project* (Cambridge, Mass.: Belknap Press of Harvard University Press, 1999).

Bennington, Geoffrey, 'Double Tonguing: Derrida's Monolingualism', *Tympanum* 4 (2000), http://www.usc.edu/dept/comp-lit/tympanum/4/bennington.html.

Bennington, Geoffrey and Jacques Derrida, *Jacques Derrida* (Chicago: Chicago University Press, 1993).

Bernasconi, Robert, 'When the Real Crime Began: Hannah Arendt's *The Origins of Totalitarianism* and the Dignity of the Western Philosophical Tradition' in Richard H. King and Dan Stone (eds), *Hannah Arendt and the Uses of History: Imperialism, Nation, Race and Genocide* (Oxford and New York: Berghahn, 2007), pp. 54–67.

Bernstein, Michael, 'Homage to the Extreme: The Shoah and the Rhetoric of Catastrophe', *Times Literary Supplement* 4953 (6 March 1998), 6–8.

Bersani, Leo and Ulysse Dutoit, *Arts of Impoverishment: Beckett, Rothko, Resnais* (Cambridge, Mass.: Harvard University Press, 1993).

Beugnet, Martine, 'Blind Spot', *Screen* 48, 2 (2007), 227–231.

Blanchot, Maurice, 'Les Justes', *L'Observateur* (20 July 1950), reprinted in Jean Cayrol, *Jean Cayrol: Œuvre lazaréenne* (Seuil, 2007), pp. 759–760.

———, *Écrits politiques 1958–1993* (Gallimard, 2008).

Bonn, Charles, *Lecture présente de Mohammed Dib* (Alger: ENAL, 1988).

———, 'Les Pouvoirs du langage' in *Mohammed Dib, Itinéraires et contacts de culture*, vols 21–22 (L'Harmattan, 1996), pp. 149–168.

Britton, Celia, 'Broken Images in Resnais's *Muriel*', *French Cultural Studies* 1 (1990), 37–46.

Brossat, Alain, *L'Épreuve du désastre: Le XXe siècle et les camps* (Albin Michel, 1998).

———, 'Massacres et génocides: Les Conditions du récit' in Catherine Coquio (ed.), *Parler des camps, penser les génocides* (Albin Michel/Idées, 1999), pp. 161–168.

Burgelin, Claude, *Georges Perec* (Seuil, 1988).

———, 'Perec et la Judéité: Une Transmission paradoxale', *Revue d'Histoire de la Shoah* 176 (2002) (special issue 'La Shoah dans la littérature française'), 167–182.

Calle-Gruber, Mireille, *Assia Djebar ou la résistance de l'écriture* (Maisonneuve et Larose, 2001).

Calle-Gruber, Mireille (ed.), *Assia Djebar, Nomade entre les murs…: Pour une poétique transfrontalière* (Maisonneuve et Larose, 2005).

Caruth, Cathy, *Unclaimed Experience: Trauma, Narrative and History* (Baltimore and London: Johns Hopkins University Press, 1996).

Castant, Alexandre, 'Histoire(s) du (son du) cinéma' in 'Où en est le God-Art?', *CinémAction* 109 (2003), 206–210.

Cayrol, Jean, 'Nous avons conçu *Nuit et Brouillard* comme un dispositif d'alerte', *Lettres françaises*, 15 February 1956, reprinted in Jacques Gerber, *Anatole Dauman, Argos Films: Souvenir d'écran* (Centre Georges Pompidou, 1989), p. 101.

_____, 'De la vie à la mort' in *Nuit et brouillard* (Fayard, 1997), pp. 45–114.

_____, 'Nuit et brouillard (commentaire)' in *Nuit et brouillard* (Fayard, 1997), pp. 17–43.

_____, *Jean Cayrol: Œuvre lazaréenne* (Seuil, 2007).

_____, 'Préambule' to 'Les Rêves lazaréens' in *Lazare parmi nous* in *Jean Cayrol: Œuvre lazaréenne* (Seuil, 2007).

Cayrol, Jean and Claude Durand, *Le Droit de regard* (Seuil, 1963).

Césaire, Aimé, *Discours sur le colonialisme* (Présence Africaine, 2004 [1955]) / *Discourse on Colonialism*, trans. Joan Pinkham (New York: Monthly Review Press, 2000 [1972]).

Chambers, Iain and Lidia Curti, 'Migrating Modernities in the Mediterranean', *Postcolonial Studies* 11, 4 (2008), 387–399.

Chamoiseau, Patrick and Rodolphe Hammadi, *Guyane: Traces-mémoires du bagne* (Caisse nationale des monuments historiques et des sites, 1994).

Chaumont, Jean-Michel, *La Concurrence des victimes: Génocide, identité, reconnaissance* (La Découverte, 1997).

Cheyette, Bryan, 'Jews and Jewishness in the Writings of George Eliot and Frantz Fanon', *Patterns of Prejudice* 29, 4 (1995), 3–17.

_____, 'Frantz Fanon and the Black Jewish Imaginary' in Max Silverman (ed.), *Frantz Fanon's Black Skin White Masks* (Manchester: Manchester University Press, 2005), pp. 74–99.

Chraibi, Driss, *Les Boucs* (Denoel, 1955).

Cixous, Hélène, 'Pieds nus' in *Une Enfance algérienne, textes inédits recueillis par Leïla Sebbar* (Gallimard, 1997), pp. 53–63 / 'Bare Feet' in *An Algerian Childhood: A Collection of Autobiographical Narratives*, trans. Marjolijn de Jager (Minnesota: Ruminator Books, 2001), pp. 49–59.

_____, 'Mon Algériance' in *Les Inrockuptibles* 115 (20 August–2 September 1997), 71–74.

Cixous, Hélène and Jacques Derrida (chaired by Jacqueline Rose), 'The Language of Others', Jewish Book Week (March 2004), http://jewishbookweek.com/archive/010304e/transcripts2.php.

Colombat, André-Pierre, *The Holocaust in French Film* (Metuchen, New Jersey: Scarecrow Press, 1993).

Conan, Eric and Henry Rousso, *Vichy: Un Passé qui ne passe pas* (Fayard, 1994).

Cooke, Dervila, 'Hollow Imprints: History, Literature and the Biographical in Patrick Modiano's *Dora Bruder*', *Journal of Modern Jewish Studies* 3, 2 (2004), 131–145.

Cooper, Sarah, *Chris Marker* (Manchester: Manchester University Press, 2008).

Coquio, Catherine, 'Parler au camp, parler des camps: Hurbinek à Babel' in Catherine Coquio (ed.), *Parler des camps, penser les génocides* (Albin Michel/Idées, 1999), pp. 609–648.

———, 'La Tendresse d'Antigone: Charlotte Delbo, un témoignage au féminin' in *Témoigner entre histoire et mémoire: Dossier Charlotte Delbo*, vol. 105 (Kimé, 2009), 145–162.

Coquio, Catherine and Irving Wohlfarth, 'Avant-propos' in Catherine Coquio (ed.), *Parler des camps, penser les génocides* (Albin Michel/Idées, 1999), pp. 11–15.

Coulthard, Lisa, 'Negative Ethics: The Missed Event in the French Films of Michael Haneke', *Studies in French Cinema* 11, 1 (2011), 71–82.

Daeninckx, Didier, *Meurtres pour mémoire* (Gallimard, 1984) / *Murder in Memoriam*, trans. Liz Heron (London: Serpent's Tail, 2005).

Dall'Asta, Monica, 'The (Im)possible History' in Michael Temple, James S. Williams and Michael Witt (eds), *For Ever Godard* (London: Black Dog Publishing, 2004), pp. 350–363.

Dallenbach, Lucien, *Le Récit spéculaire* (Seuil, 1977).

Davis, Colin, *Haunted Subjects: Deconstruction, Psychoanalysis and the Return of the Dead* (Basingstoke, Hampshire: Palgrave Macmillan, 2007).

de Baecque, Antoine, 'L'Histoire qui revient: La Forme cinématographique de l'histoire dans *Caché* et *La Question humaine*', *Annales. Histoire, Sciences sociales* 63, 6 (2008), 1275–1301.

de Beauvoir, Simone, *Les Mandarins* (Gallimard, 1954).

———, *La Force des choses*, vol. 2 (Gallimard, 1963) / *Force of Circumstance*, trans. Richard Howard (Harmondsworth: Penguin 1968).

———, *Les Belles images* (Gallimard, 1966).

Delage, Christian and Vincent Guigeuno, *L'Historien et le film* (Gallimard, 2004).

Delbo, Charlotte, *Aucun de nous ne reviendra (Auschwitz et après 1)* (Minuit, 1970) / *None of Us Will Return* in *Auschwitz and after*, trans. Rosette C. Lamont (New Haven and London: Yale University Press, 1995), pp. 1–114.

———, *Une Connaissance inutile (Auschwitz et après 2)* (Minuit, 1970) / *Useless Knowledge* in *Auschwitz and after*, trans. Rosette C. Lamont (New Haven and London: Yale University Press, 1995), pp. 115–231.

———, *Mesure de nos jours (Auschwitz et après 3)* (Minuit, 1971) / *The Measure of our Days* in *Auschwitz and after*, trans. Rosette C. Lamont (New Haven and London: Yale University Press, 1995), pp. 233–354.

Deleuze, Gilles, *Cinéma 2: L'Image-temps* (Minuit, 1985) / *Cinema 2: The Time-image*, trans. Hugh Tomlinson and Robert Galeta (London: Athlone Press, 1989).

Derrida, Jacques, *L'Écriture et la différence* (Seuil, 1967) / *Writing and Difference*, trans. Alan Bass (London: Routledge, 2011).

_____, *Spectres de Marx* (Galilee, 1993).

_____, *Le Monolinguisme de l'autre, ou le prothèse de l'origine* (Galilée, 1996) / *Monolingualism of the Other; or, The Prosthesis of Origin*, trans. Patrick Mensah (Stanford, California: Stanford University Press, 1998).

_____, *Le Droit à la philosophie du point de vue cosmopolitique* (Éditions Verdier/UNESCO, 1997).

_____, *Cosmopolites de tous les pays, encore un effort!* (Galilée, 1997) / *On Cosmopolitanism* (trans. Mark Dooley) in *On Cosmopolitanism and Forgiveness* (London: Routledge, 2001).

Derrida Jacques and Hélène Cixous, 'From the Word to Life: A Dialogue Between Jacques Derrida and Hélène Cixous', *New Literary History* 37, 1 (2006), 1–13.

Dib, Mohammed, *Qui se souvient de la mer* (Éditions de la différence, 2007 [1962]).

Didi-Huberman, Georges, *Images malgré tout* (Minuit, 2003) / *Images in Spite of All*, trans. Shane B. Lillis (Chicago and London: University of Chicago Press, 2008).

_____, 'Opening the Camps, Closing the Eyes: Image, History, Readability' in Griselda Pollock and Max Silverman (eds), *Concentrationary Cinema: Aesthetics as Political Resistance in Alain Resnais's 'Night and Fog' (1955)* (Oxford and New York: Berghahn, 2011), pp. 84–125.

Dine, Philip, 'The Inescapable Allusion: The Occupation and the Resistance in French Fiction and Film of the Algerian War' in H.R. Kedward and Nancy Wood (eds), *The Liberation of France: Image and Event* (Oxford: Berg, 1995), pp. 269–282.

Djebar, Assia, *Femmes d'Alger dans leur appartement* (Des Femmes, 1980) / *Women of Algiers in their Apartment*, trans. Marjolijn de Jager (Charlottesville and London: University Press of Virginia, 1992).

Einaudi, Jean-Luc, *La Bataille de Paris: 17 octobre 1961* (Seuil, 1991).

Elsaesser, Thomas, 'Freud as Media Theorist: Mystic Writing-pads and the Matter of Memory', *Screen* 50, 1 (2009), 100–113.

Emmanuel, François, *La Question humaine* (Stock, 2000).

Evrard, Franck, 'Mythologies et écriture du sport' in Louis Arsac (et al), *Analyses et réflexions sur Georges Perec: W ou le souvenir d'enfance* (Ellipses, 1997), pp. 119–125.

Ezra, Elizabeth and Jane Sillars, 'Hidden in Plain Sight', *Screen* 48, 2 (2007), 215–221.

Fanon, Frantz, *Peau noire masques blancs* (Seuil, 1952) / *Black Skin, White Masks*, trans. Charles Lamm Markmann (London: Pluto, 2008).

_____, *Les Damnés de la terre* (Gallimard/Folio, 1991 [1961]).

———, 'Racisme et culture' in *Pour la révolution africaine: Écrits politiques* (La Découverte, 2001 [1956]), pp. 37–51 / 'Racism and Culture' in *Toward the African Revolution*, trans. Haakon Chevalier (New York: Grove Press, 1967), pp. 29–44.

———, 'Unité et solidarité effective sont les conditions de la libération africaine' in *Pour la révolution africaine: Écrits politiques* (La Découverte, 2001 [1956]), pp. 197–200.

Felman, Shoshana and Dori Laub, *Testimony: Crises of Witnessing in Literature, Psychoanalysis and History* (New York and London: Routledge, 1992).

Ffrench, Patrick, 'The Memory of the Image in Chris Marker's *La Jetée*', *French Studies* 59, 1, (2005), 31–37.

Finkielkraut, Alain, *Le Juif imaginaire* (Seuil, 1980).

———, *La Défaite de la pensée* (Gallimard, 1987).

Fleischer, Alain, *L'Art d'Alain Resnais* (Éditions du Centre Pompidou, 1998).

Forsdick, Charles and David Murphy, 'Introduction: Situating Francophone Postcolonial Thought' in Charles Forsdick and David Murphy (eds), *Postcolonial Thought in the French-speaking World* (Liverpool: Liverpool University Press, 2009), pp. 1–27.

Freud, Sigmund, 'A Note upon the "Mystic Writing Pad" (1925)' in *General Psychological Theory* (New York: Touchstone, 1997), pp. 207–212.

———, *Introductory Lectures on Psychoanaysis*, vol. 1 (Harmondsworth: Penguin, 1978).

Friedlander, Saul (ed.), *Probing the Limits of Representation: Nazism and the 'Final Solution'* (Cambridge, Mass.: Harvard University Press, 1992).

Genette, Gérard, *Palimpsestes: La Littérature au second degré* (Seuil, 1982).

Gilloch, Graham, *Walter Benjamin: Critical Constellations* (Cambridge: Polity, 2002).

Gilman, Sander, *Difference and Pathology: Stereotypes of Sexuality, Race and Madness* (Ithaca: Cornell University Press, 1985).

———, *Inscribing the Other* (Lincoln: University of Nebraska Press, 1991).

Gilroy, Paul, *The Black Atlantic: Modernity and Double Consciousness* (London: Verso, 1993).

———, 'Afterword: Not Being Inhuman' in Bryan Cheyette and Laura Marcus (eds), *Modernity, Culture and 'the Jew'* (Cambridge: Polity, 1998), pp. 282–297.

———, *Between Camps: Nations, Cultures and the Allure of Race* (London: Routledge, 2004 [2000]).

Glissant, Édouard, *La Cohée du Lamentin: Poétique V* (Gallimard, 2005).

Golsan, Richard, *Vichy's Afterlife: History and Counterhistory in Postwar France* (Lincoln: University of Nebraska Press, 2000).

Greene, Naomi, *Landscapes of Loss: The National Past in Postwar French Cinema* (Princeton, New Jersey: Princeton University Press, 1999).

Griffiths, Kate and David Evans (eds), *Haunted Presences: Ghosts in French Literature and Culture* (Cardiff: University of Wales Press, 2009).

Grimbert, Philippe, *Le Secret* (Grasset, 2004).

Halbwachs, Maurice, *Les Cadres sociaux de la mémoire* (Presses Universitaires de France, 1952).

———, *La Topographie légendaire des évangiles en terre sainte: Étude de mémoire collective* (Presses Universitaires de France, 1941) / *On Collective Memory* (Chicago: University of Chicago Press, 1992).

Hall, Stuart, '"When Was the Post-colonial?" Thinking at the Limit' in Iain Chambers and Lidia Curti (eds), *The Post-colonial Question: Common Skies, Divided Horizons* (London and New York: Routledge, 1996), pp. 242–260.

Hallward, Peter, *Absolutely Postcolonial: Writing between the Singular and the Specific* (Manchester and New York: Manchester University Press, 2001).

Hammerschlag, Sarah, *The Figural Jew: Politics and Identity in Postwar French Thought* (Chicago: Chicago University Press, 2010).

Hamon, Hervé and Patrick Rotman, *Les Porteurs de valises: La Résistance française à la guerre d'Algérie* (Seuil, 1982).

Haneke, Michael, 'Collective Guilt and Individual Responsibility: An Interview with Michael Haneke', *Cinéaste* (2005), http://www.thefreelibrary.com/Collective+guilt+and+individual+responsibility:+an+interview+with...-a0144567341 (accessed 2 September 2008).

———, 'Interview: Michael Haneke, réalisateur de "Caché"', *Arte* (2006), http://www.arte-tv.com/fr/Impression/4982,CmC=876864,CmStyle+98682.html (accessed 2 September 2008).

Harbord, Janet, *La Jetée* (London: Afterall Books, 2009).

Harrison, Nicholas, 'Learning from Experience: Hélène Cixous's "Pieds nus"', *Paragraph* 27 (2004), 21–32.

———, 'Assia Djebar: Fiction as a Way of "Thinking"' in Charles Forsdick and David Murphy (eds), *Postcolonial Thought in the French-speaking World* (Liverpool: Liverpool University Press, 2009), pp. 65–76.

Hartje, Hans, 'W et l'histoire d'une enfance en France' in *Georges Perec et l'histoire*, Actes du colloque international de l'Institut de littérature comparée Université de Copenhague du 30 avril au 1er mai 1998, recueillis et publiés par Steen Bille Jorgensen et Carsten Sestoft (Copenhagen: Museum Tusculanum Press, 2000), pp. 53–66.

Hartman, Geoffrey (ed.), *Holocaust Remembrance: The Shapes of Memory* (Oxford: Blackwell, 1994).

Hebard, Andrew, 'Disruptive Histories: Toward a Radical Politics of Remembrance in Alain Resnais's *Night and Fog*', *New German Critique* 71 (1997), 87–113; reproduced in Griselda Pollock and Max Silverman (eds), *Concentrationary Cinema: Aesthetics as Political Resistance in Alain Resnais's 'Night and Fog' (1955)* (Oxford and New York: Berghahn, 2011), pp. 214–237.

Hiddleston, Jane, 'Derrida, Autobiography and Postcoloniality', *French Cultural Studies* 16 (2005), 291–304.

———, *Assia Djebar: Out of Algeria* (Liverpool: Liverpool University Press, 2006).

———, 'Jacques Derrida: Colonialism, Philosophy and Autobiography' in Charles Forsdick and David Murphy (eds), *Postcolonial Thought in the French-speaking World* (Liverpool: Liverpool University Press, 2009), pp. 53–64.

Higgins, Lynn, *New Novel, New Wave, New Politics: Fiction in the Representation of History in Postwar France* (Lincoln and London: University of Nebraska Press, 1996).

Hill, Leslie, 'Perec à Warwick' in Mireille Ribière (ed.), *Parcours Perec* (Lyon: Presses Universitaires de Lyon, 1990), pp. 25–30.

Hilliard, Aouicha, 'Discourse and Language of the Mother in Mohammed Dib's *Qui se souvient de la mer*' in Kamal Sahli (ed.), *Francophone Studies: Discourse and Identity* (Exeter: Elm Bank Publications), pp. 173–188.

Hirsch, Joshua, *Afterimage: Film, Trauma and the Holocaust* (Philadelphia: Temple University Press, 2004).

———, '*Night and Fog* and Posttraumatic Cinema' in Griselda Pollock and Max Silverman (eds), *Concentrationary Cinema: Aesthetics as Political Resistance in Alain Resnais's 'Night and Fog' (1955)* (Oxford and New York: Berghahn, 2011), pp. 183–198.

Hirsch, Marianne, *Family Frames: Photography, Narrative and Postmemory* (Cambridge, Mass.: Harvard University Press, 1997).

Hodgkin, Katherine and Susannah Radstone, 'Introduction: Contested Pasts' in Katherine Hodgkin and Susannah Radstone (eds), *Contested Pasts: The Politics of Memory* (London and New York: Routledge, 2003), pp. 1–21.

Hori, Junji, 'Godard's Two Historiographies' in Michael Temple, James S. Williams and Michael Witt (eds), *For Ever Godard* (London: Black Dog Publishing, 2004), pp. 334–349.

Horkheimer, Max and Theodor Adorno, *Dialectic of Enlightenment* (New York: Continuum, 2001 [1944]).

House, James, 'Memory and the Creation of Solidarity during the Decolonization of Algeria' in Michael Rothberg, Debarati Sanyal and Max Silverman (eds), '*Noeuds de mémoire*: Multidirectional Memory in Post-war French and Francophone Culture', *Yale French Studies* 118/119 (2010), 15–38.

House, James and Neil Macmaster, *Paris 1961: Algerians, State Terror and Memory* (Oxford and New York: Oxford University Press, 2006).

Huyssen, Andreas, *Present Pasts: Urban Palimpsests and the Politics of Memory* (Stanford, California: Stanford University Press, 2003).

Huston, Nancy, *L'Empreinte de l'ange* (Actes Sud, 1998).

Jacobson, Howard, *Kalooki Nights* (London: Jonathan Cape, 2006).

Jakobson, Roman, 'Two Aspects of Language and Two Types of Aphasic Disturbances' in Roman Jakobson and Morris Halle (eds), *Fundamentals of Language* (The Hague: Mouton, 1971 [1956]), pp. 67–96.

John, Matthew, 'Concentrationary Cinema', unpublished Ph.D. thesis (University of Leeds, 2012).

Johnson, Christopher, *System and Writing in the Philosophy of Jacques Derrida* (Cambridge: Cambridge University Press, 1993).

Jurgenson, Luba, 'L'Identité narrative chez Charlotte Delbo: Un Modèle chorale' in *Témoigner entre histoire et mémoire: Dossier Charlotte Delbo*, vol. 105 (Kimé, 2009), 65–75.

Keller, Richard Charles, *Colonial Madness: Psychiatry in French North Africa* (Chicago and London: University of Chicago Press, 2007).

Khadda, Naget, *Mohammed Dib: Cette impestive voix recluse* (Aix-en-Provence: Édisud, 2003).

Khatibi, Abdelkebir, *La Mémoire tatouée: Autobiographie d'un décolonisé* (Denoel, 1971).

King, Richard H. and Dan Stone, 'Introduction' in Richard H. King and Dan Stone (eds), *Hannah Arendt and the Uses of History: Imperialism, Nation, Race and Genocide* (Oxford and New York: Berghahn, 2007), pp. 1–17.

Kristeva, Julia, *Étrangers à nous-mêmes* (Fayard, 1988).

LaCapra, Dominic, *History and Memory after Auschwitz* (Ithaca and London: Cornell University Press, 1998).

Landsberg, Alison, *Prosthetic Memory: The Transformation of American Remembrance in the Age of Mass Culture* (New York: Columbia University Press, 2004).

Levy, Daniel and Natan Sznaider, 'Memory Unbound: The Holocaust and the Formation of Cosmopolitan Memory', *European Journal of Social Theory* 5, 1 (2002), 87–106.

———, *The Holocaust and Memory in the Global Age* (Philadelphia: Temple University Press, 2006).

Lindeperg, Sylvie, *Les Écrans de l'ombre: La Seconde guerre mondiale dans le cinéma français (1944–1969)* (CNRS Éditions, 1997).

———, *'Nuit et brouillard', un film dans l'histoire* (Odile Jacob, 2006).

———, 'Night and Fog: A History of Gazes' in Griselda Pollock and Max Silverman (eds), *Concentrationary Cinema: Aesthetics as Political Resistance in Alain Resnais's 'Night and Fog' (1955)* (Oxford and New York: Berghahn, 2011), pp. 55–70.

Lindeperg, Sylvie and Annette Wieviorka, *Univers concentrationnaire et génocide: Voir, savoir, comprendre* (Mille et une nuits/Arthème Fayard, 2008).

Lindkvist, Sven, *Exterminate All the Brutes: One Man's Odyssey into the Heart of Darkness and the Origins of European Genocide* (London: Granta, 2002 [1997]).

Lionnet, Françoise, 'Afterword: *Francophonie*, Postcolonial Studies, and Transnational Feminisms' in H. Adlai Murdoch and Anne Donadey (eds), *Postcolonial Theory and Francophone Literary Studies* (Gainesville: University Press of Florida, 2005), pp. 258–269.

———, '"Dire *exactement*": Remembering the Interwoven Lives of Jewish Deportees and Coolie Descendants in 1940s Mauritius' in Michael Rothberg, Debarati Sanyal and Max Silverman (eds), '*Noeuds de mémoire*: Multidirectional Memory in Post-war French and Francophone Culture', *Yale French Studies* 118/119 (2010), 111–135.

Lundemo, Trond, 'The Index and Erasure: Godard's Approach to Film History' in Michael Temple, James S. Williams and Michael Witt (eds), *For Ever Godard* (London: Black Dog Publishing, 2004), pp. 380–395.

Macey, David, *Frantz Fanon: A Life* (London: Granta, 2000).

Macmaster, Neil, '"Black Jew: White Negro": Antisemitism and the Construction of Cross-racial Stereotypes', *Nationalism and Ethnic Politics* 6, 4 (2000), 65–82.

Mamdani, Mahmood, *When Victims Become Killers: Colonialism, Nativism and the Genocide in Rwanda* (Princeton, NJ: Princeton University Press, 2001).

Maspero, François, *Les Passagers du Roissy-Express* (Seuil, 1990).

Mazower, Mark, 'Foucault, Agamben: Theory and the Nazis', *Boundary 2* 35, 1 (2008), 23–34.

———, *Hitler's Empire: Nazi Rule in Occupied Europe* (London: Allen Lane, 2008).

McCusker, Maeve, *Patrick Chamoiseau: Recovering Memory* (Liverpool: Liverpool University Press, 2007.

Memmi, Albert, *Portrait du colonisé* (Gallimard, 1957).

———, *Portrait d'un juif* (Gallimard, 1962).

Mesnard, Philippe, 'Pourquoi Charlotte Delbo?' in *Témoigner entre histoire et mémoire: Dossier Charlotte Delbo*, vol. 105 (Kimé, 2009), 17–23.

Michael, Robert, 'Night and Fog', *Cineaste* 13, 4 (1984), 36–37.

Milne, Lorna, *Patrick Chamoiseau: Espaces d'une écriture antillaise* (Amsterdam and New York: Rodopi, 2006).

Modiano, Patrick, *Dora Bruder* (Gallimard, 1997).

———, *Des Inconnues* (Gallimard, 1999).

———, *Un Pedigree* (Gallimard, 2005).

Molden, Berthold, 'Vietnam, the New Left and the Holocaust: How the Cold War Changed Discourse on Genocide' in Aleida Assmann and Sebastian Conrad (eds), *Memory in a Global Age: Discourses, Practices and Trajectories* (London and New York: Palgrave Macmillan, 2010), pp. 79–96.

Monaco, James, *Alain Resnais* (Oxford and New York: Oxford University Press, 1979).

Morin, Edgar, *Les Stars* (Seuil, 1972).

Moses, A. Dirk, 'Conceptual Blockages and Conceptual Dilemmas in the "Racial Century": Genocides of Indigenous Peoples and the Holocaust', *Patterns of Prejudice* 36, 4 (2002), 7–36.

Motte, Warren, 'Georges Perec and the Broken Book', in Lawrence D. Kritzman (ed.), *Auschwitz and After: Race, Culture and 'the Jewish Question' in France* (London: Routledge, 1995), pp. 235–249.

Mufti, Aamir, *Enlightenment in the Colony: The Jewish Question and the Crisis of Postcolonial Culture* (Princeton and Oxford: Princeton University Press, 2007).

Nora, Pierre (ed.), *Les Lieux de mémoire* (Gallimard, 3 volumes: 1984, 1986, 1992).

Olivier, Laurent, 'L'Impossible archéologie de la mémoire: À propos de *W ou le souvenir d'enfance* de Georges Perec', *European Journal of Archaeology* 3, 3 (2000), 387–406.

Oster, Daniel, *Jean Cayrol et son oeuvre* (Seuil, 1967).

Ostrowska, Dorota, 'Dreaming a Cinematic Dream: Jean Cayrol's Writings on Film', *Studies in French Cinema* 6, 1 (2006), 17–28.

Owens, Craig, 'The Allegorical Impulse: Toward a Theory of Postmodernism', *October* 12 (1980), 67–86.

Parrau, Alain, *Écrire les camps* (Belin, 1995).

Perec, Georges, *W ou le souvenir d'enfance* (Denoel, 1975) / *W, or the Memory of Childhood*, trans. David Bellos (Jaffrey, New Hampshire: David R. Godine, 1988).

Perrot, Michelle, 'Histoire et mémoire des femmes dans l'oeuvre d'Assia Djebar' in Mireille Calle-Gruber (ed.), *Assia Djebar, Nomade entre les murs…: Pour une poétique transfrontalière* (Maisonneuve et Larose, 2005), pp. 33–42.

Pollock, Griselda, *Vision and Difference: Femininity, Feminism and the Histories of Art* (London: Routledge, 1988).

———, 'Dreaming the Face, Screening the Death: Reflections for Jean Louis Schefer on *La Jetée*', *Journal of Visual Culture* 4, 3 (2005), 287–305.

———, Death in the Image: The Responsibility of Aesthetics in *Night and Fog* (1955) and *Kapo* (1959)' in Griselda Pollock and Max Silverman (eds), *Concentrationary Cinema: Aesthetics as Political Resistance in Alain Resnais's 'Night and Fog' (1955)* (Oxford and New York: Berghahn, 2011), pp. 258–301.

Pollock, Griselda and Max Silverman, 'Introduction: Concentrationary Cinema' in Griselda Pollock and Max Silverman (eds), *Concentrationary Cinema: Aesthetics as Political Resistance in Alain Resnais's 'Night and Fog' (1955)* (Oxford and New York: Berghahn, 2011), pp. 1–54.

Prédal, René, *L'Itinéraire d'Alain Resnais* (Lettres Modernes, 1996).

Proust, Marcel, *Le Temps retrouvé* (Gallimard, 1954) / *Time Regained*, trans. Andreas Mayor (London: Chatto and Windus, 1972).

Rancière, Jacques, 'L'Historicité du cinéma' in Antoine de Baecque and Christian Delage (eds), *De l'histoire au cinéma* (Éditions Complexe, 1998), pp. 45–60.

———, *Le Destin des images* (La Fabrique, 2003) / *The Future of the Image*, trans. Gregory Elliott (London and New York: Verso, 2007).

———, 'S'il y a de l'irreprésentable?' in *Le Destin des images* (La Fabrique, 2003), pp. 123–153 / 'Are Some Things Unrepresentable?' in *The Future of the Image*, trans. Gregory Elliott (London and New York: Verso, 2007) (first published in *Genre Humain* 36 (2001), 81–102).

Raskin, Richard, *Nuit et brouillard by Alain Resnais: On the Making, Reception and Functions of a Major Documentary Film* (Aarhus: Aarhus University Press, 1987).

Raymond, Hélène, *Poétique du témoignage: Autour du film 'Nuit et brouillard' d'Alain Resnais* (L'Harmattan, 2008).

Ricœur, Paul, 'Histoire et mémoire' in Antoine de Baecque and Christian Delage (eds), *De l'histoire au cinéma* (Éditions Complexe, 1998), pp. 17–28.

Rioux, Jean-Pierre and Jean-François Sirinelli (eds), *La Guerre d'Algérie et les intellectuels français* (Brussels: Éditions Complexe, 1991).

Roche, Anne, 'Perec et le monde arabe' in *Georges Perec et l'histoire*, Actes du colloque international de l'Institut de littérature comparée, Université de Copenhague, du 30 avril au 1er mai 1998, recueillis et publiés par Steen Bille Jorgensen et Carsten Sestoft (Copenhagen: Museum Tusculanum Press, 2000), pp. 159–168.

Rose, Gillian, *Mourning Becomes the Law: Philosophy and Representation* (Cambridge and New York: Cambridge University Press, 1996).

Ross, Kristin, *Fast Cars, Clean Bodies: Decolonization and the Reordering of French Culture* (Cambridge Mass.: MIT Press, 1995).

———, *May '68 and its Afterlives* (Chicago and London: University of Chicago Press, 2002).

Rothberg, Michael, *Traumatic Realism: The Demands of Holocaust Representation* (Minneapolis: University of Minnesota Press, 2000).

———, *Multidirectional Memory: Remembering the Holocaust in the Age of Decolonization* (Stanford: Stanford University Press, 2009).

———, 'Introduction: Between Memory and Memory. From *Lieux de mémoire* to *Noeuds de mémoire*' in Michael Rothberg, Debarati Sanyal and Max Silverman (eds), '*Noeuds de mémoire*: Multidirectional Memory in Post-war French and Francophone Culture', *Yale French Studies* 118/119 (2010), pp. 3–12.

Rousset, David, *L'Univers concentrationnaire* (Minuit, 1965 [1946]) / *The Other Kingdom*, trans. Ramon Guthrie (New York: Reynal and Hitchcock, 1947).

Rousso, Henry, *Le Syndrôme de Vichy (1944–198…)* (Seuil, 1987).

Said, Edward, 'Raymond Schwab and the Romance of Ideas' in *The World, the Text, and the Critic* (London: Faber and Faber, 1984 [1983]), pp. 248–267.

_____, *Culture and Imperialism* (London: Chatto and Windus, 1993).

Saint, Nigel, 'Drame de juillet, tragédie de l'été: Perec et Roland-Garros', *French Cultural Studies* 10 (1990), 173–178.

Salgas, Jean-Pierre, 'Shoah, ou la disparition' in Denis Hollier (ed.), *De la littérature francaise* (Bordas, 1993), pp. 1005–1013.

Santner, Eric, *Stranded Objects: Mourning, Memory and Film in Postwar Germany* (Ithaca and London: Cornell University Press, 1990).

Sanyal, Debarati, 'Crabwalk History: Torture, Allegory and Memory in Sartre' in Michael Rothberg, Debarati Sanyal and Max Silverman (eds), *'Noeuds de mémoire*: Multidirectional Memory in Post-war French and Francophone Culture', *Yale French Studies* 118/119 (2010), 52–71.

_____, 'Auschwitz as Allegory in *Night and Fog*' in Griselda Pollock and Max Silverman (eds), *Concentrationary Cinema: Aesthetics as Political Resistance in Alain Resnais's 'Night and Fog' (1955)* (Oxford and New York: Berghahn, 2011), pp. 152–182.

Sartre, Jean-Paul, *Réflexions sur la question juive* (Gallimard, 1954 [1946]) / *Anti-semite and Jew*, trans. George J. Becker (New York: Schocken Books, 1948).

_____, *Situations, V: Colonialisme et néo-colonialisme* (Gallimard, 1964).

Saxton, Libby, 'Secrets and Revelations: Off-screen Space in Michael Haneke's *Caché* (2005)', *Studies in French Cinema* 7, 1 (2007), 5–17.

_____, *Haunted Images: Film, Ethics, Testimony and the Holocaust* (London and New York: Wallflower Press, 2008).

_____, 'Horror by Analogy: Paradigmatic Aesthetics in Nicolas Klotz and Elisabeth Perceval's *La Question humaine*' in Michael Rothberg, Debarati Sanyal and Max Silverman (eds), *'Noeuds de mémoire*: Multidirectional Memory in Post-war French and Francophone Culture', *Yale French Studies* 118/119 (2010), pp. 209–224.

Scemama, Céline, *'Histoire(s) du cinéma' de Jean-Luc Godard: La Force faible d'un art* (L'Harmattan, 2006).

Scharfman, Ronnie, 'Cixous, Derrida, and the Vichy Years in Algeria' in H. Adlai Murdoch and Anne Donadey (eds), *Postcolonial Theory and Francophone Literary Studies* (Gainesville: University Press of Florida, 2005), pp. 87–101.

Schefer, Jean Louis, 'À propos de *La Jetée*' in *Images mobiles: Récits, visages, flocons* (P.O.L., 1999), pp. 131–137.

Sebbar, Leïla, *La Seine était rouge* (Thierry Magnier, 1999).

Sheringham, Michael, *French Autobiography: Devices and Desires* (Oxford: Oxford University Press, 1993).

Silverman, Max, *Deconstructing the Nation: Immigration, Racism and Citizenship in Modern France* (London and New York: Routledge, 1992).

————, 'Re-figuring "the Jew" in France' in Bryan Cheyette and Laura Marcus (eds), *Modernity, Culture and 'the Jew'* (Cambridge: Polity, 1998), pp. 197–208.

————, 'Reflections on the Human Question' in Max Silverman (ed.), *Frantz Fanon's Black Skin White Masks* (Manchester: Manchester University Press, 2005), pp. 112–127.

————, 'Horror and the Everyday in Post-Holocaust France: *Nuit et brouillard* and Concentrationary Art', *French Cultural Studies* 17, 1 (2006), 5–18.

————, 'The Empire Looks Back', *Screen* 48, 2 (2007), 245–249.

————, '"Killing me softly": Racial Ambivalence in Jean-Paul Sartre's *Réflexions sur la question juive'* in Phyllis Lassner and Lara Trubowitz (eds), *Antisemitism and Philosemitism in the Twentieth and Twenty-first Centuries: Representing Jews, Jewishness and Modern Culture* (Newark: University of Delaware Press, 2008), pp. 47–62.

————, 'Hybrid Memory in the City', *Moving Worlds*, special issue on 'Postcolonial Europe', Graham Huggan (ed.), 11, 2 (2011), 57–66.

Sontag, Susan, *Regarding the Pain of Others* (London: Penguin, 2003).

Stafford, Andrew, 'Patrick Chamoiseau and Rodolphe Hammadi in the Penal Colony: Photo-text and Memory-traces', *Postcolonial Studies* 11, 1 (2008), 27–38.

Sternhell, Zeev, *The Anti-Enlightenment Tradition* (New Haven and London: Yale University Press, 2009).

Stone, Dan, *Histories of the Holocaust* (Oxford and New York: Oxford University Press, 2010).

Suk, Jeannie, *Postcolonial Paradoxes in French Caribbean Writing: Césaire, Glissant, Condé* (Oxford: Oxford University Press, 2001).

Suleiman, Susan Rubin, *Crises of Memory and the Second World War* (Cambridge, Mass.: Harvard University Press, 2006).

Syrotinski, Michael, *Deconstruction and the Postcolonial: At the Limits of Theory* (Liverpool: Liverpool University Press, 2007).

Temple, Michael, 'Big Rhythm and the Power of Metamorphosis: Some Models and Precursors for *Histoire(s) du cinéma'* in Michael Temple and James S. Williams (eds), *The Cinema Alone: Essays on the Work of Jean-Luc Godard 1985–2000* (Amsterdam: Amsterdam University Press, 2000), pp. 77–95.

Terdiman, Richard, *Present Past: Modernity and the Memory Crisis* (Ithaca, NY: Cornell University Press, 1993).

Thatcher, Nicole, *A Literary Analysis of Charlotte Delbo's Concentration Camp Re-presentation* (Lampeter: Edwin Mellen, 2000).

Thomas, Dominic, 'Intersections and Trajectories: Francophone Studies and Postcolonial Theory' in H. Adlai Murdoch and Anne Donadey (eds), *Postcolonial Theory and Francophone Literary Studies* (Gainesville: University Press of Florida, 2005), pp. 235–257.

Todorov, Tzvetan, *Mémoire du mal, tentation du bien: Enquête sur le siècle* (Robert Laffont, 2000).

———, *Les Abus de la mémoire* (Arléa, 2004).

Traverso, Enzo, 'La Singularité d'Auschwitz: Hypothèses, problèmes et dérives de la recherche historique' in Catherine Coquio (ed.), *Parler des camps, penser les génocides*, (Albin Michel/Idées, 1999), pp. 128–140.

———, *La Violence nazie: Une Généalogie européenne* (La Fabrique, 2002).

———, *Le Passé, modes d'emploi: Histoire, mémoire, politique* (La Fabrique, 2005).

Trigg, Dylan, 'The Place of Trauma: Memory, Hauntings, and the Temporality of Ruins', *Memory Studies* 2, 1 (2009), 87–101.

Ungar, Steven, *Scandal and Aftereffect: Blanchot and France since 1930* (Minneapolis: University of Minnesota Press, 1995).

———, 'In the Thick of Things: Rouch and Morin's *Chronique d'un été* Reconsidered', *French Cultural Studies* 14, 1 (2003), 5–22.

Virilio, Paul, *Guerre et cinéma 1: Logistique de la perception* (Éditions de l'Étoile, 1984).

Wheatley, Catherine, 'Secrets, Lies and Videotape', *Sight and Sound* 16, 2 (2006), 32–36.

———, *Michael Haneke's Cinema: The Ethics of the Image* (Oxford and New York: Berghahn, 2009).

Wieviorka, Annette, *L'Ère du témoin* (Plon, 1998).

Wieviorka, Olivier, *La Mémoire désunie: Le Souvenir politique des années sombres, de la Libération à nos jours* (Seuil, 2010).

Wilson, Emma, 'Material Remains: *Night and Fog*', *October* 112 (2005), 89–110.

———, *Alain Resnais* (Manchester: Manchester University Press, 2006).

Witt, Michael, 'Montage, My Beautiful Care, or Histories of the Cinematograph', in Michael Temple and James S. Williams (eds), *The Cinema Alone: Essays on the Work of Jean-Luc Godard 1985–2000* (Amsterdam: Amsterdam University Press, 2000), pp. 33–50.

Wood, Nancy, 'Remembering the Jews of Algeria' in *Vectors of Memory: Legacies of Trauma in Postwar Europe* (Oxford: Berg, 1999).

Woodhull, Winifred, 'Mohammed Dib and the French Question', *Yale French Studies* 98 (2000), 66–78.

Wolff, Janet, 'The Invisible *Flâneuse*: Women and the Literature of Modernity', *Theory, Culture and Society* 2, 3 (1985), 37–48.

Zimmerer, Jurgen, 'Colonialism and the Holocaust: Towards an Archaeology of Genocide' in A. Dirk Moses (ed.), *Genocide and Settler Society: Frontier Violence and Stolen Indigenous Children in Australian History* (Oxford and New York: Berghahn Books, 2004), pp. 49–76.

———, 'The Birth of the *Ostland* out of the Spirit of Colonialism: A Postcolonial Perspective on the Nazi Policy of Conquest and Extermination', *Patterns of Prejudice* 39, 2 (2005), 202–224.

INDEX